# Logical Data Base Design

# Logical Data Base Design

### Robert M. Curtice
Staff Member
Arthur D. Little, Inc.

and

### Paul E. Jones, Jr.
Staff Member
Arthur D. Little, Inc.

**Van Nostrand Reinhold Data Processing Series**

**VNR** VAN NOSTRAND REINHOLD COMPANY
NEW YORK CINCINNATI TORONTO LONDON MELBOURNE

Library of Congress Catalog Card Number: 81-10465
ISBN: 0-442-24501-7

Manufactured in the United States of America

Published by Van Nostrand Reinhold Company Inc.
135 West 50th Street, New York, N.Y. 10020

Van Nostrand Reinhold Australia Pty, Ltd.
17 Queen Street
Mitcham, Victoria 3132, Australia

Van Nostrand Reinhold Company Limited
Molly Millars Lane
Wokingham, Berkshire, England

15  14  13  12  11  10  9  8  7  6  5  4  3  2

**Library of Congress Cataloging in Publication Data**

Curtice, Robert M.
  Logical data base design.

  (Van Nostrand Reinhold data processing series)
  Includes bibliographical references and index.
  1. Data base management.   I. Jones, Paul E.
II. Title.   III. Series.
QA 76.9.D3C877       001.64        81-10465
ISBN 0-442-24501-7                 AACR2

# Series Introduction

Helpful diagrams and a workable approach—those are keys to logical data-base design. But diagrams alone are not enough, and the authors are aware of that. Directions are provided to help you recognize and be sensitive to the elements of logical data-base design. Then diagram representations of the important design aspects are given. Thus, taken together, the approach and the diagrams provide a basis for creating and describing the logical design of a data base.

The examples are especially helpful in this book. They are broad enough to approach the realism of actual data-base design situations. They illustrate how the authors' approach yields a useful, logical data-base design. The diagrams that describe the resulting design communicate what that design is, and give insight into the way the data are to act in the systems that will access the data base.

An aspect of this book that will endear it to many readers is its emphasis on the practical aspects of logical data-base design. This is not a book on theory. This is a book for people who want to do logical data-base design.

NED CHAPIN, Ph.D
Series Editor

THE VAN NOSTRAND REINHOLD DATA PROCESSING SERIES

Edited by Ned Chapin, Ph.D.

IMS Programming Techniques: A Guide to Using DL/1
   Dan Kapp and Joseph L. Leben

Reducing COBOL Complexity Through Structured Programming
   Carma L. McClure

Composite/Structured Design
   Glenford J. Myers

Reliable Software Through Composite Design
   Glenford J. Myers

Top-Down Structured Programming Techniques
   Clement L. McGowen and John R. Kelly

Operating Systems Principles
   Stanley Kurzban, T. S. Heines and A. P. Sayers

Microcomputer Handbook
   Charles J. Sippl

Strategic Planning of Management Information Systems
   Paul Siegel

Flowcharts
   Ned Chapin

Introduction to Artificial Intelligence
   Philip C. Jackson, Jr.

Computers and Management for Business
   Douglas A. Colbert

Evaluating Data Base Management Systems
  Judy King

Network Systems
  Roshan Lal Sharma, Ashok D. Inglé and Paulo T. De Sousa

Logical Data Base Design
  Robert M. Curtice and Paul E. Jones, Jr.

Decision Tables in Software Engineering
  Richard B. Hurley

CICS/VS Command Level with ANS Cobol Examples
  Pacifico A. Lim

# Preface

In 1968, Arthur D. Little, Inc., conducted a major study on behalf of 20 large U.S. corporations entitled, "Fast Response Data-Based Systems." As participants in that study, we were exposed to the problems which all these companies were having in trying to apply the emerging technology of data-base management. The design of the data base seemed to be a common stumbling block. It took many, many months to achieve an acceptable design, no matter how many intelligent people were applied to the problem. Separating physical from logical design considerations had not as yet been recognized as a way to simplify the problem. And, in general, there were no methodologies or ground rules to guide the design process.

The ideas and methods presented in this book had their origin during the 1968 study. They have been in continuous use and under continuous development during the intervening years. Our experiences have given us an unshakeable conviction about the process of data-base design that places extraordinary emphasis on discovering the coherent organizing principles of the data problem *first*. We believe the following: Once you "see" the data fall into place, everything else is easy. The whole trick is to have the design "crystallize." Making this happen quickly has always been our goal. As a consequence, we strip away every consideration that might stand in the way. The notation we use is *lean*: leaner today than it was when we began.

We are indebted to our colleagues at Arthur D. Little, Inc., and Corporate-Tech Planning, Inc. Their intense analysis of the methods, as they learned to use them, forced us to find better ways to explain and to justify the discipline. With help from these colleagues, our logical design methodology has been applied to some truly enormous data bases; it has also been used—in stripped-down form—in the design of small data structures and even a manual filing system. (See Stankard, M., *Successful Management of Large Clerical Operations,* McGraw Hill, 1981). It continues to be applied to practical data-base design problems. Though it is not treated in this book, some readers will be interested to know that computer programs have been developed—not only by us but by our clients—to support and aid in the design process.

Chapter 1 describes and introduces the problem of logical data-base design. The basic notation is defined as part of the introduction. The reader who is willing to accept the definitions at face value will gain the ability to "read" a logical design. Chapter 2 is devoted in its entirety to exhibiting a fragment of real data-base design. We present this realistic picture because the "toy" data bases usually found in books about data bases are inadequate to convey the real problem. It simply is not very difficult to figure out the qualities of the toy problems (STUDENT, COURSE, TEACHER for example), though it is important to know the structural building blocks. Our interest is directed one step earlier in the process—a time when it is *unclear* whether students, courses, or teachers exist, *unclear* what they are, and *unclear* how they are related. Is a "student" always a person or could a machine (an industrial robot, for example) take a "course"? Can a person who takes *no* courses for credit be a "student"? (Remember there are programs for "special students.") Can a videotape be a "teacher"? Do students and teachers really have to be located in the same room? We urge the reader to think about how easy it is to study STUDENT, TEACHER, COURSE when we know what they are, versus how hard it is to crystallize a design when these basic elements are fuzzy. Chapter 2 illustrates a portion of a solid data problem and gives our solution.

In Chapter 3 we discuss the process of logical design with emphasis on the way entities are discovered and the need to factor entities and relationships into their constituent parts. Chapter 4 concentrates on data elements and their familiar and unfamiliar properties. Then, in Chapter 5, the notation is re-examined with the aim of imparting a deeper understanding of the characteristics of logical data structures. A "writing knowledge" of the language for defining logical data structures can be obtained by studying this chapter and adhering to the rules and guidelines that are recommended. Finally, in Chapter 6, some more advanced properties of data relationships are developed, an approach to documenting a design is outlined, and we compare this approach with the CODASYL and Relational Models.

ROBERT M. CURTICE
PAUL E. JONES

Cambridge, Mass.

# Contents

# 1
# Fundamentals of Logical Data Base Design

## INTRODUCTION

A data base is, fundamentally, a body of information contained in a mechanism that facilitates the use of the information. A data base must be distinguished from the many mechanisms available for managing records—the envelopes in which information is carried. Record management systems range from visible filing systems for cards through complex secondary storage devices and associated software for large computer applications. Record management systems provide for the storage and retrieval of information-bearing envelopes; little attention is paid to the contents.

Data bases are different. They are also complex mechanisms of hardware and software, but with added capabilities that are concerned with the information itself. The distinction made here is crucial, and one which distinguishes data base from file management or an access method. A data base is capable of relating pieces of information to one another, and in general is affected by the meaning of the information it manages.

How is the meaning of the information within a data base recorded and transmitted among people? This is an interesting question, for if one were to look inside a data base, the only thing observable would be a profusion of symbols. The information stored in any physical data base is thus bound into the symbol structures found there. Combinations of symbols are perfectly capable of carrying information as these examples show:

"The doctor is out."
"$2^5 + 1 = (5 - 2) \times (5 \times 2 + 1)$"
"*Cogito ergo sum.*"

But unless one knows the rules of interpretation, there is no way to grasp the kind of information being conveyed—no way to tell if the symbol string is meant to convey a fact, theorem, conclusion, etc., or to study the meaning of the symbols. Since a data base contains information (and is *not* a meaningless system of symbols), it is important to understand the relationship between the symbols and the abstract ideas they presume to represent.

The 'X' in 'X = X' can refer to anything and is nevertheless true. In formal systems like mathematics, attention is focused on the form of the symbol strings, not their interpretation. Not so with the symbols stored in data bases. Almost every one is richly endowed with meaning or draws meaning from its context. The digit pair '26,' adroitly stored in the correct position relative to other symbols, could easily mean:

— The 26th letter, i.e., Z.
— There are 26 students assigned to this classroom.
— There are 26 students in class on Thursday (though 35 are assigned).
— Somebody owes somebody 26 drachmas.
— An event took place 26 time units after (before) another identified event.
— Something else.

It would be quite difficult to identify a boundary that restricts what a symbol string in a data base might mean (or denote, connote, represent, signify, stand for). After all, those who cause information to be stored in data bases have certain privileges:

"When *I* use a word," Humpty Dumpty said, in rather a scornful tone, "it means just what I choose it to mean—neither more nor less."

"The question is," said Alice, "whether you *can* make words mean so many different things."

"The question is," said Humpty Dumpty, "which is to be master—that's all."

For a data base to be useful then, it must be associated with a set of rules of interpretation, which along with the symbol strings, provide the meaning.

The rules of interpretation may be provided in many different ways. Certainly the definitions of the individual units of information convey a large part of the meaning. The appearance of related units of information within the same context likewise indicates a certain meaning. And the overall structure of the data base, in the form of relationships among certain units of information conveys additional meaning. Sometimes more subtle embodiments are employed—like the interpretation given to one piece of information appearing in sequence prior to another, or more dramatically, by a single bit indicating that the data to follow is to be interpreted as the location of certain information and not the information itself.

A data base may be interpreted, and hence designed or described, on several levels. The following levels of description are widely recognized

- *Physical.* The physical, or internal level of data base description reflects how the information is embodied physically in the data storage mechanism. This level of description is concerned with formats (binary vs. BCD), encoding methods (EBCDIC vs. ASCII), lengths of data items, and allocation of information units to physical storage (e.g., cylinder 42, block 7). It is also concerned with describing the record management subsystem of a data base—for although a data base is more than a record management system, it subsumes one to accomplish its function. Thus the access methods which the *data base* uses for the purposes of storage and retrieval of *records* are described at the physical level. Note that since encoding, storage and retrieval are the major resource-consuming components of a data base, physical characteristics will largely determine its performance or efficiency.
- *Application.* The application, or external, level of data base description presents a particular view of the information which is geared to a specific purpose. The particular perspective is often oriented towards a given application program, but

the application view may be oriented towards answering a set of end-user inquiries as well. Thus there are numerous application descriptions (views) of a data base, each supplying the perspective required. An application view must be derivable from the physical data base, but conversions, subsets, and other alterations and transformations which provide the needed perspective are allowed. Moreover, the purely physical characteristics of the data base are not supplied to an application view until they are needed—i.e., when data is actually being utilized. Tailoring the view of the data base, and omitting physical characteristics until needed, enables an application view (and hence the programs which make use of it) to achieve a degree of data independence.

• *Conceptual.* The conceptual, or logical, level of description of a data base provides the rules for interpretation of the meaning of a data base. It is minimally concerned with the physical aspects of the data base, concentrating instead on identifying the real world objects which will be represented in the data base, and detailing how these representations are to be related to one another.

This book is about data base design at the conceptual level, i.e., about logical data base design. The logical level of data base description is the most recent to be recognized as having an important role in the overall data base development process. In large part, logical design represents a critical transition in which a perception of the world gets formulated and translated into "a design." It is an important step, because if the perception or the translation is in error, no hardware or software will be able to correct it.

If a logical data base design is to be successful, it must meet several important criteria.

### Reflection of the Real World

A data base is meant to reflect conditions which exist outside of itself, i.e., in the real world, and which are of interest to an organization. Thus the symbols within the data base, their relation to one another, and the rules for their interpretation must reflect the real world conditions of interest. This doesn't mean, of course, that any data base *will* reflect real world conditions. Two kinds of errors can be identified which would cause the data base to reflect something other than what we wish. Data errors are always possible: if someone inputs a value of '14' for the number of items withdrawn from stock, when in fact 15 were withdrawn, then the data base will not reflect reality. This certainly is an error in data base content. However, it can be identified and rectified with relative ease. It is important to distinguish such data content errors from the second type of error. Consider the case in which only two digits have been allowed for inventory balances, and in fact the inventory for an item turns out to be 137. This data base not only does not reflect reality, it cannot. To rectify the situation is far more costly than correcting data errors. Even more egregious errors are possible. Consider a data base which allows a receipt to show one purchase order number (indicating the purchase order under which the received items were ordered). If in fact a receipt may contain items from several different purchase orders, or maybe even several vendors, the data base is incapable of showing certain real world cases. And what happens when the purchase order number is unknown at the time of receipt? How is "unknown" reflected in the data base? Errors of this sort have nothing to do with the values of data items; they are different in kind. They are logical data base design errors.

When a data base is capable of reflecting real world conditions, it can be said to model reality. A successful data base will provide a better model than an unsuccessful one, remembering that any data base will in all probability not be able to reflect every possible condition or every piece of information of interest.

## Flexibility

Reality changes over time—not only in content, but in form. Business conditions, legislation, procedures, and practices are all changing and many of these touch upon the information stored within the data base. So a data base which is capable of reflecting reality today may not provide a good model of the reality of tomorrow. To some degree, likely future changes can be incorporated directly into today's model, but only to the degree that we can anticipate them. On the other hand, as will be shown later, some data bases can be extended, altered and modified more easily than others. This property—the flexibility of the logical data base design—has nothing to do with the services offered by generalized data management software. It is concerned with the "hooks" provided for future possibilities and the design's provisions for localizing the impact of minor redefinitions.

## Clarity

Clarity is a property of a data base which enables us to apply the rules of interpretation in an understandable and unambiguous way. It means that complexity has not been introduced where none is warranted. Remember that the developers of data bases are free to represent information and provide the rules of interpretation as they see fit. A misguided developer might provide for a data item called "special condition flag," which is to be interpreted as follows: a value of 1 means the next data item is not the inventory balance as we have defined it to be elsewhere, but the inventory balance plus the sum of the withdrawals over the last week. If the value is 2, some other rule applies, and so forth. One could forcefully argue that this data base was indeed capable of reflecting actual conditions. But not clearly.

## Efficiency

Efficiency suggests many things when applied to a data base and as pointed out earlier, most of them have to do with physical characteristics. However, the logical design of a data base can be efficient as well. A design which minimizes the number of logical constructs (logical records, data elements, relationships) and yet preserves the other important characteristics of clarity and representation can be considered efficient. Even "logical" access to the data base can be measured, and certain designs will achieve more efficiency in this respect than others. Efficient designs often turn out to be the most general and yet succinct solutions to the data problems.

## Semantic Integrity

Finally, the capability of the data base to support the development of meaningful inferences reflects its semantic integrity. In many ways, the concept of semantic integrity resembles the concept of logical consistency—a global property of many assertions taken together. But it is important to note at once that a data base is quite capable of holding inconsistent and contradictory facts, so that the requirement for semantic integrity is far more subtle than the requirements levied by logic alone.

In using a data base, we wish to be able to compound simple relationships into long complex ones—and to be able to do so meaningfully. For example, if A is related to B, and B is related to C, and X is a datum about C, then we want to be able to attach X to ABC and affirm some meaningful assertion that relates A and X. More significantly, it is essential to be able to do this without losing confidence that the resulting complex assertion is meaningful.

## BASIC NOTATION AND PRINCIPLES

The logical structure of a data base needs to be expressed in an appropriate language before it can be studied, refined and communicated to interested technical and non-technical people concerned with data base development. In this section, a subset of such a language for describing logical data structures is introduced. Called the "basic notation," this subset is nevertheless expressive enough to cover many of the data structuring problems one is likely to encounter in practice. The remaining cases are treated in Chapter 5, where the notation is approached from a more advanced point of view and extended to deal with several new classes of data structuring problems.

A language (or in this case a notation) for recording logical data structures provides a vehicle for jotting down certain selected facts about the data. As noted earlier, logical structuring is concerned with stipulating facts about the data that are far more fundamental than questions of the physical storage of the data. Consequently, the facts that are selected for expression in a logical design notation exclude, as much as possible, considerations of physical layout. Much of the responsibility for selecting the facts properly rests on the user of the language, as is true of any language. But the logical design notation helps out a little by failing to provide any notational support for such physical storage concepts as records, record delimiters, files, areas, format controls, pictures, addresses, blocks, tracks, devices, etc. It also makes no provision for the length or size of data items, for this too is a physical property. Finally, the notation is insensitive to "how many" items there are and regards them all as being of variable length.

Given that the notation excludes physical considerations and that data is abstracted from its physical embodiment, then what is there of substance to jot down? The best place to begin is with the acknowledgment that the data base will contain some reference to things in the real world: people, vehicles, parts, etc. Assume we wish to associate a height measure with each person, i.e., we wish to provide for recording each person's height in a logical data structure. The intention to associate each person with his/her height remains in force no matter how we choose to identify the people—by name, using a combination of date of birth and address, by Social Security number, by employee number, etc. The objective is also unaffected by the units used to measure height—feet and inches, feet and tenths, millimeters, deviation from the mean, and so on. And it is unaffected by how we elect to arrange the data (e.g., segregating files by sex, age, or height). All of these additional details rest on the basic strategic decision, which we record in the notation as:

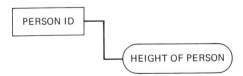

This is the decision to store, for each PERSON ID, the height of that person.

In developing logical data structures, the focus of attention is placed—with considerable discipline and rigor—on the fundamental strategic statements of intent, such as the one above. The substance of logical data base design involves the scrutiny of innocent-looking decisions like the one recorded above to make sure they accurately reflect the correct decisions relative to the problem at hand. This particular relationship has two serious (logical) omissions that would ordinarily need to be addressed and clarified. Ideally, the deficiencies can be detected during the early stages of analysis and design, for they are likely to cause trouble later.

To illustrate the concerns of logical data base design, let us probe the two flaws in this example.

## Time Dependency

The most important flaw is the failure to recognize that the height of a person is something that changes. If the data base contains data about young people, especially children, then their heights need to be associated with a date of measurement. Otherwise, the data base might store the idiotic notion that person X, now 18, is four feet tall because the last measurement was made at age 11. The changing relation between person and height forces attention to:

- The need to recognize that the relationship is not fixed but variable.
- The need to identify what the factors are on which the variation is dependent (date of measurement in this case).
- The need to devise possible remedies and decide upon one of them.

Observe that there are several remedies, each of which raises problems:

- Restrict the data base to adults only.
- Decide against maintaining the height, after all.
- Require that everyone be measured annually—perhaps possible in paramilitary contexts.
- Introduce date of measurement, keep most recent.
- Introduce date of measurement, keep them all as a history.

These remedies have far-reaching effects; they raise questions about the future flexibility of the data base, the purpose and justification for storing this data, the character of the environment in which the system operates, and the requirement for keeping a historical record of changes. These questions were raised by analyzing the *logical* properties of the requirement to store the height of the person.

## The Person Identifier

A second possible flaw in the PERSON ID–HEIGHT OF PERSON example is one which will receive considerable attention in later chapters as well. It concerns the PERSON ID that was used. We all know, without any doubt whatsoever, that we mean to associate a height like 5′ 10″ with the ID of the person just measured and who therefore possesses that height. If every person has a unique ID and no person has two ID's and no ID has been assigned to two persons and we can detect unassigned ID's, then (maybe) this record-keeping process will work.

However, at this level of logical data structuring, there is reason to be quite skeptical of such numbering systems. Logically, what the statement prescribes is an effort to associate a datum about a (real) person, his or her height, with another datum about a (real) person, the ID number. (There is no pretense that the ID number is 5′ 10″ tall.) Consequently, the processes of assigning ID numbers to people, of reusing and reassigning them, of deleting them, etc., have to be scrutinized and then controlled to validate the inference that the height and the ID number refer to the same person.

The severity of the issues raised in the logical design process (illustrated above by one of the most trivial relations imaginable) suggests the need for a notational scheme that keeps track of the design issues that have been faced and resolved, and which organizes the attack on the more complex issues that develop when simple relationships are combined.

In the discussion which follows, a series of definitions, notational conventions, and rules is developed. The basic notation is composed of very few notational elements:

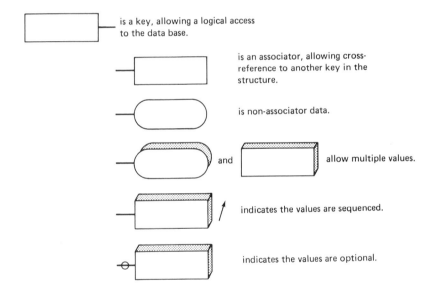

The names of data variables are placed inside these shapes and they are connected together to form diagrams of the data structure. These six elements, plus a "double-entry bookkeeping" rule that requires cross-references to be reversed (*See, See From*), are the totality of the basic notational system.

Only three claims are made for the notational scheme: (a) that it is reasonably free from nonlogical considerations, (b) that it has proved easy for people to understand, and (c) that it encourages the designer to build up data structures *rapidly*. The rules impart regularity and consistency of practice to the structures that result. They are rather like the rules of meter and rhyme for sonnets and limericks. Violation of the rules by a novice or an amateur usually leads to a result that is awkward. On the other hand, a skilled artist can break the rules and still create a powerful expression. We encourage the reader to test the rules and to explore what happens when departures are made. For the objective of logical data base design is to achieve understanding, insight, and clarity, *not* to force the problem into this or any other system of notation.

In the method of logical data base design presented here, we insist that each data variable takes on values chosen from a well-defined set of possible data values. Data variables like PERSON ID, LOAN NO., HEIGHT, and DATE take on data values appropriate to the variable: for example, LOAN NO. takes on data values that are loan numbers—not dates, not Social Security numbers, not uncontrolled strings of alphabetic text. In later chapters, rules governing how variables take on data values will be formulated more precisely. However, these more precise rules are only needed to cope with fine points of data definition, like the case in which "12-28-80" is both a date (December 28, 1980) and also a loan number (loan type 12, agency 28, the 80th loan).

Strictly speaking, the data variables being used should be defined with appropriate formality. Recall that in solving algebra problems, the first step is to write down a well-structured definition of the variables: "Let X be the number of dollars borrowed from John by Joe." Most teachers stress the need to state that X is a *number* and to include the units of measure in the definition. In working with data, we will have no need to represent data variables by single letters like X. Long names are used for data variables (strings like DATE OF BIRTH) instead of short ones (like D). Naturally, use of D would demand a definitional statement explaining that D is a data variable that takes on the value *date* and is used to signify the date of birth of some thing. On the other hand, use of the string DATE OF BIRTH to denote the variable conveys much of this information all by itself. Other information about the data variable may be recorded on separate forms (or in an automated data dictionary).

The logical design of a data base is recorded as a set of pictures in this notation. The pictures are called assertion templates, each relates two or more data variables. While the data variables play the role of "nouns" in the logical design language, the assertion templates can be thought of as sentences that relate the variables in a general way.

The simplest example of an assertion template, one containing but two data variables, has already been introduced:

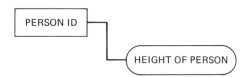

In this example, PERSON ID is the subject of the assertion, the verb "possesses a height measurement, with shoes on, of" is understood, and HEIGHT OF PERSON functions as the direct object. Assertion templates are built up from this basic form—just as compound and complex sentences are built up from simple constituents.

A single variable begins each assertion template, and is called the *key* of that assertion template. By a convention introduced below, this variable appears only once as the key of any assertion template in the data base design. The key is written in the upper left-hand corner of the picture, and is always outlined by a rectangular shape.

The key of an assertion template is generally a well-controlled identifier which identifies things about which there is to be substantial information recorded in the data base—information thoroughly detailed in the assertion template itself.

The example above which relates a PERSON ID to a HEIGHT OF PERSON shows a primitive assertion template. A primitive assertion template is a relationship declared between two data variables. The interpretation of the primitive two-variable template establishes the pattern for all the data structures covered by the basic notation. It reads: "To each and every value of [data-variable-1] (the key), there must be associated exactly one value of [data-variable-2], and the resulting pair of values is an assertion that the external world object identified by the first value bears the [relation-name] relationship to the external world object identified by the second value." The relation name is usually obvious from the context and the definition of the second element, so it does not need to be spelled out in most cases. In this notation, the relation is represented by the rightmost part of the connecting line between the two data variables.

There are four variants of this basic assertion template which it is useful to present side-by-side using the notation's conventions. These conventions, which concern optional and multiple values, are:

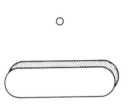

A small circle placed in front of the second (nonkey) variable means that values of the second variable are optional. Otherwise, as in the example above, a value must be present for each value of the key.

The use of a solid, three-dimensional figure signifies that multiple values of the variable are allowed. A plane shape, on the other hand, signifies that at most one value is allowed.

Allowing multiple values does *not* mean the same value may be repeated. These solid shapes represent sets of values—sets in the mathematical sense.

Note that at least one value of the second variable must always be present when a variable is mandatory, i.e., when there is no small circle.

The four combinations of the foregoing symbols exhibit slight differences in the markings on the second variable:

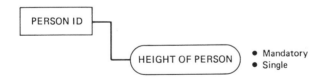

Every person *must* have *exactly one* height (the example previously used).

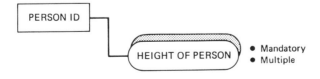

Every person *must* have *at least one* height but may have more than one. (Multiple heights could be due to taking a set of measurements, to study the measurement error, for example.)

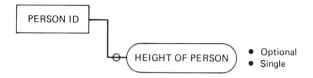

Every person *may* have *up to one* height. (Some people have none, but there are never multiple measurements.)

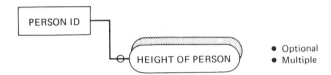

Every person *may* have *any number of* heights—from zero up to many. (This is the variant that allows the greatest freedom, since there are no restrictions on the second variable.)

Later on, we will introduce a variation on the shape of the figure surrounding the second variable name, allowing it to be a plane or solid rectangle instead of the rounded shapes shown above. This change in appearance in no way alters the interpretation of the small o (optional) and solid figure (multiple) conventions. The four basic forms shown above are exhaustive of all possible primitive assertion templates that can be defined.

As previously mentioned, more complex assertion templates can be built up. Other data variables which are related to the same first data variable (the key) can be attached to the vertical part of the connecting line, without limit.

The result is a set of assertions combined in coordination like this:

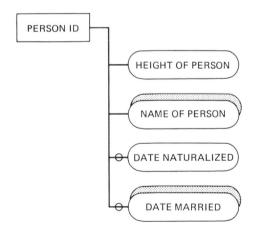

All possible patterns of optional and multiple coding are shown. The four cases exhibit, respectively, provisions for:

- Exactly one height
- One or more names (for stage names, aliases)

- Possibly at most one date of naturalization
- Zero to many marriage dates

The vertical sequence of presentation has no significance; the arrangement is arbitrary.

This "compound" structure is the result of combining four primitive assertion templates that begin with the same data variable in the subject position. Once compounded, the template reads (in short form) "Each $V_1$ is related to certain $V_2$ *and also* to certain $V_3$ *and also*. . . ." Thus, for a given value of the subject, all the primitive assertions hold independently, subject to the restrictions that the small o and the solid shading prescribe.

The compound structure makes it easy to obey the following rule in using the notation:

> Combine assertion templates whenever possible so that the same data variable is never written more than once on the top left-hand side of the page. When combining (i.e., compounding) two assertions templates, be certain that the subject data variable is really the same in the two assertions.

The final sentence form creates assertion templates that invoke more than two data variables in one relationship. The resulting structures increase both the expressive power and the complexity of the notation. In this form, called a cascade, a variable may be subsumed under any "higher" variable.

Here is a cascade containing six data variables.

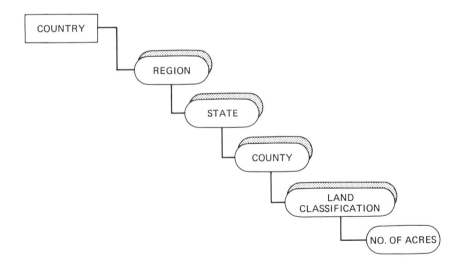

It indicates that: "Each country is broken into regions, each of which is made up of states, each of which is made up of counties, each of which has land in various classes, for each of which the number of acres is supplied." Naturally, given the fact that the lower values appear "for each" value above, all the variables in the cascade except the key and the last one are generally in solid outlines.

A final remark concerns "optional" variables in a cascade. Suppose COUNTY is optional and LAND CLASSIFICATION is subsumed under COUNTY as above. A declaration that LAND CLASSIFICATION is mandatory applies to its relationship to COUNTY and the rest of the cascade above COUNTY. If COUNTY (which is now shown as optional) does not appear, then LAND CLASSIFICATION will not appear. If, however, COUNTY does appear, then at least one LAND CLASSIFICATION *must* appear. Thus, an optional variable early in the cascade affects all the lower level variables subordinate to it.

The cascaded template structure and the compound template structure can be used together to form elaborate structures like the following.

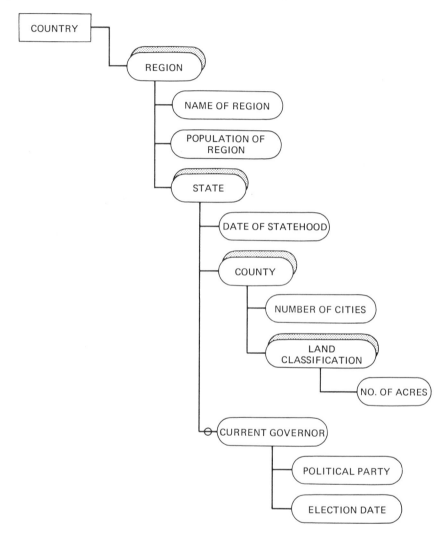

The last notational element to be discussed is both the simplest and the most powerful. An associator is a data variable, other than the key, which is placed in a plane or solid rectangle. It takes on values of a data variable which (almost always) occurs as a key in another assertion in the structure. All or any part of the data recorded under the cited key is "incorporated by reference" whenever the associator is used. The associators provide cross-referencing "pointers" that link assertion templates together, establishing the rich relational structure of the data base design. Remember, in a logical design, an associator is a cross-referencing *means*; there is no physical implication.

The use of associators as cross-reference mechanisms leads to an imposing increase in the capability of the basic notation. Indeed, the associator mimics the ability of a random access storage device to jump elsewhere to pick up data. Both the physical jump and the associator's implied logical jump are enormously useful when used judiciously. On the other hand, both can easily be misused. Consequently, the constraints placed on the use of associators need to be introduced immediately.

It is a general rule to reverse all associators: "If A points to B, then B points to A." This requires that the following pattern be established.

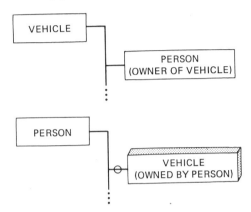

Actually, the reversal rule is exceedingly demanding, for it requires that each individual pair of *values* related by the associator be reversed. If Jim Myers owns a given green Chevrolet and an associator is used as above, then the logical data structure stipulates that:

Green Chevrolet "points to" Jim Myers (as owner Person).

Jim Myers "points to" the green Chevrolet (and to other specific vehicles he owns).

The rule states:

If an associator B appears in a template whose key is A, then an associator A must also appear in the template whose key is B, in such a fashion that the first relationship is expressed in inverse form by the second relationship (and vice versa) for all values of A and B that are so related.

The primary purpose of the associator reversal rule is to require consideration of the relationship that exists in the reverse direction. The vehicle-to-owner relationship, asserting that every vehicle has exactly one person who is owner (in this example) fails to inform us of some useful facts which are also known: that some persons are not vehicle owners, that some people own several vehicles. The reversal rule is first a discipline for making sure all the facts are recorded.

Adherence to the reversal rule provides a further benefit in that each assertion template (by virtue of "pointing back") exhibits all the keys that cite it as well as all those that are cited. Thus the assertion template shows all its linkages with other keys. This is particularly useful when one has occasion to consider amending or deleting the contents of an assertion template.

But the ultimate force of the reversed associators is that they set up a bidirectional *correspondence* between the two keys, whereas a reference in one direction only is a *mapping* from one key to the other. These correspondences are explored more fully in Chapter 6. Given these correspondences, which hold between the keys (i.e., between the entire set of persons and the entire set of vehicles in the data base), it becomes the responsibility of the data base to maintain the correspondence as defined, in the face of changes, disruptions, and the evolution of the data base. There are 16 different correspondences that can be set up between two keys, ranging from a one-to-one correspondence between all the A's and all the B's, to a many-to-many correspondence between some of the A's and some of the B's.

## USE OF THE NOTATION

As can be seen from the foregoing discussion, the result of developing a set of assertion templates is a set of pictures or charts that depict the relationships among the data variables. It is useful to summarize the notational elements in this section for reference. Attention will then turn to:

- Populating the data base, in which data values are substituted for the data variables.
- Executing transactions, in which data retrieval and update operations are illustrated.

### Review of Notational Elements

The elements of the notation are summarized as follows:

**Key**. A single data variable name written in a box on the left-hand side of the page, e.g.,

is the *key* of an assertion template. The key is the subject of all the primitive assertions in the assertion template. A given key appears no more than once on the left-hand side in a set of charts. The key plus data portrayed to its right comprise an assertion template. Each assertion template has exactly one key.

**Associator**. A data variable name written at the right and placed in a box is (almost always)* a reference to some key located on the charts.

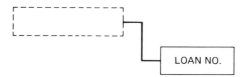

A data variable name which is used as an associator will appear elsewhere in the charts on the left-hand side as the key of an assertion template. The associator signifies that more data is available via logical access to the cited key.

*Exceptions to this provision which provide for reference to nonkeys are described in Chapter 2.

**Data**. On the other hand, some data is depicted as stored on the right-hand side without any need to look elsewhere, e.g.,

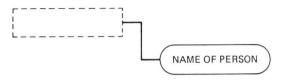

This is shown by rounded ends around the data variable name. This data variable will not appear on the left-hand side as a key.

**Sets**. Solid figures are used to make provision for more than one value of a data variable:

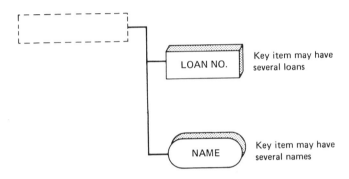

Unless explicit provisions are made, all these sets are assumed to be unordered, and never contain duplicate values.

**Mandatory/Optional**. A small circle that stands for "optional" may be placed on the horizontal connecting line to indicate that the data variable which follows does not need to be present:

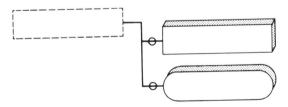

**Sequence**. It is standard practice to assume the variable values are stored in random order. If their sequence has significance, the practice is to show an arrow next to the solid shape.

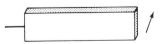

In a logical design, the use of sequence should be avoided. Where possible, leave the sequence unspecified.

## A Toy Data Base

With the notational elements established, it is useful next to combine them into a unified example, to illustrate how the templates relate to a data base populated with data, and to show how operations of access and processing can be performed on the result.

Consider the following three assertion templates that are concerned with people who obtain loans from various issuing agencies:

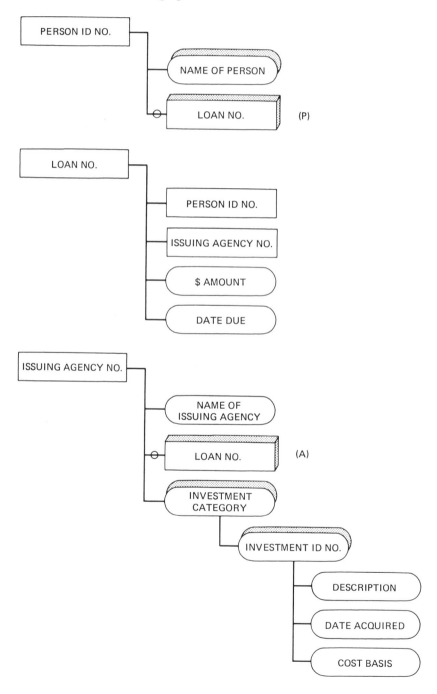

The first assertion template has PERSON ID NO. as its key and declares that there must be one (or maybe more than one) NAME OF PERSON associated with a given PERSON ID NO. It also provides for a set of LOAN NO.'s representing funds that the person has borrowed.

The second assertion template has LOAN NO. as its key and covers four types of primitive assertions with which the data base is concerned. The first assertion type relates each LOAN NO. to one PERSON ID NO., and its intent is to identify the party responsible for repaying the loan. The second assertion type relates each LOAN NO. to one ISSUING AGENCY NO., and its intent is to identify the office that issued the loan. The third assertion type records the face $ AMOUNT of the loan; the last one records the DATE DUE, on which the loan is to be repaid.

The final template in this small data base has ISSUING AGENCY NO. as its key, and it is a template for two primitive assertion types and a cascade. The first assertion type indicates the NAME OF ISSUING AGENCY in text form. The second assertion type identifies the loans that have been issued by the agency. Finally, the cascade is provided to encompass a list of the agency's portfolio of investments. These are first broken down by INVESTMENT CATEGORY (consisting here of the categories stocks, bonds, real estate, and others). Then each investment (which is identified by an internal INVESTMENT ID NO.) is characterized by a description, the date it was acquired, and its cost basis.

The various assertion templates that describe a logical data base are, of course, expressed in terms of data variables. When values are substituted for the variables, the structure is said to be "populated." A populated assertion template is called an *assertion instance* (or just an assertion).

The illustration pursued here is a straightforward process of supplying (fabricated) data that meets the foregoing specification. The result is presented in Figure 1-1 to exhibit how the specification relates to the details.

When the logical data structure is assumed to be populated with sample data in the fashion shown in Figure 1-1, it is possible to visualize a set of operations on the resulting data base.

The most important step is the *logical access*. To accomplish this, one must be in possession of a *value* of a particular key. Thus, to begin to use the populated data base, one must have either a PERSON ID NO., a LOAN NO. or an ISSUING AGENCY NO. When such a value is supplied, all of the information in the assertion for that key value is made available by a single logical access. Inspection of the contents of the assertion, no matter how complex it might be, does not involve another logical access. Only an access to a key is so counted.

Operations against the logical data base make extensive use of the associators and act upon them as sets. To illustrate, first make a single logical access for the loans outstanding to person 234-56-7890 using the PERSON ID as the access argument:

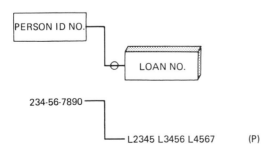

This yields the set P of three loans outstanding to this person.

Next, make a second logical access using Agency Number 42, looking for the loans they have issued:

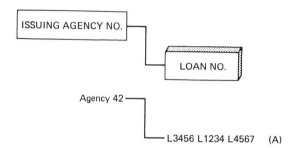

This yields the set A of three loans they have issued.

These two lists of loan numbers (associators) can now be intersected to obtain the LOAN NO.'s that are in *both* sets, namely L3456 and L4567.

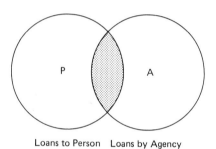

Loans to Person   Loans by Agency

The LOAN NO's (associators) appearing in both lists of LOAN NO.'s would be "loans to the given person by the given agency." Because these loan numbers are values of associators, and appear as keys, it is now possible to access the assertion which has LOAN NO. as the key in order to:

• Add up the total dollar amount of the loans to the given person by the agency. For L3456 and L4567, this total is $11,000.
• Find the earliest loan due. L4567 is due April 3, 1981.
• Print out all the loan data.

In summary, then, a logical data base permits access via key to any assertion instance, unlimited capability to select the data within an assertion instance, the ability to follow any associator by making a logical access to the key (with the guarantee that the value will be found), and the ability to perform unlimited set intersection and related operations on associator sets. While adding and deleting nonassociator data can also be accomplished, the rules for deleting or modifying associators and/or keys are complex enough that they must await the advanced discussions in Chapter 5.

PERSON ID NO.
    123-45-6789:  Smith, Alan     Smith, A. Marcus  ;  L1234
    234-56-7890:  Dow, Jane                      ;  L2345 L3456 L4567
    456-78-9012:  Drake, Susan                 ;

LOAN NO.
    L1234  :  123-45-6789  ;  Agency 42  ;  $1000  ;  Jan. 28, 1980
    L2345  :  234-56-7890  ;  Agency 36  ;  $2000  ;  Mar. 16, 1981
    L3456  :  234-56-7890  ;  Agency 42  ;  $8000  ;  Jun. 21, 1982
    L4567  :  234-56-7890  ;  Agency 42  ;  $3000  ;  Apr. 3, 1981

ISSUING AGENCY NO.
Agency 36  :  Comprehensive National Bank  ;  L2345

            Stocks:
                    ATT  (2000)  ;  Jan. 3, 1970  ;  $   64,410.77
                    UVW  (6000)  ;  Jun. 8, 1978  ;  $   120,010.31

            Bonds:
                    GM   (6199)  ;  Mar.3, 1975  ;  $ 1,627,125.20

            Real Estate:
                Star Bank
                Building         ;  Dec. 1, 1977  ;  $23,100,000.17

Agency 42  :  The Fisherman's Bank  ;  L3456 L1234 L4567
           (Investments Truncated)

Agency 43  :  The Star Bank       ;
           (Investments Truncated)

Figure 1-1. Populated assertion templates.

## SUMMARY

A data base is a body of information stored in a highly manipulable form. While a physical data base contains nothing but symbols, various levels of interpretation are provided. The physical level is concerned with the arrangement of the symbols in the storage media. The application level is intended to support various points-of-view. The conceptual (logical) level, which is the subject of this book, describes the entities and the relationships among them in a fashion that is more general than that of projects (application level) or implementations (physical level).

A logical design must reflect the external world. It must also exhibit flexibility, clarity, and efficiency and exhibit ways to preserve the semantic integrity of the data. To achieve these goals, data objects and relationships need to be examined with a critical eye.

In the notation for logical design used in this book, linking elements (keys and associators) are shown in boxes, while other data elements are shown in ovals. Shading is used to declare multiple valued elements; optional and sequenced data may also be declared. The notation is designed to facilitate rapid progress through the process of logical design. (This process is treated in Chapter 3; the notation is expanded in Chapter 5.)

From the basic elements listed above, complex data structures can be formed, including multilevel cascades and coordinated structures (in which many elements are related to the same key). The use of the notation was illustrated by designing and then populating a toy data base. These basic concepts and notational tools are sufficient for an understanding of the sample data base to be studied in Chapter 2.

## REFERENCES

1. Fry, James P., and Sibley, Edgar. "Evolution of Data-Base Management Systems," *Computing Surveys,* **8**: 1, March 1976.

   A useful background study of the history of data base management concepts and technology.

2. Tsichritzis, Dennis, and Klug, Anthony (eds.) "The ANSI/X3/SPARC DBMS Framework—Report of the Study Group on Database Management Systems," reprinted in *Information Systems*, **3**: 3, 1978.

   The X3/SPARC study group of the American National Standards Institute is charged with investigating issues of standardizing data base management systems. As a first step, the group has been developing a prototypical framework for data base management in which over 40 interfaces among DBMS components, activities, and organizational roles have been identified. These interfaces are then regarded as candidates for standardization.

   One of the most significant ideas supported by the study group is the need to define explicitly and manage a "conceptual" level description or schema of an organization's data base, in addition to the internal and external descriptions. The study group's report envisions an organizational function called the enterprise administrator being responsible for "systems synthesis" (determining what information flows and needs there are within the organization) leading to the definition of the Conceptual Schema. The Conceptual Schema contains:

   — definitions of information to be managed
   — security, integrity, and availability requirements
   — definitions of the relationship among the "information objects."

3. Nijssen, G. M. "Current Issues in Conceptual Schema Concepts," in *Architecture and Models in Data Base Management Systems*, North-Holland Publishing Company, 1977.

   This work provides additional commentary on the idea of a conceptual schema and the requirements for suitable conceptual schema framework. In the second half of the paper, the author introduces a proposed method and notational system for the conceptual schema. Many such systems have been proposed in the recent past, and the reader will want to become familiar with them. Some are similar to the scheme presented in this book, others differ considerably. Additional comparisons to other schemes are presented in Chapter 6.

4. Fry, J., and Teorey, T. "The Logical Record Access Approach to Database Design," *Computing Surveys*, **12**: 2, June 1980.

   This paper provides a perspective on logical data base design which differs from the presentation in this book. The authors define logical design as the design of a logical data base structure that is processable by the DBMS and describes the user's view of the data, while physical design is the selection of a physical structure such as the indexed sequential or direct access method.

   The presentation in this book, of course, excludes all considerations of a DBMS in logical design; moreover, it encourages the development of a single unified design from the start; other methods emphasize the integration of distinct "user views." The bulk of this paper is concerned with measuring the performance of a logical design according to three metrics:

   Logical Record Access—the sum of all accesses to all logical records required for all applications.

   Transport Values—the product of Logical Record Access for each record type and the raw data size of each record, summed over all record types.

   Storage Space—the product of raw data size for each record and the number of expected records in the data base, summed over all record types.

   Notice that the first two of these measures are very application-dependent. As such, they can only measure the performance of a design relative to a specific set of applications. Since a logical design is meant to transcend any specific set of applications (which will change over time), these measures are of limited use in logical design. But they can be used effectively during physical design.

5. Jones, Paul E. *Data Base Design Methodology: A Logical Framework*, QED Monograph Series, No. 3, 1976.

   Introduces the notation developed in this book.

# 2

# The New Plants Division Data Base—
# An Example

## INTRODUCTION

One of the characteristics of modern data bases, especially so-called integrated, corporate data bases, is the variety of detail they contain and therefore the variety with which the data base designer must contend. This chapter describes a fairly comprehensive example of a logical data base design and endeavors both to portray this detail and to convey a sense of typical design complexity to the reader. Other authors have tended to make use of simplified data examples to illustrate specific points about data base design—indeed we shall do so later on, drawing where appropriate from portions of the larger example about to be described. But if we were to rely *only* on such simplified examples, we would miss two significant lessons. One is that the data base designer must be prepared to deal with a high degree of complexity and detail. The other is that subtle but difficult design issues arise only when we look at real, complex problems, and not when we restrict discussion to hypothetical, simplified examples. The reader is therefore urged to avoid the natural temptation of skimming over the example; instead we urge the reader to study it in some detail before proceeding to the next chapter.

First, we will describe the overall situation which the data base example is meant to address; this description will cycle through the problem several times, in increasing levels of detail. Following this, at the end of the chapter, are a set of schematic diagrams which depict the logical data base design. In these schematics, we utilize the notational scheme which was presented in Chapter 1, although a few advanced features are included which will not be fully explained until Chapter 5.

As noted in Chapter 1, data elements appearing in rectangular figures are to be considered keys, those in oval figures are not. In either case, the appearance of depth to the figures indicates multiple occurrences. Explicit definitions of data element, key, and other terminology will be delayed until a later chapter. And discussion of the initial processes by which a problem statement is translated into a design, a process we call factoring, is addressed in the next chapter. This chapter is restricted to an explanation of the design itself.

The example is based on a real (but anonymous) company's data base plans. In practice, the facts and objectives so conveniently summarized here must first be culled from hundreds of sources—some of which are documents, most of which are experienced people who need to be interviewed. Except for editorial condensation and selective changes to preserve the company's anonymity, the example is quite real. It is representative, in its complexity, of the kind of problems a data base design team is expected to analyze.

## THE NEW PLANTS DIVISION

The illustrative company is a large U.S.-based conglomerate, headquartered in New Jersey, which does a significant amount of overseas business. This is especially true of the New Plants Division which concerns us in this example.

The New Plants Division designs and builds factories (plants) for client companies. The other divisions of the conglomerate are occupied with other kinds of work that has little to do with factory construction (like transporting cotton on barges, building farm machinery, etc.). Yet we cannot ignore the existence of the other divisions completely. There is, first of all, a strong, centralized corporate accounting system in place. This automated system must interface with the sample data base. Other centralized services, like Purchasing, also cross divisions. It is fortunate for this example that, except for these centralized control and service functions, the division has few current contacts with other divisions. But it must be acknowledged that the conglomerate has a strong history of growth and has a record of making successful acquisitions. Consequently, a new company could be acquired at any time, presumably to become another division. Such an acquisition might lead to a situation requiring heavy cross-divisional linkages at some future time. But there are few now.

The New Plants Division, which is in the business of designing and constructing factories, specializes in constructing factories that are materials-processing operations. The business involves major contracts with client companies. First, the client company decides it is ready to go into production with a new chemical process. Naturally, this decision follows a significant amount of research, pilot plant testing, and analysis regarding the plant location. The client company has a clear idea of the factory or plant it needs—typically a huge industrial complex which will consume trainloads of ingredient raw materials and produce large amounts of the product. (We shall have no need here to know about the interior chemical process in detail.) This client company enters into a contract with the New Plants Division to design and build a carefully specified plant in the stated place. The New Plants Division contracts to design and then to deliver a plant in working order on a targeted date for an appropriate fee. The price of such a contract is in the tens of millions of dollars. The design and construction work typically takes several years to complete.

While the design phase of the contracted work is heavily paper-oriented (the development of drawings, blueprints, diagrams, specification sheets, materials lists, etc.), the construction phase, like any typical construction project, is concerned with the management of physical things. Construction crews will be at work laying concrete, setting up girders, connecting up pipes, wiring the lighting system, and installing hundreds of motors throughout the plant. Units of heavy machinery (bulldozers, cranes, etc.) will need to be deployed. All of this vigorous construction activity needs to be scheduled and carefully managed on an hour-by-hour basis.

The New Plants Division has a dozen such contracts in progress at any given time— some in design, others in various stages of construction—in the U.S. Use of a data base is contemplated in part because there are observable similarities across projects, both current projects and past projects already completed. Some of these similarities are similarities of design. (Two plants that perform substantially the same process can easily be so similar that experience with building the first one is an excellent basis for estimating the next one.) Other similarities arise in the construction phase—since every factory has a foundation, a roof, a ventilation system, etc. Because the New Plants

Division has standard approaches to most such tasks, these large units are often comparable even though the factories they go into have radically different purposes.

A data base is needed that will support the entire process of factory construction, collecting data on the design of the factory, planned efforts and actual costs, materials needed and actually used, etc. This is to be done in such a way that past experience can be used in estimating (or evaluating) current efforts.

## DATA BASE REQUIREMENTS

### Plant Design Data

The data base needs to contain, in great detail, the information considered to be the *design* of a plant. This plant design should include the various systems, be they material-handling systems (e.g., conveyor belts), piping systems (for water, chemicals, steam, gas, fuel oil, etc.), or wiring systems (lighting, power, alarm, and control circuits). In principle, the plant *design* states in detail *what* is to be constructed at the customer's site.

Naturally, such a plant design identifies various parts and assemblies that go into the plant (motors, valves, circuit boxes, light fixtures, floor gratings, and vessels in which the chemicals are mixed, heated, etc.). These are all identified by "item numbers" of various kinds. Similarly, materials (pipe, I-beams, concrete) are required and called for in the design. Again, established numbering systems exist. Since many of the parts, fixtures, machines and other items in a plant are purchased from vendors, the New Plant Division's number often needs to be supplemented by the vendor's number. Also the client company (who will, after all, be running and maintaining the plant for 30–50 years) has his *own* numbering system too. Thus the items in a plant design are rather thoroughly numbered, as are the drawings which depict appropriate portions of the plant. The drawings are considered to be part of the plant design.

### Other Requirements

Four very serious requirements are overlaid on the foregoing body of design-related data.

- First, the data base is meant to handle not just one plant design but all the ongoing projects. This is required (a) because of similarities between projects, (b) because of their interference patterns in competing for resources and (c) because the value of the information in the data base is maximized by completeness of coverage.
- The system has to support such plant designs through all stages of the project cycle. Obviously, in the early stages of project planning, only a preliminary, embryonic sketch of the plant is available. Later, there is a partial plant design in which, for example, the detailed characteristics—even the item numbers—of some equipment items have been decided, while others remain unspecified. Much later, during construction, new problems arise, especially those of tracking changes to the design. Though the components have all been detailed, there are still changes being made. (A steam pipe too close to a ladder is relocated for safety reasons, an important pump proves to be unavailable and the subsystem is redesigned to use two smaller ones; the client company changes the specification to

comply with a new pollution-control regulation, etc.). The plant *design* must be perceived as dynamic, a fact which has technical impact on the data base. However, there is no requirement for the data base to retain (on line, so to speak) a history of the design changes. It just has to keep up with the current state of the design.

- The New Plants Division is highly advanced in the use of computers to assist in the massive engineering calculations required to undertake such projects. Programs for calculating pipe stress and for the "automated design" of piping systems, electrical systems, edifices, structures, and concrete members are in common use. The data base must admit the continued use of such programs. Notice that such programs are used most heavily in the early stages when the plant design details are most meager. But they may also be used very late in the project's life-cycle when a redesign problem comes up.

- Finally, the data base must tie into a scheduling system. (The users need to know that a particular motor ought to arrive at the site on day 10, which means that it should be shipped on day 9, inspected and accepted for shipment on day 8, ordered on day 3, based on bids evaluated on day 2, which were solicited on day 1, etc.) The business is conducted with detailed schedules of this kind; obviously thunderstorms, strikes and unforeseen delays cause the schedule, too, to be dynamic. Scheduling is already highly automated, and the New Plants Division (like many construction companies) is staffed by qualified virtuosi who keep the project moving along smoothly no matter what happens. For various reasons, the data base is to *link* to the scheduling system and is not expected to encompass the schedule.

## OVERVIEWS OF THE NEW PLANTS DIVISION DATA BASE

The New Plants Division data base which meets the foregoing requirements is extensive, detailed, and complicated even at the logical level. In order to cope with the many details, the description of the data base contents is preceded by a series of introductory overviews, each of which explains the data base in increasing depth. The final subsection, which contains the fine structure of the data base at the data element level, relies on these overviews for providing the context and the rationale for the logical arrangement that was chosen.

### Broadest Overview (First Level)

At the broadest level, which we call the first level, the data base is an integrated collection of data about six kinds of things (Figure 2-1).

- PLANTS and their Sites
- CONTRACTS—their Administration
- PLAN of Work and Actuals
- COMPONENTS used in building the plant, including items, drawings, materials, etc.
- VENDORS and related Purchasing activity, especially related to items
- SYSTEMS in a Plant, also especially related to items

All of the data contained within one or another of these groupings is usually linked and related to data appearing in other groupings. The connecting lines in the figure show only the "principal" connections between the groupings.

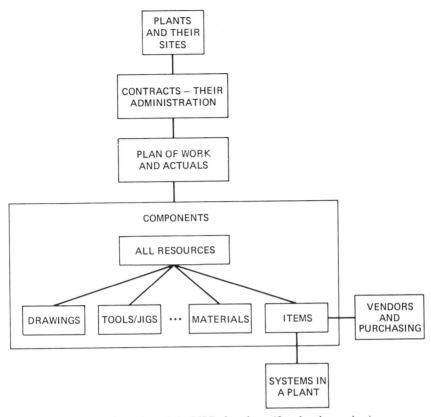

Figure 2-1. Overview of the NPD data base (first level overview).

Each data grouping shown in the first level diagram contains answers to some very broad questions.

*What kind of plants do we build, and where?*
The data base contains a grouping of data concerning "PLANTS and their Sites." This is primarily data about the various types of plants which the division is prepared to construct. It includes standard approaches and past experience and serves to organize the historical record. It also includes demographic, geographic and economic data about the various locations where plants have been or may be built. The fact that a particular kind of plant is right now being constructed at a given site provides the natural linkage to Contracts shown in the diagram.

*What contracts are there? Where do they stand?*
In the grouping called "CONTRACTS—their Administration," one finds data for each of the contracts that the New Plants Division is concerned with. Administrative data covers: stages of authorization (needed if the work proceeds in phases or if there are changes and amendrnents to the original contract), the status of various design, engineering and construction activities in progress, and the records of the task assignments that have been apportioned to the Division's managers at various levels. The data needed for these administrative purposes is highly important, but it is not voluminous.

*What is the Plan of Work? The schedule? Projected resource needs?*
A voluminous body of data called "PLAN of Work and Actuals" is shown at the middle of the figure. For each contract, as covered above, there may actually be several plans for how to accomplish it. It will be shown later that the contract is finely subdivided into a network of "work packages," each of which is likely to need items, drawings, and other resources when the plan of work is executed. The plan of work for each contract is organized to provide strong support to decision makers concerned with scheduling and those concerned with planning resource requirements. Actual expenditures of resources and money are held in relation to the approved plan (budget).

*What are the Components used in building a plant?*
The subgroups labeled "Drawings," "Items," "All Resources," etc., contain additional facts and details appropriate to these "components" of the plant-construction process. They are shown as separate groups because they have notably distinct data qualities. Drawings, for example, are related to each other in a (so-called) drawing tree, with lower-level drawings showing details within higher-level ones. Some drawings cross contracts, most do not. The data about items, on the other hand, has a more complex set of data qualities. First, the items are actually constructed from other items which may or may not be purchased from vendors, may or may not be late, etc. Second, the items are physically placed in the plant. Third, they are hooked together to make systems. For these reasons, it is useful to discuss items and drawings differently. Observe that "Materials" (like bar stock, concrete) have no assembly structure like that just discussed for drawings and items, while "Tools/Jigs" are not fully consumed and may be reused. The subgroup "All Resources" covers all these various types. As noted earlier, these resources are planned very carefully by the Division, and it is routine for a given resource to be needed across most, if not all, of the contracts.

*Where can we get items?*
"Vendors and Purchasing" contains extensive data on the sources (vendors) from which an item could be obtained as well as details of the purchasing, ordering, follow-up, expediting, and payment processes that follow once the item has been ordered.

*How is the plant put together?*
"SYSTEMS in a Plant" is a very complicated structure that carries information on how all the items in the plant are hooked together. For overview purposes, it is useful to perceive this block as containing the entire Plant Design. Because of its intricacy, the discussion of its contents is postponed until later.

### Restricted Overview (Second Level)

The example which we shall develop in this book does not cover the entire data base introduced in the preceding section. The grouping that pertains to PLANTS and their Sites has been truncated. So have Drawings and the grouping called VENDORS and Purchasing. The reader needs to be aware that these data groups are part of the data base, and there will be occasional mention of the connections that exist to such data. But the contents of the data groupings will not be detailed further. This permits attention to focus on a smaller number of data groupings.

Figure 2-2 shows the data groupings that remain in the restricted (second-level) overviews. There are four major groupings shown:

- CONTRACTS—their Administration
- PLAN of Work and Actuals
- COMPONENTS—especially Resources and Items
- SYSTEMS in a Plant

The first three of these provide the cornerstone of the data base design, and they will be discussed during this second-level overview. The Plant Design (SYSTEMS in a Plant) will be discussed in the third-level overview which follows.

The second level overview diagram is redrawn in Figure 2-3 to show the three major keys that are contained within these groupings: CONTRACT, RESOURCE, and WORK PACKAGE.

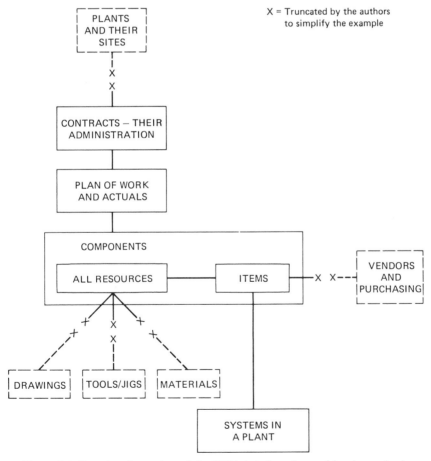

Figure 2-2. Restricted overview of the NPD data base (second level overview).

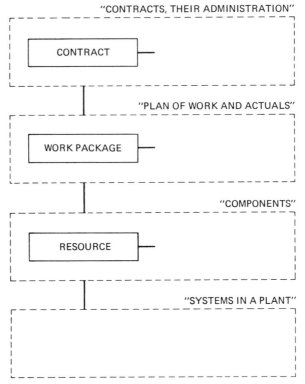

Figure 2-3. The most important keys in the second level overview of the NPD data base.

- CONTRACT is the set of all past, current, and future contracts in the New Plants Division. Each contract, as previously noted, covers the design, engineering, and construction of an entire factory or plant.
- RESOURCE signifies the set of all resources used in executing such contracts. Each distinct resource is uniquely identified. Included in the resources are:

  — Individual drawings and other documents needed
  — The various items (both manufactured and purchased items)
  — Various categories of skilled and unskilled labor, including specific crews
  — Raw materials (concrete, beams, etc.)
  — Selected units of heavy machinery
  — Tools and jigs (like scaffolding, for instance)

  These resources also fall into classes which the data base recognizes.
- WORK PACKAGES represent a subdivision of the work to be done under a contract. To a first approximation, WORK PACKAGES have the following properties:

  — When they are all marked "finished" then the CONTRACT is "finished"
  — Most WORK PACKAGES "produce" a specific thing, be it a drawing or a well-defined numbered item (part)

These three major keys (CONTRACT, RESOURCE, WORK PACKAGE) are havily interrelated and have a great deal of effect on each other. Each CONTRACT is made up of a set
of WORK PACKAGES. Most WORK PACKAGES "produce" drawings or items. But every
WORK PACKAGE uses resources: Figure 2-3 shows a link to RESOURCE. Notice that the
set of CONTRACTS would be considered company-wide information while the WORK
PACKAGES are "within contracts." Notice also that the RESOURCE data is important both
within CONTRACTS and across CONTRACTS, for management is interested both in

- Amount of material used so far in this contract (RESOURCE within CONTRACT)
- Utilization or projected need, over all contracts, of the material (RESOURCE across
  CONTRACTS)

It is useful to show, from the perspective of an overview, the specific relationships
that the data base maintains among these major keys. These relationships, which have
been stated before in different words, are as follows:

- A CONTRACT is subdivided into a set of WORK PACKAGES. In the notation used for
  showing the logical data base design in detail, this relationship is portrayed by:

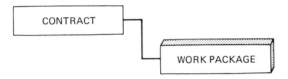

  The CONTRACT is shown in the key position, since CONTRACT *bears* the relationship
  in question. The relationship name is "is subdivided into." WORK PACKAGE is borne
  this relationship.* The three-dimensional box around WORK PACKAGE is to show
  that there may be many WORK PACKAGES per CONTRACT.
- Each WORK PACKAGE makes use of a set of RESOURCES.
  This is portrayed by:

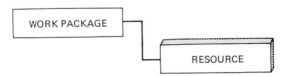

  The figure is to be interpreted similarly. Each of the RESOURCES needed by the
  WORK PACKAGE is listed in the solid box, and it will be natural, later on, to qualify
  the relationship by showing "how much" of each RESOURCE is needed.
- Each WORK PACKAGE belongs to exactly one CONTRACT.
  This relationship, which is the reverse of the first one presented, is portrayed by:

*Of course, there is also a reverse relationship which will be duly noted later.

Notice that the right-hand box is not three-dimensional, to signify that there are not many CONTRACTS per WORK PACKAGE.

• Finally, each RESOURCE is used by many WORK PACKAGES (both within and across CONTRACTS).

This is portrayed by:

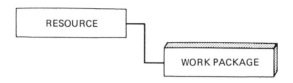

When these elementary relationships are combined, the result is:

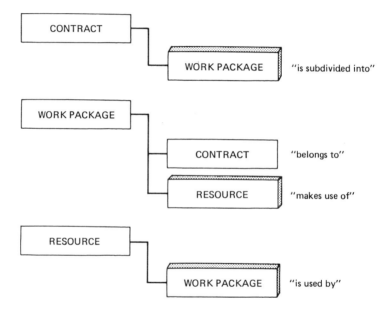

In narrative form: A CONTRACT is subdivided into many WORK PACKAGES. A WORK PACKAGE, in turn, belongs to one CONTRACT and makes use of many RESOURCES. A RESOURCE, in turn, is used by many WORK PACKAGES.

In the detailed logical data base definition presented at the end of this chapter, these major organizing relationships are not so clearly visible. First, there are hundreds of other relationships also present in the data base. Second, there is a need to make these relationships less direct than they appear at the summary level. For example, the set of WORK PACKAGES in a CONTRACT needs to be subdivided in several ways. One of these criteria is STATUS, differentiating the completed work from work in progress and from future activities. Similarly, there are several sets of RESOURCES needed for accomplishing a WORK PACKAGE, depending on which plan is followed. The introduction of these indirect relationships is a necessary refinement. But the overview shows the fundamental linkages that the data base maintains.

### Key-Level Overview (Third Level)

Figure 2-4 provides a "key-level overview" of the data base. That is, it shows all the keys (except those that have been truncated by the authors to simplify the example) including the more important associators. The individual items of data stored under the keys—like accounts payable data under CONTRACT, or AMOUNT OF RESOURCE under RESOURCE are omitted. The diagram shows all the direct connections between these keys that the data base maintains.

The nature of the relationship that exists between two keys connected by a line in the key-level overview is indicated by the direction of the arrow at one end of the line. The relationship is such that the entity represented by the box at the end of the line without the arrow stands in a one-to-many relationship with the entity represented by the box pointed to by the arrow. Thus, there is a one-to-many relationship between RESOURCE CLASS and RESOURCE. Note also that relationships between an entity and itself may be depicted on the key-level overview, and many-to-many relationships are indicated by arrows at both ends of a connecting line.

As will be clear from the complete logical design to come, each box in the overview corresponds to a key or an associator in the detailed design; the boxes are numbered in a fashion consistent with the numbering scheme used in the assertion charts at the end of this chapter.

Unlike previous overviews presented in this chapter, whose purpose was wholly introductory, the key-level overview can be considered a *summary* of the definition in the logical data base. In practice, the key-level overview should be constructed *after* the detailed assertions have been developed, never before. Rules for doing this are given in Chapter 6.

CONTRACTS—Their Administration. This major data grouping contains the four major keys itemized below that are shown in Figure 2-4. It reflects the breakdown of a contract into physical components (AREA and SUBAREA of a plant) and into administrative components (CONTRACT and CONTRACT AUTHORIZATION).

CONTRACT (1.0)
Each CONTRACT (1.0) is divided into a number of CONTRACT AUTHORIZATIONS (1.14) which authorize a phase of work to proceed. It is also composed of a number of AREAS (1.9).

CONTRACT AUTHORIZATION (1.14)
The WORK PACKAGES (2.0) are grouped and separated by CONTRACT AUTHORIZATION (1.14). The CONTRACT AUTHORIZATION (1.14) represents a stage in the funding of the effort by the customer. Each CONTRACT (1.0) generally consists of several CONTRACT AUTHORIZATIONS (1.14)—for planning, design, site preparation, and construction. In later phases of the contract, "authorized additions" representing an authorized change to the plant are common. The CONTRACT AUTHORIZATIONS (1.14) form mutually exclusive, collectively exhaustive subsets of the WORK PACKAGES (2.0) under a CONTRACT (1.0).

AREA (1.9)
Each CONTRACT represents a construction site which, early in the design process, is surveyed and subdivided into three-dimensional AREAS (1.9). They are actually "volumes" which extend upward at least one story. The AREAS (1.9) tend to be quite large: a plant has from 3 to 20 AREAS (1.9).

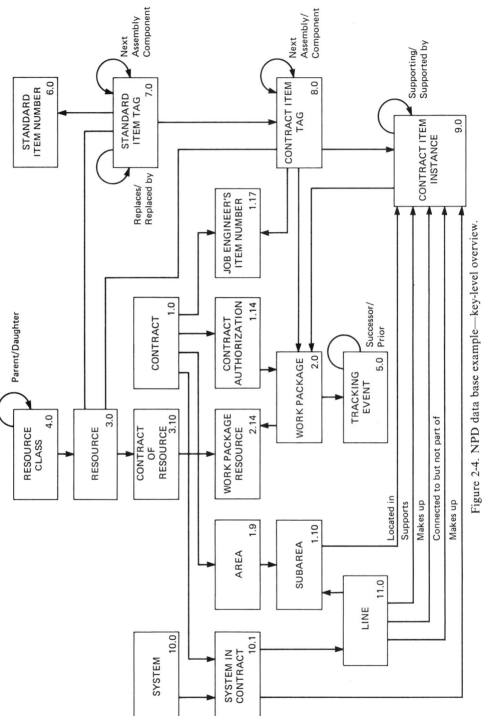

Figure 2-4. NPD data base example—key-level overview.

SUBAREA (1.10)

Each AREA (1.9) is subdivided into as many SUBAREAS (1.10) as needed. Usually a SUBAREA (1.10) is a physical compartment like a room, but large open spaces may also be subdivided for administrative convenience.

PLAN of Work and Actuals. Data about plans for the usage of resources to accomplish the work, as well as the actual resources consumed, is contained in the keys RESOURCE (3.0) WORK PACKAGE (2.0) and TRACKING EVENT (5.0). Of particular importance is the ability to record several different plans for utilizing resources, and the need to examine resource projections across an entire contract (or all contracts) by plan type.

Before examining each of the keys, the following example will illustrate the kinds of plans and departures from plans that are carried in a work package, and it will also clarify what sort of things these resources are.

Consider a WORK PACKAGE (2.0) devoted to the installation of the front door on the main office building—a task we want to describe in terms any homeowner would recognize. Here is the data, recorded under the "budget" Resource Plan Type.

RESOURCE PLAN TYPE—BUDGET

| Resource | Amount |
|---|---|
| Door, 3′ × 7′, wood #6BJ-25-36B | 1 |
| Installation Kit, door, #6BJ-25-36B-IK | 1 |
| Crew #36B (Door installers) | 1.4 (hours) |
| Primer, gray, #PJ3-24-8 | 1 (pint) |
| Paint, blue, #XB3 (Special pigment) | 1 (quart) |
| Crew #8 (Exterior Trim Finishers) | 2.5 (hours) |
| Security Kit, exterior door, #6BJ-13-2796 | 1 |
| Crew #12J (Security) | 1.2 (hours) |

For illustrative purposes, the various *types* of resources (labor, paint, kits, items) are distinguished in the item description text. Actually, the resource type is coded and is held "centrally" as a property of each of the listed RESOURCES (3.0). Also held "centrally" is the unit of measure, though it is included above in parentheses in the descriptive text.

In this data base, one Resource Plan Type coded "current official plan" has additional data attached to show what actually happened. By design, the "actual" data is held right along with the "plan" data since it is obviously necessary to make frequent comparisons of the plan against the actuals. But there are several differences in the data. First, the actuals (unlike a plan) contain figures both for the amount of the resource expended and for its dollar value. This is because prices change with time and the New Plants Division has a policy of accruing the costs at (and as of) the date they are incurred. The second difference also relates to the treatment of time: each expenditure of a resource may represent a small time period (e.g., a day) within the span of the WORK PACKAGE (2.0). The plan covers the entire interval, but the actuals are broken down more finely into specific time periods.

Actual work to install the door pursuant to the plan shown above will now be illustrated to suggest the logical data structure involved.

*Narrative:* There was no work performed on the given WORK PACKAGE (2.0) until Week 32. The prior weeks were devoted to preparing the site, constructing the building, fitting the door jamb, allowing the mortar to set, and waiting for the arrival of the needed resources. No updates were recorded through the end of Week 31. During Week 32, the following entry was made.

ACTUALS (WEEK 32)

| Resource | Amount | $ Value |
|---|---|---|
| Door, 3′ × 7′, wood, #6BJ-25-36B | 1 | 28.50 |
| Installation Kit, door, #6BJ-25-36B-IK | 1 | 7.95 |
| Door, 3′ × 6′11″, wood, #6BJ-25-34J | 1 | 31.98 |
| Crew #36B (Door Installers) | 6.2 (hr) | 162.00 |

*Narrative:* In Week 32, the crew tried to install the first listed door as planned, found it to be too large and attempted to trim it to size. Apparently, the door jamb opening had set on a slight tilt. Too much material needed to be trimmed from the door and it split. The door was discarded in favor of a smaller door. The same installation kit was reused, however. The process of fitting the door took far more labor than was planned. No additional entry was made until Week 35.

ACTUALS (WEEK 35)

| Resource | Amount | $ Value |
|---|---|---|
| Paint, blue, #XB3 (Special Pigment) | 1 (pt) | 3.75 |
| Crew #8 (Exterior Trim Finishers) | 1.0 (hr) | 5.00 |

*Narrative:* After waiting two weeks for good weather, the door was painted blue. The substitute door was already preprimed, so there was no need to apply the gray primer that was planned. The next entry appeared in Week 38.

ACTUALS (WEEK 38)

| Resource | Amount | $ Value |
|---|---|---|
| Security Kit, exterior door, #6BJ-13-2796 | 1 | 95.00 |
| Crew #12J (Security) | 1.2 (hr) | 27.80 |
| Crew #8 (Exterior Trim Finishers) | 0.5 (hr) | 8.00 |

*Narrative:* This week, the security kit was applied exactly in accordance with the plan's expectations. On completion, the Exterior Trim Finishing crew returned to touch up the paint and complete the job. Notice that the painters were granted a raise since Week 35: the crew is now billed at $16 per hour instead of $15 per hour.

The work package has had an interesting history. It began as an ill-defined chunk of work that became quite specific when the plan (the budgeted resources) was decided. We skipped over the process of plan revision, and the work package began to accumulate actuals. These resource expenditures departed from the plan for obvious reasons, and the exercise illustrated some of the things to be expected: parts were substituted for parts in the plan, quantities different from the plan were used, some resources (the original door) were destroyed during the activity described by a work package, and certain stable parameters that ordinarily change rather infrequently (like the wage rate) showed their habit of undergoing impromptu change in the middle of a work package. Naturally, the example is a simplified portrayal of the work package used in the NPD data base, but it serves to give the general idea.

WORK PACKAGE (2.0)

The work required to fulfill a CONTRACT (1.0) is subdivided into small manageable units represented by WORK PACKAGES (2.0). The WORK PACKAGE (2.0) is a task or activity which can cover any phase of the work, though it must be wholly contained within an CONTRACT AUTHORIZATION (1.14), and hence within a CONTRACT (1.0). Often, a WORK PACKAGE (2.0) produces a tangible item within the plant: a CONTRACT ITEM identified by its TAG (8.0) or a CONTRACT ITEM INSTANCE (9.0). The tag applies in the case where the item is produced but not installed, and the instance applies in the case where the product is installed at the appropriate location in the plant.

In addition to producing outputs, the WORK PACKAGE (2.0) also consumes inputs, i.e., RESOURCES (3.0). In practice, several lists of these RESOURCES are carried which show different resource requirements. One listing may reflect the current official plan—if it has been prepared. Others may reflect the original estimate, the final estimate, the budget, and various contingency plans.

Notice that these plans can employ *different resources* in different quantities to accomplish the same work. The original estimate for site preparation provides for bulldozers, dynamite and a blasting crew on the assumption that ledge may be encountered; the later plan shows no need for the blasting crew, but there is instead a need for trucks and imported fill to even out the site. Such differences between resource requirements for the same task are seldom radical, and the primary difference appears in the amount of each of the resources needed.

An inventory of all the RESOURCES (3.0) used by a particular plan type is kept by CONTRACT (1.0) (across all WORK PACKAGES (2.0)) under CONTRACT OF RESOURCE (3.10). The same type of data is also held for each WORK PACKAGE (2.0). In each case, the resource usage data are subdivided by Resource Plan Type to separate firm estimates from various other kinds of plans. Thus the individual RESOURCES (3.0) required for the WORK PACKAGE (2.0) are listed according to the planning assumptions conveyed by the Resource Plan Type.

TRACKING EVENT (5.0)

An ordered set of TRACKING EVENTS (5.0) is attached to each WORK PACKAGE (2.0). These are basically transactions which track the status of the WORK PACKAGE (2.0) and which are needed for historical purposes. Other lesser transactions which report the expenditure of labor and other resources are not TRACKING EVENTS (5.0); they are simply posted to the appropriate data elements in the data base. Notice that it is logically necessary to examine previous TRACKING EVENTS (5.0) in order to reconstruct the chronology of events. It is not logically necessary to reconstruct how much labor had been expended up to an arbitrary previous date. Thus the TRACKING EVENT (5.0) series is a logical construct which is above and beyond the audit trails, transaction logs, rollback capabilities and similar features of data base management systems. Indeed, the same audit trails, etc., would apply to the TRACKING EVENT (5.0) itself as to any other key under discussion here.

Components. The New Plants Division data base contains a large number of keys that refer to components needed for the construction of a plant. The major ones are listed here.

RESOURCE CLASS (4.0)

Across all CONTRACTS (1.0), RESOURCES (3.0) are grouped into standard classes by a hierarchical coding system of the following general form

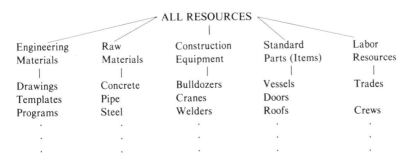

Individual RESOURCES (3.0) belong to the lowest level classes in this generalization hierarchy. Notice that it is an important purpose of this data base to support inquiries both across CONTRACTS (1.0) or within a CONTRACT (1.0). "What is the total amount (or $ value of) certain RESOURCES (3.0) expended—or planned—in a given time period?" This question is interesting both within CONTRACTS and divisionwide. The primary purpose of the RESOURCE CLASS (4.0) is to support the framing of such broad questions of management interest.

RESOURCE (3.0)

Each individual RESOURCE (3.0) is an item in one of the above classes and each is uniquely identified. Several examples of these RESOURCES (3.0) appear in the illustrations above. Sometimes a STANDARD ITEM TAG (7.0), which is a standard part used across contracts, is declared to be a RESOURCE (3.0). Such a part, like the door in the earlier example, may be needed as one of the inputs to the execution of a WORK PACKAGE (2.0). Similarly, a CONTRACT ITEM TAG (8.0), which is a specialized item applicable only to one contract, may also be declared a RESOURCE (3.0).

The data base maintains a significant amount of information about each of the thousands of RESOURCE (3.0) items being administered. Though it is not shown in Figure 2.4, the data base maintains by week within CONTRACT (1.0), a summary of the amount of the RESOURCE (3.0) actually expended across all WORK PACKAGES. In addition, the planned amount for that week is also held, and provisions are made for holding several planned amounts if several plans are under consideration.

Other data held "centrally" with each RESOURCE (3.0) include the items mentioned earlier: the text description of the RESOURCE (3.0), its unit of measure (hours, pints, quarts, etc.), and the current figures needed for establishing the standard cost of using the RESOURCE (3.0).

STANDARD ITEM NUMBER (6.0)

This is a standard part number—sometimes several part numbers for the same item—used across CONTRACTS (1.0) throughout the New Plants Division to identify commonly used (and most often purchased) parts. It is not a unique item identifier for reasons noted immediately below, but it is almost unique.

STANDARD ITEM TAG (7.0)

The STANDARD ITEM TAG represents one of the items used across contracts. A product structure is defined among the STANDARD ITEMS (7.0), by next assembly and component relationships: the blower may be a standard part, the motor may be a standard part, and the blower-motor assembly may also be a standard part. Furthermore, with the passage of time, the same STANDARD ITEM TAG (7.0) may accidentally be given different STANDARD ITEM NUMBERS (6.0).

When a STANDARD ITEM (7.0) is selected for inclusion in a plant by a plant designer, the STANDARD ITEM TAG (7.0) is linked to the CONTRACT (1.0) in the data base by defining a new object CONTRACT ITEM TAG (8.0). The CONTRACT ITEM (8.0) reflects the facts surrounding the usage of this standard part in the given contract. The STANDARD ITEM TAG (7.0) in contrast, represents facts that pertain to the item from a global, cross-contract point of view. Naturally, there are STANDARD ITEMS (7.0) not used on a given CONTRACT (1.0), and there are a great many CONTRACT ITEMS (8.0) that are not used across CONTRACTS (1.0), but are designed for only one CONTRACT (1.0). Thus they are not STANDARD ITEMS (7.0).

In this data base, the "global" object, STANDARD ITEM (7.0) is treated as a different object from the "local" object, CONTRACT ITEM (8.0). In another design, one might find the "local" object treated as a facet of the "global" one and carrying the same ID number, qualified by CONTRACT (1.0). Two factors made this alternate (and possibly more intuitive) approach inappropriate in the present case. One factor was related to the purchasing practices of the New Plants Division: they have a rule that only STANDARD ITEMS (7.0) could be purchased from vendors. Since these considerations have been truncated from the example, we merely note the influence in passing. Additionally, there is a need to delete "very old" CONTRACTS (1.0) and also to delete some "very new" CONTRACTS (1.0) that were estimated in depth but never consummated. The rigorous separation pursued here makes it evident that data associated with the CONTRACT ITEM (8.0) is to be deleted while data associated with the STANDARD ITEM (7.0) is to be retained.

Finally, each STANDARD ITEM TAG (7.0) may be declared to be a RESOURCE (3.0). As such, it may be an input to a WORK PACKAGE (2.0); it is never an output. This is a further difference between the STANDARD ITEMS (7.0) and the CONTRACT ITEMS (8.0) to be discussed further below.

JOB ENGINEER'S ITEM NUMBER (1.17)
Every item in the plant is assigned an external ID by the Job Engineer. The numbering system varies among CONTRACTS (1.0) and is only valid within a CONTRACT (1.0), reflecting the needs of the client's numbering schemes. These numbers appear routinely on work orders and other documents, and most items in the plant have markings on them that show the JOB ENGINEER ITEM NUMBER (1.17). Again, there exists the possibility that the Job Engineer will assign different JOB ENGINEER'S ITEM NUMBERS (1.17) to the same CONTRACT ITEM TAG (8.0).

CONTRACT ITEM TAG (8.0)
CONTRACT ITEM TAG (8.0) is a unique identifier for each component item in the plant. CONTRACT ITEMS (8.0) are organized in an extensive product structure: the component next-assembly relationships which hold between CONTRACT ITEMS (8.0) are part of the Plant Design. The complete "product structure" or design of a plant is thus represented as follows. At the highest levels of the design are CONTRACT ITEMS (8.0) which are unique to the CONTRACT (1.0). These may have component CONTRACT ITEMS (8.0) which also tend to be designed and hence manufactured to suit an individual CONTRACT (1.0). At lower levels of the design, we encounter CONTRACT ITEMS (8.0) which are (purchased or manufactured) standard parts. In this case, the CONTRACT ITEM TAG (8.0) refers to a unique STANDARD ITEM TAG (7.0). The lower level of the design is reflected by the component structure of the STANDARD ITEMS. An example is provided in Figure 2-5.

CONTRACT ITEMS (8.0) may act as RESOURCES (3.0), i.e., inputs to WORK PACKAGES (2.0), and they are also often outputs or by-products of WORK PACKAGES (2.0).

It is important to see that a CONTRACT ITEM (8.0) is covering a set of identical things—a set of electric motors that are indistinguishabie replicas, for example. The fact that 16 motors are needed in the plant is a property of the CONTRACT ITEM (8.0). The data base has another key, CONTRACT ITEM INSTANCE (9.0), in which each of the 16 motors is treated as an individual. The fact that a motor is placed at coordinates X, Y, Z is a property of the CONTRACT ITEM INSTANCE (9.0), as is the fact that this particular one has now been tested.

SYSTEMS in a Plant. In addition to being manufactured or fabricated into subassemblies and assemblies, the items in a factory are interconnected by "lines" (e.g., piping, conveyors, electrical circuits) into various operating "systems" (e.g., waste disposal, air-conditioning). This aspect of the plant design is represented by the three keys discussed below.

CONTRACT ITEM INSTANCE (9.0)
As noted above, the CONTRACT ITEM INSTANCE (9.0) represents one individual instance of the set of objects covered by CONTRACT ITEM TAGS (8.0). Most are products of WORK PACKAGES (2.0). All the CONTRACT ITEM INSTANCES (9.0) eventually refer to things that are physically present in the completed plant. When so located, each has an XYZ COORDINATE within a SUBAREA (1.10) of an AREA (1.9) within the CONTRACT (1.0), representing the plant as a whole.

The connections from one CONTRACT ITEM INSTANCE (9.0) to another in the data base reflect another aspect of the Plant Design. The connections are very detailed, and they cover a broad

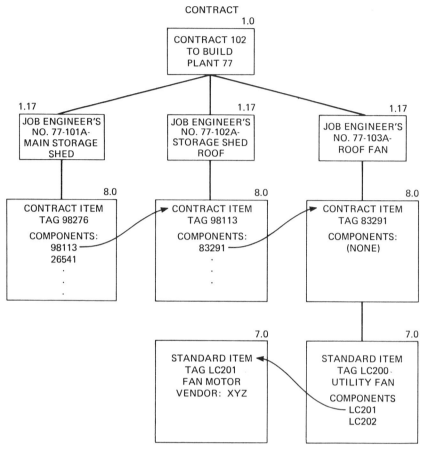

Figure 2-5. Plant design example.

range of "hookups" that exist between physical objects in a factory environment. These "hook-ups" reflect the operation of certain plant systems, or of the operational relationships among component items rather than the way the items are manufactured or assembled. Remember that a CONTRACT ITEM INSTANCE (9.0) could be a length of pipe, a beam, a ladder, a motor, a switch, a connection box, a lighting fixture, a huge factory door, a conveyor belt, a large vessel, a crusher, a light fixture, a valve, or practically any object in the plant. In addition to the "component of" relationship noted above under CONTRACT ITEM TAG (8.0), the data base maintains four different relationships between CONTRACTS ITEM INSTANCE (9.0) and related constructs.

- Being part of a SYSTEM IN CONTRACT (10.1) (like the materials handling, electrical, or fresh air system). Note that the CONTRACT ITEM INSTANCE (9.0) may be connected to this or other SYSTEMS IN CONTRACT (10.1) through LINES (11.0), although strictly speaking it is not part of any LINE (11.0).
- Being one of the components that actually make up the LINE (11.0).
- Being a support for another CONTRACT ITEM INSTANCE (9.0) (like the base of a vessel, or a stanchion supporting a catwalk).
- Being a support for a LINE (11.0) (like a pipe hanger).

The Plant Design is built up from CONTRACT ITEM INSTANCES (9.0), SYSTEMS IN CONTRACT (10.1), LINES (11.0), from relationships among them, and from the product structures noted under CONTRACT ITEM TAG (8.0) and STANDARD ITEM TAG (7.0).

SYSTEM (10.0)
The method for identifying SYSTEMS (10.0) is standard across different CONTRACTS (1.0) and so it is possible to make certain gross comparisons across CONTRACTS (1.0). For example, it is possible to compare the cost of the fresh water system across two CONTRACTS (1.0) or to compare the number of valves used, the amount of pipe, etc. Nevertheless, most of the data associated with a SYSTEM (10.0) as shown on the diagram is data for one plant and is held under SYSTEM IN CONTRACT (10.1).

SYSTEM IN CONTRACT (10.1)
For each SYSTEM IN CONTRACT (10.1), the data base holds a list of all the CONTRACT ITEM INSTANCES (9.0) that make up the SYSTEM IN CONTRACT (10.1). It also holds a list of all the LINES (11.0) that make up the SYSTEM IN CONTRACT (10.1).

LINE (11.0)
The LINES (11.0) are generally conduits, like pipes, ducts, and cables. A LINE (11.0) belongs to exactly one SYSTEM IN CONTRACT (10.1). Each LINE (11.0) is made up of a sequence of CON-TRACT ITEM INSTANCES (9.0), and may also be supported at various points by CONTRACT ITEM INSTANCES (9.0). Furthermore, a line may be connected to other CONTRACT ITEM INSTANCES (9.0) which are strictly speaking components of a SYSTEM (10.0) but not of any LINE (11.0). The coordinates of these connections are stored, as are the coordinates of the path followed by the LINE (11.0) between these end points. Much of the effort in detailed plant design consists in routing and rerouting LINES (11.0). Hence, these paths are quite variable. Finally, in support of various computer-aided design processes, the direction of flow of the contents through the line is also noted, as are the SUBAREAS (1.10) through which the LINE (11.0) passes.

The concepts of SYSTEMS and LINES are further clarified by the example of Figure 2-6. In studying this example, note that:

- The entire diagram represents the mixing system in the factory.
- This system is composed of two vessels (the mixing Vats) and two lines.
- The Piping Layout line goes from Vat #2 to Vat #3, and is made up of three pipe sections and two elbow connections.
- The piping line is supported by hangers at two locations (these are not part of the line).
- The Vats are different instances of the same CONTRACT ITEM. The Vats are part of the system, but not part of any line. Vat #3 is supported by two tank supports (these are not part of the system nor of any line).
- The Electric Circuit line is made up of two lengths of wire and a switch. It connects Vat #3 to the Circuit Breaker. The Circuit Breaker is part of the Master Electrical System. It is an example of an item which is part of a system, but which is also connected to a number of different lines in different systems.

## DETAILS OF THE NEW PLANTS DIVISION DATA BASE

The series of charts in this section show the detailed logical design of the New Plants Division data base. The overview discussion in preceding sections help to explain the context to which these details apply. The basics of the notation were introduced in Chapter 1.

In these charts, we have included a sentence or two opposite each data element. This

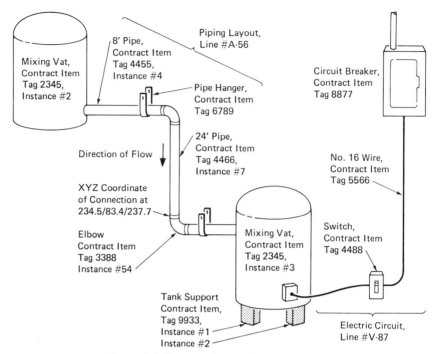

Figure 2-6. Systems, lines and items example.

explanation is far too brief for a real data base design; generally several paragraphs are required to discuss and explain a data element. Here, a sentence summarizes the major function of the element in question.

The numbers on the charts are locators. The key number precedes the decimal point and the elements are numbered in the order encountered within a key. These reference numbers have no other purpose except to identify explicit data elements on the charts.

Some shapes are marked ★ . These represent linkages to data groupings that have been truncated by the authors to simplify the example. The data element name in each associator box contains a **boldface** portion. The text so highlighted is the exact name of the key to which the associator refers. The remaining text is included to help delimit the role of the data element. Thus, in entry 2.14 the data element name WORK PACKAGE RESOURCE refers to the key called RESOURCE (entry 3.0).* The descriptive prefix, WORK PACKAGE, is a reminder that data element 2.14 identifies a specific resource which has been planned in connection with a given WORK PACKAGE.

Finally, note that there are several places in the example where a data variable in a box does not in fact appear as a key with its own data structure, as the general rules would suggest (other than the truncated keys marked with ★ ). One of these is CONTRACT AUTHORIZATION (1.14). In this case, the key (or subkey) CONTRACT AUTHORI-

---

*The reader who is already familiar with domains (see Chapter 4) will recognize in this practice that the domain of the associator WORK PACKAGE RESOURCE, is declared to be a subdomain of the key element RESOURCE.

ZATION (1.14) appears totally within another key, CONTRACT (1.0). Strictly speaking, the design (at the key-level overview) looks like this:

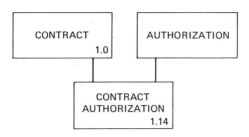

However, AUTHORIZATIONS, in and of themselves, are meaningless. There is no use at all for grouping all authorizations that are identified by "-1"; the identification schemes even differ by CONTRACT. Nonetheless, AUTHORIZATION is a frequently referenced qualifier within CONTRACT, and so we have chosen to treat it as a subkey. Notice that compound keys (such as CONTRACT + AUTHORIZATION) are not permitted as a single key. Further elaboration of these topics will be found later on in the book.

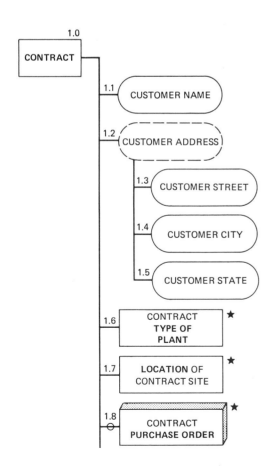

Each active or historical contract is uniquely identified by a well-controlled number.

The legal name of the customer for whom the plant is to be designed and constructed is listed here. Note that since relatively few contracts are active, most customer information is handled outside the system.

The customer address data group stands for the combination of street, city, and state.

The street address of the customer is recorded here.

The city of the customer's address is recorded here.

Finally, the state of the customer's address completes the data group.

This data item is valid across contracts and is established when the contract is first set up. It provides access to lists of standard parts which can be used to develop an initial skeleton design for the new plant.

Identifies the place where the new plant is to be constructed. For each location, the data base would indicate such information as labor rates, average material cost, environmental factors, and so on.

This associator provides a reversal of the purchase order to contract reference. As such, it is an index to all Purchase Orders for this contract.

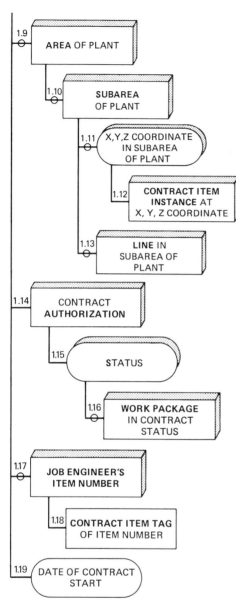

Each plant is subdivided into areas and sub-areas for purposes of reference, breakdown of work, cost estimating, and so forth. Note that each plant is subdivided in a different way, and therefore area identification is not consistent across plants.

Sub-areas are subdivisions of areas. They generally correspond to room-size volumes.

Points in space within the plant are identified by X, Y, Z, distances from a given reference point.

Identifies a specific instance of a part (item) which is located at this point. Since X, Y, Z coordinates are only accurate to several inches, we must allow for multiple items at the same point.

Identifies the (plumbing, electrical, air conditioning, etc.) lines which run through this sub-area of the plant.

Most contracts are divided up into phases, where a separate contract authorization is required before beginning each phase. The authorizations or phases are identified differently within each contract.

The status of each work package is recorded e.g., whether it is pending, in process, behind schedule, completed, etc. Within each contract all the work packages which are in a particular status are grouped together.

Lists the work packages which are currently in the given status.

Provides an inventory of all item numbers which have been uniquely defined for this contract.

Each unique item is assigned an internal identifier or 'tag'.

The start date of the contract is needed because in some instances activities are measured in elapsed days from contract start. This allows comparisons with similar projects, for example.

2.0

```
WORK
PACKAGE
```

A work package is a well defined activity which results in a specific product or accomplishment as part of the plant design or construction.

**2.1**  **CONTRACT** OF WORK PACKAGE

Each work package is part of one and only one contract.

**2.2**  **AUTHORIZATION** OF WORK PACKAGE

Each work package is contained wholly within an authorization of the contract.

**2.3**  DESCRIPTION OF WORK PACKAGE

This is a textual description of the work to be performed under the work package. It could be to "design the materials handling system" or to "build the mixing vat", etc.

**2.4**  **DISCIPLINE** RESPONSIBLE ★

Indicates the organization within the New Plants Division which is responsible for the work, such as Electrical, Mechanical, Structural, etc.

**2.5**  CUSTOMER'S WORK PACKAGE IDENTIFICATION

Optionally, the customer may have his own method of identifying portions of the work, and may wish to have progress reports reference his numbering scheme.

**2.6**  **DRAWING TAG** OF WORK PACKAGE RESULT ★

If the work package is to produce a drawing, it is referenced here.

**2.7**  CONTRACT ITEM TAG OF WORK PACKAGE RESULT

Alternatively, a particular item may be produced by the work package.

**2.8**  CONTRACT ITEM **INSTANCE** OF WORK PACKAGE RESULT

Or, a specific instance of an item may be installed in the plant as a result of the work package.

**2.9**  BEGINNING **NODE** OF WORK PACKAGE ★

Reference is made to a node within another portion of the data base specifying the beginning point of the work package activity used in a network scheduling program (e.g., PERT).

**2.10**  ENDING **NODE** OF WORK PACKAGE ★

Likewise the ending node of the work package is referenced.

**2.11**  STATUS OF WORK PACKAGE

The current status of the work package is recorded.

**2.12**  LATEST **TRACKING EVENT** TAG OF WORK PACKAGE

Tracking events are transactions which indicate the progress of a work package. Each is linked to the event which occurred immediately previously. The most recent event is referenced here.

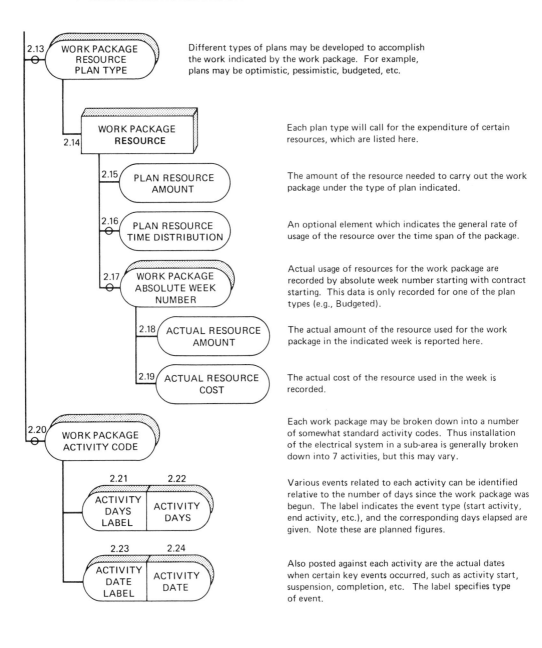

**2.13 WORK PACKAGE RESOURCE PLAN TYPE**

Different types of plans may be developed to accomplish the work indicated by the work package. For example, plans may be optimistic, pessimistic, budgeted, etc.

**2.14 WORK PACKAGE RESOURCE**

Each plan type will call for the expenditure of certain resources, which are listed here.

**2.15 PLAN RESOURCE AMOUNT**

The amount of the resource needed to carry out the work package under the type of plan indicated.

**2.16 PLAN RESOURCE TIME DISTRIBUTION**

An optional element which indicates the general rate of usage of the resource over the time span of the package.

**2.17 WORK PACKAGE ABSOLUTE WEEK NUMBER**

Actual usage of resources for the work package are recorded by absolute week number starting with contract starting. This data is only recorded for one of the plan types (e.g., Budgeted).

**2.18 ACTUAL RESOURCE AMOUNT**

The actual amount of the resource used for the work package in the indicated week is reported here.

**2.19 ACTUAL RESOURCE COST**

The actual cost of the resource used in the week is recorded.

**2.20 WORK PACKAGE ACTIVITY CODE**

Each work package may be broken down into a number of somewhat standard activity codes. Thus installation of the electrical system in a sub-area is generally broken down into 7 activities, but this may vary.

**2.21 ACTIVITY DAYS LABEL    2.22 ACTIVITY DAYS**

Various events related to each activity can be identified relative to the number of days since the work package was begun. The label indicates the event type (start activity, end activity, etc.), and the corresponding days elapsed are given. Note these are planned figures.

**2.23 ACTIVITY DATE LABEL    2.24 ACTIVITY DATE**

Also posted against each activity are the actual dates when certain key events occurred, such as activity start, suspension, completion, etc. The label specifies type of event.

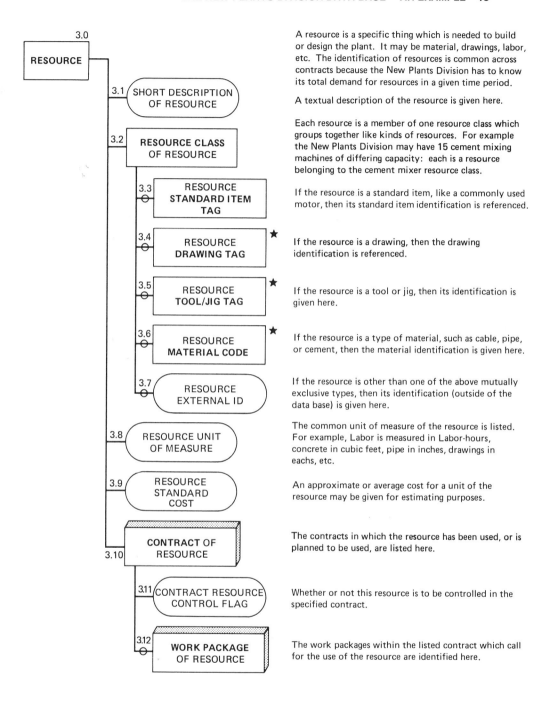

**3.0 RESOURCE**

A resource is a specific thing which is needed to build or design the plant. It may be material, drawings, labor, etc. The identification of resources is common across contracts because the New Plants Division has to know its total demand for resources in a given time period.

**3.1 SHORT DESCRIPTION OF RESOURCE**

A textual description of the resource is given here.

**3.2 RESOURCE CLASS OF RESOURCE**

Each resource is a member of one resource class which groups together like kinds of resources. For example the New Plants Division may have 15 cement mixing machines of differing capacity: each is a resource belonging to the cement mixer resource class.

**3.3 RESOURCE STANDARD ITEM TAG**

If the resource is a standard item, like a commonly used motor, then its standard item identification is referenced.

**3.4 RESOURCE DRAWING TAG** ★

If the resource is a drawing, then the drawing identification is referenced.

**3.5 RESOURCE TOOL/JIG TAG** ★

If the resource is a tool or jig, then its identification is given here.

**3.6 RESOURCE MATERIAL CODE** ★

If the resource is a type of material, such as cable, pipe, or cement, then the material identification is given here.

**3.7 RESOURCE EXTERNAL ID**

If the resource is other than one of the above mutually exclusive types, then its identification (outside of the data base) is given here.

**3.8 RESOURCE UNIT OF MEASURE**

The common unit of measure of the resource is listed. For example, Labor is measured in Labor-hours, concrete in cubic feet, pipe in inches, drawings in eachs, etc.

**3.9 RESOURCE STANDARD COST**

An approximate or average cost for a unit of the resource may be given for estimating purposes.

**3.10 CONTRACT OF RESOURCE**

The contracts in which the resource has been used, or is planned to be used, are listed here.

**3.11 CONTRACT RESOURCE CONTROL FLAG**

Whether or not this resource is to be controlled in the specified contract.

**3.12 WORK PACKAGE OF RESOURCE**

The work packages within the listed contract which call for the use of the resource are identified here.

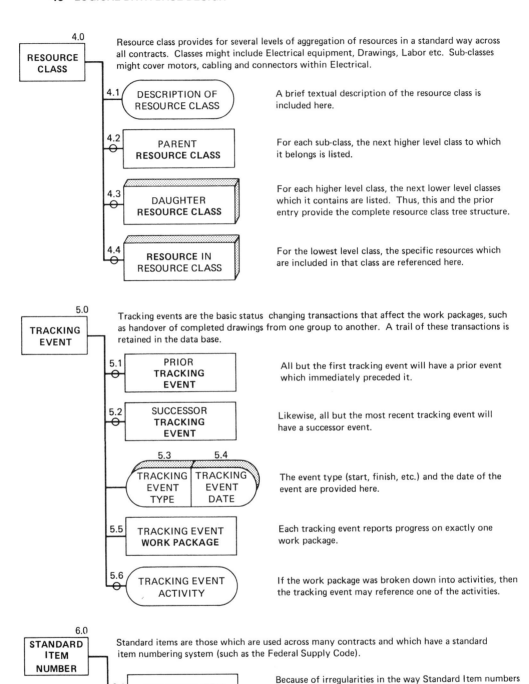

**4.0 RESOURCE CLASS**

Resource class provides for several levels of aggregation of resources in a standard way across all contracts. Classes might include Electrical equipment, Drawings, Labor etc. Sub-classes might cover motors, cabling and connectors within Electrical.

**4.1 DESCRIPTION OF RESOURCE CLASS**

A brief textual description of the resource class is included here.

**4.2 PARENT RESOURCE CLASS**

For each sub-class, the next higher level class to which it belongs is listed.

**4.3 DAUGHTER RESOURCE CLASS**

For each higher level class, the next lower level classes which it contains are listed. Thus, this and the prior entry provide the complete resource class tree structure.

**4.4 RESOURCE IN RESOURCE CLASS**

For the lowest level class, the specific resources which are included in that class are referenced here.

**5.0 TRACKING EVENT**

Tracking events are the basic status changing transactions that affect the work packages, such as handover of completed drawings from one group to another. A trail of these transactions is retained in the data base.

**5.1 PRIOR TRACKING EVENT**

All but the first tracking event will have a prior event which immediately preceded it.

**5.2 SUCCESSOR TRACKING EVENT**

Likewise, all but the most recent tracking event will have a successor event.

**5.3 TRACKING EVENT TYPE    5.4 TRACKING EVENT DATE**

The event type (start, finish, etc.) and the date of the event are provided here.

**5.5 TRACKING EVENT WORK PACKAGE**

Each tracking event reports progress on exactly one work package.

**5.6 TRACKING EVENT ACTIVITY**

If the work package was broken down into activities, then the tracking event may reference one of the activities.

**6.0 STANDARD ITEM NUMBER**

Standard items are those which are used across many contracts and which have a standard item numbering system (such as the Federal Supply Code).

**6.1 STANDARD ITEM TAG**

Because of irregularities in the way Standard Item numbers are assigned, the data base assigns its own unique standard item tag to each.

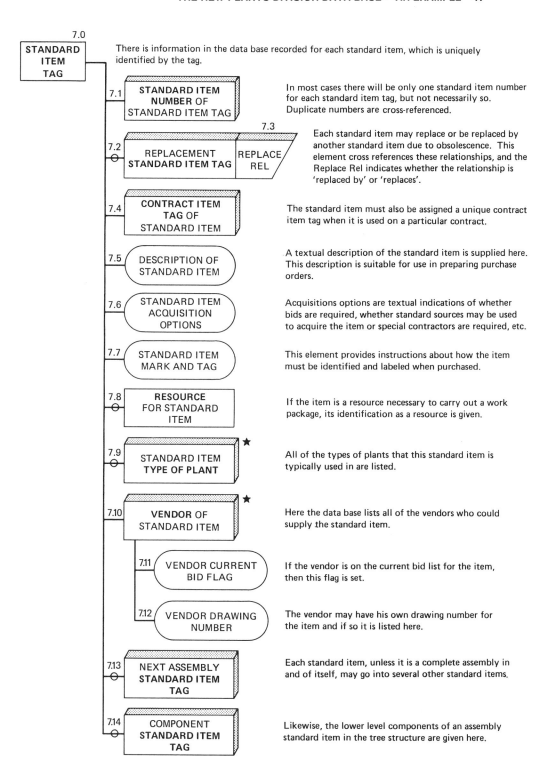

**7.0 STANDARD ITEM TAG**

There is information in the data base recorded for each standard item, which is uniquely identified by the tag.

**7.1 STANDARD ITEM NUMBER OF STANDARD ITEM TAG**

In most cases there will be only one standard item number for each standard item tag, but not necessarily so. Duplicate numbers are cross-referenced.

**7.2 REPLACEMENT STANDARD ITEM TAG / 7.3 REPLACE REL**

Each standard item may replace or be replaced by another standard item due to obsolescence. This element cross references these relationships, and the Replace Rel indicates whether the relationship is 'replaced by' or 'replaces'.

**7.4 CONTRACT ITEM TAG OF STANDARD ITEM**

The standard item must also be assigned a unique contract item tag when it is used on a particular contract.

**7.5 DESCRIPTION OF STANDARD ITEM**

A textual description of the standard item is supplied here. This description is suitable for use in preparing purchase orders.

**7.6 STANDARD ITEM ACQUISITION OPTIONS**

Acquisitions options are textual indications of whether bids are required, whether standard sources may be used to acquire the item or special contractors are required, etc.

**7.7 STANDARD ITEM MARK AND TAG**

This element provides instructions about how the item must be identified and labeled when purchased.

**7.8 RESOURCE FOR STANDARD ITEM**

If the item is a resource necessary to carry out a work package, its identification as a resource is given.

**7.9 STANDARD ITEM TYPE OF PLANT** ★

All of the types of plants that this standard item is typically used in are listed.

**7.10 VENDOR OF STANDARD ITEM** ★

Here the data base lists all of the vendors who could supply the standard item.

**7.11 VENDOR CURRENT BID FLAG**

If the vendor is on the current bid list for the item, then this flag is set.

**7.12 VENDOR DRAWING NUMBER**

The vendor may have his own drawing number for the item and if so it is listed here.

**7.13 NEXT ASSEMBLY STANDARD ITEM TAG**

Each standard item, unless it is a complete assembly in and of itself, may go into several other standard items.

**7.14 COMPONENT STANDARD ITEM TAG**

Likewise, the lower level components of an assembly standard item in the tree structure are given here.

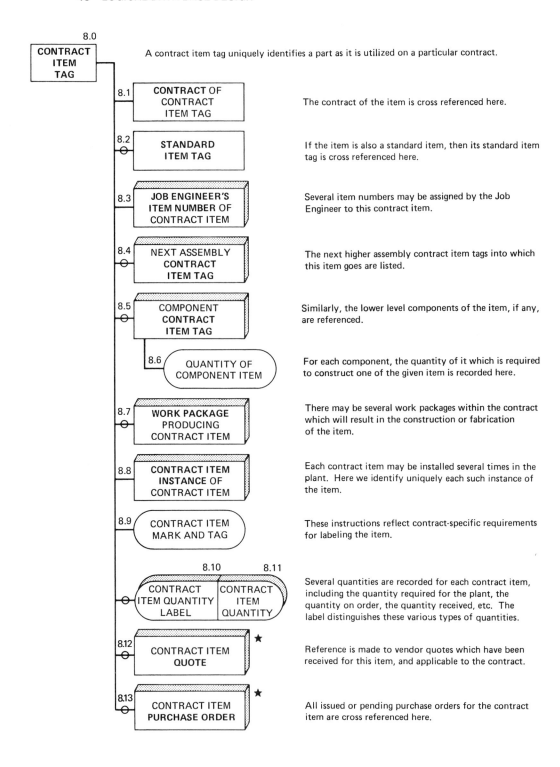

**8.0 CONTRACT ITEM TAG**

A contract item tag uniquely identifies a part as it is utilized on a particular contract.

**8.1 CONTRACT OF CONTRACT ITEM TAG**

The contract of the item is cross referenced here.

**8.2 STANDARD ITEM TAG**

If the item is also a standard item, then its standard item tag is cross referenced here.

**8.3 JOB ENGINEER'S ITEM NUMBER OF CONTRACT ITEM**

Several item numbers may be assigned by the Job Engineer to this contract item.

**8.4 NEXT ASSEMBLY CONTRACT ITEM TAG**

The next higher assembly contract item tags into which this item goes are listed.

**8.5 COMPONENT CONTRACT ITEM TAG**

Similarly, the lower level components of the item, if any, are referenced.

**8.6 QUANTITY OF COMPONENT ITEM**

For each component, the quantity of it which is required to construct one of the given item is recorded here.

**8.7 WORK PACKAGE PRODUCING CONTRACT ITEM**

There may be several work packages within the contract which will result in the construction or fabrication of the item.

**8.8 CONTRACT ITEM INSTANCE OF CONTRACT ITEM**

Each contract item may be installed several times in the plant. Here we identify uniquely each such instance of the item.

**8.9 CONTRACT ITEM MARK AND TAG**

These instructions reflect contract-specific requirements for labeling the item.

**8.10 CONTRACT ITEM QUANTITY LABEL  8.11 CONTRACT ITEM QUANTITY**

Several quantities are recorded for each contract item, including the quantity required for the plant, the quantity on order, the quantity received, etc. The label distinguishes these various types of quantities.

**8.12 CONTRACT ITEM QUOTE** ★

Reference is made to vendor quotes which have been received for this item, and applicable to the contract.

**8.13 CONTRACT ITEM PURCHASE ORDER** ★

All issued or pending purchase orders for the contract item are cross referenced here.

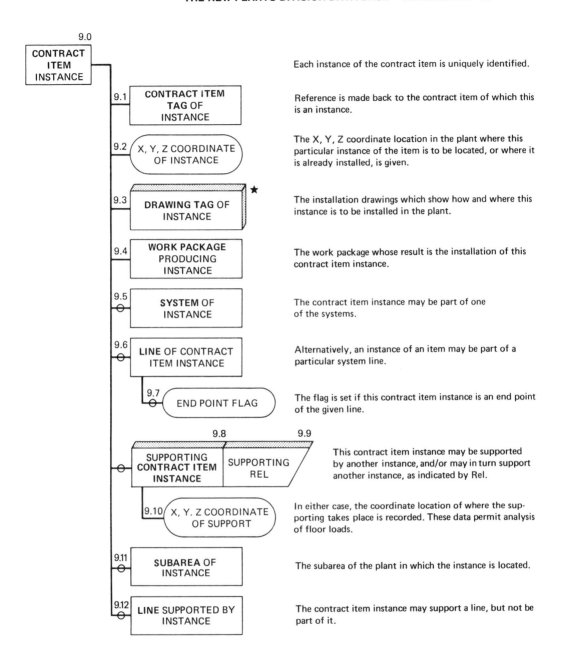

**9.0 CONTRACT ITEM INSTANCE**

Each instance of the contract item is uniquely identified.

**9.1 CONTRACT ITEM TAG OF INSTANCE**

Reference is made back to the contract item of which this is an instance.

**9.2 X, Y, Z COORDINATE OF INSTANCE**

The X, Y, Z coordinate location in the plant where this particular instance of the item is to be located, or where it is already installed, is given.

**9.3 DRAWING TAG OF INSTANCE** ★

The installation drawings which show how and where this instance is to be installed in the plant.

**9.4 WORK PACKAGE PRODUCING INSTANCE**

The work package whose result is the installation of this contract item instance.

**9.5 SYSTEM OF INSTANCE**

The contract item instance may be part of one of the systems.

**9.6 LINE OF CONTRACT ITEM INSTANCE**

Alternatively, an instance of an item may be part of a particular system line.

**9.7 END POINT FLAG**

The flag is set if this contract item instance is an end point of the given line.

**9.8 SUPPORTING CONTRACT ITEM INSTANCE   9.9 SUPPORTING REL**

This contract item instance may be supported by another instance, and/or may in turn support another instance, as indicated by Rel.

**9.10 X, Y, Z COORDINATE OF SUPPORT**

In either case, the coordinate location of where the supporting takes place is recorded. These data permit analysis of floor loads.

**9.11 SUBAREA OF INSTANCE**

The subarea of the plant in which the instance is located.

**9.12 LINE SUPPORTED BY INSTANCE**

The contract item instance may support a line, but not be part of it.

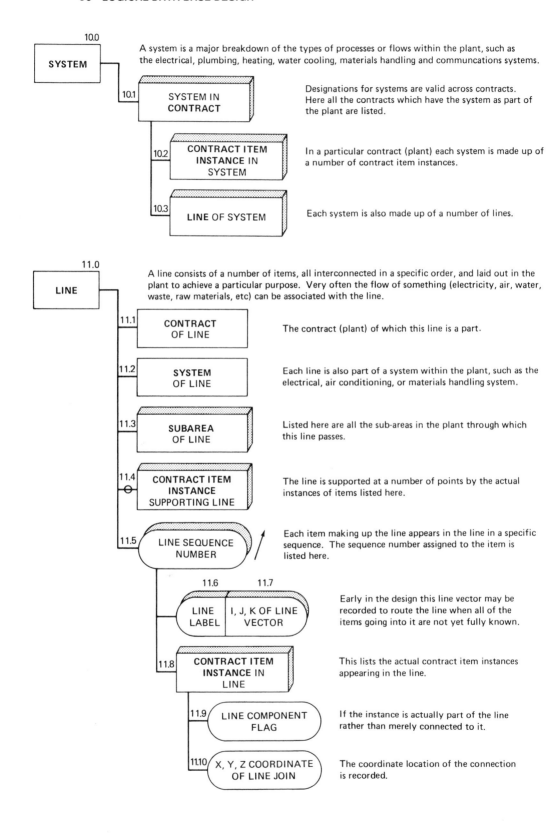

**10.0 SYSTEM**

A system is a major breakdown of the types of processes or flows within the plant, such as the electrical, plumbing, heating, water cooling, materials handling and communcations systems.

**10.1 SYSTEM IN CONTRACT**

Designations for systems are valid across contracts. Here all the contracts which have the system as part of the plant are listed.

**10.2 CONTRACT ITEM INSTANCE IN SYSTEM**

In a particular contract (plant) each system is made up of a number of contract item instances.

**10.3 LINE OF SYSTEM**

Each system is also made up of a number of lines.

**11.0 LINE**

A line consists of a number of items, all interconnected in a specific order, and laid out in the plant to achieve a particular purpose. Very often the flow of something (electricity, air, water, waste, raw materials, etc) can be associated with the line.

**11.1 CONTRACT OF LINE**

The contract (plant) of which this line is a part.

**11.2 SYSTEM OF LINE**

Each line is also part of a system within the plant, such as the electrical, air conditioning, or materials handling system.

**11.3 SUBAREA OF LINE**

Listed here are all the sub-areas in the plant through which this line passes.

**11.4 CONTRACT ITEM INSTANCE SUPPORTING LINE**

The line is supported at a number of points by the actual instances of items listed here.

**11.5 LINE SEQUENCE NUMBER**

Each item making up the line appears in the line in a specific sequence. The sequence number assigned to the item is listed here.

**11.6 LINE LABEL**   **11.7 I, J, K OF LINE VECTOR**

Early in the design this line vector may be recorded to route the line when all of the items going into it are not yet fully known.

**11.8 CONTRACT ITEM INSTANCE IN LINE**

This lists the actual contract item instances appearing in the line.

**11.9 LINE COMPONENT FLAG**

If the instance is actually part of the line rather than merely connected to it.

**11.10 X, Y, Z COORDINATE OF LINE JOIN**

The coordinate location of the connection is recorded.

# 3

# The Logical Design Process

OVERVIEW

The process of logical data base design is an activity that relates the two portions of Chapter 2, i.e., the statement of the problem and the logical data base design that emerges. During this process, in the case of the New Plants Division example, the data base designer decided

- To define the 11 keys shown in Chapter 2, plus all the other keys which the authors have truncated from the example
- To define 129 data elements, shown in the charts, plus those truncated by the authors
- To define 68 associators reflecting key-to-key relationships of significance

In order to understand how those decisions were made, it is useful to emphasize how the process of logical data base design unfolds.

First of all, the designer usually has little advance knowledge of the problem which the organization (e.g., the New Plants Division) is facing. Even if the designer does have advance knowledge—by being a member of the organization, for instance—that knowledge is probably unreliable; it is probably knowledge of how things are done now, rather than insight into how they are to be done in the future. Additionally, the knowledge is likely to be in terms of the design and constraints of existing information systems. Thus, the process of logical data base design begins with study and learning about the problem at hand.

People have their own learning styles. Some learn best by hearing, and these designers prefer to interview knowledgeable people in the organization. Designers who learn best by reading will tend to devour all available written material first. Some people were born with the talent to translate concepts into orderly mental pictures that fall easily into data structures. Others have trained or are training their minds to do this. But whatever the combination of learning mode and mental set, there are two things which good data base designers seem to have in common: their tolerance for detail is exceptional, and they have a knack for working out problems that are not stated clearly.

Given a problem, like that of the New Plants Division, which is stated very incompletely, the designer sets out to achieve a logical data base design comparable in completeness and specificity to the charts presented in Chapter 2. Some readers who have studied the subject of logical data base design before will recognize that the notion of a "conceptual schema" in the ANSI/SPARC model closely resembles the idea of a logical data base presented here. First, it is very enterprise-oriented, or problem-oriented, at least with respect to the data processing sense of "solution." It is understandable by nontechnical user personnel, and it has value beyond merely being a step on the way to physical design. Moreover, it is not geared to a specific application processing requirement, but rather depicts the natural data and relationships to be shared by many applications. And lastly, it is conceptual: it assumes nothing about the physical aspects of the data base. Yet, the conceptual design incorporates many requirements and constraints to which the physical designer must adhere because they are deemed to be important to the data problem.

When viewed in this way, the reader will observe that logical data base design in current practice falls short of the objectives described above. There is no logical design step in many data base development efforts, and hence there is no logical design (other than a default one which would be equivalent to the physical design). Even in data base projects, which may have a logical design step, it is quite different from the logical design discussed here. For instance, many IMS data base projects go through a "logical design" phase in which the logical views for each application are combined into an overall DL/I data base capable of generating each view. This is equivalent to generating the internal schema from the external schemas in the ANSI model; it is not at all comparable to the logical design process in this book.

Similarly, one can observe that many data base design methodologies are *bottom-up*. They begin by gathering all the data of interest in sight, putting it into data dictionaries and other manipulating programs, and then generating cross-references, matrices, and the like in order to produce *the* design. There are grave consequences to such an approach, particularly in the logical design stage. First of all, there is never only *one* design. Rather, there are many, each having its own strengths and costs, flexibilities and complexities. A good design methodology should permit (and even encourage) differing designs to emerge and be judged in the process, rather than zeroing in on one. Secondly, the bottom-up methodologies are very mechanistic: plug all this data about data in one end and the design comes out the other. In the process, no one sees the design as a whole, or gets a chance to weigh completely different approaches. Such a methodology also gives the misleading impression that anyone is capable of good data base design with very little training. Finally, bottom-up methodologies are very restrictive. By the time anyone gets an appreciation of the final overall design, all the details have already been determined. Much work has already been put into data definitions, input/output cross-references, and so on. To change something significant at this stage is a major undertaking.

The *top-down* approach discussed here avoids these pitfalls. It does require design personnel who are familiar with the data problem, and who can conceptualize an overall data base structure with little hard data, zeroing in on the important data items, identifying the major issues and formulating likely alternatives. Longer range planning objectives, which cannot be represented as input to bottom-up methods, can also be taken into account. This is not to suggest that the details are to be ignored, or that individual application requirements are taken lightly. Rather, these additional factors and levels of detail are applied in successive stages; the design is continually refined and expanded during this process.

In the top-down approach under discussion, emphasis is placed on developing the definitions of real-world things as they are characterized by the data and the relationships in the data base. Naturally, this information may not necessarily be known to the designer in advance. It must be elicited from specialists in the organization—people who understand those real world things and their relevance to the business problems the data base is meant to address. Very rarely is that understanding written down, not because organizations are sloppy, but because:

- Much of what is sought is common knowledge to people in the organization.
- People within the company are often concerned on a day-to-day basis with the current system's records about something, not with the thing itself.

For example, existing systems—including manual ones—may have voluminous documentation that describes the handling of employee numbers. But the employee number is (usually) not the real world thing we want to treat in a logical design. The *person* is.

The logical design process is an interpersonal intellectual activity of considerable psychological sensitivity. Whenever information is being elicited and facts are being recorded—it makes a great deal of difference how the question is asked. For this reason, even when the employee number is a unique identifier that can be used to refer to persons, it is harmful to use it in a logical design session. A conversation aimed at learning about persons is wholly different from one that concerns the objects identified by employee numbers. Obviously, "person" is a broader concept, and it will generally turn out that there are nonemployee persons (customers or former employees, for example) of interest to the data base. The major defect in learning about employee numbers, however, lies in learning a concept of what an employee is that is overwhelmingly biased by the organization's past practice in assigning employee numbers. Assume that the employee number has, in the past, been used quite satisfactorily for regular employees, feeding the payroll system, and so on. The reader can picture what would be learned from an effort to depict data by employee number: it would elaborate the current data structure, with a few changes to the conventions now in use. What is in danger of being missed, however, is a whole set of related requirements that pertain to people who do not meet the system's definition of "employee." These quasi-employees could easily share part of the data structure for regular employees in the new data base—though they are handled completely separately at present. Consider just two examples:

- Candidates for employment—a full employee record is available, but these people are not on the payroll yet and do not have an employee number.
- Royalty recipients—the company pays royalties to authors and inventors. Some are employees, many are not.

To summarize then, the method employed for data base design in this book is a top-down process which emphasizes critical thinking, conceptualization of new approaches, and considerable analysis of the important data items. This is in opposition to more mechanistic methods which emphasize a bottom-up, predefined process.

Organizing a mass of relationships among ill-defined things is never easy. Still, there are various characteristics of the design problem which can increase or diminish the difficulty of sorting out the underlying structure.

- If the data requirements of the enterprise have been carefully analyzed and documented in advance, it is generally easier to delineate the problem and define the data structures. The reason for the simplification is *not* found in the fact that a system analysis has already defined some of the data. That would be begging the question. The reason for the simplification lies in the fact that questions have already been posed and answered during the system analysis process which clarify what the data should mean and that delimit both the scope and the objectives of the data base. These clarifications are of outstanding importance to the logical design process for *all* the open questions of data definition and system scope need to be addressed *and resolved* during logical data base design.

- Logical data base design is made more difficult as a function of the "fuzziness" of the system's objectives. Such "fuzziness" arises routinely in all aspects of human endeavor because people are not totally precise in saying what they mean. But this routine fuzziness is not the complicating factor. The challenging situation arises when management elects not to place clear limits on the objectives of the system. The fuzziness is wanting to get "as much benefit as possible" from the data, being willing to cut back if it proves too hard to attain or too expensive. Developing a design under these circumstances is by no means impossible, nor is management's attitude necessarily wrong; they want to establish some limits in their own minds on what the data base system is capable of doing for them. But the designers' job is made more complicated since they are analyzing a problem whose boundary does not stand still. Alternatively, the problems are simplified in an environment where there is a long-range business plan, and the objectives of this plan have been related to the organization's information resources.

- "Numbers" also affect the difficulty of the problem. The more keys, the more entities, the more relationships, and the more people involved, the more complex the problem as a rule. But notice that this does not specifically relate to the *size* of the physical data base. A very large data base can have a very simple design—indeed, until recently it *had* to have a very simple design. Though it contains millions of physical items, it is much simpler to design than small data bases with complex relationships. The number of organizational units that will be sharing the data in the data base definitely aggravates the difficulty both of sorting out what is needed, and of achieving a workable design.

- Finally, the design team's limitations also affect the design process. Unfamiliarity with the kinds of data structures being uncovered is a handicap. But since everyone has to encounter a structure for the first time and work it through, it is not a fatal handicap. The more serious limitation is related to the individual designer's ability to cope with detail. Real data base problems have endless detail, and nobody has infinite capacity to absorb it. The designer needs to adopt a disciplined and purposeful strategy by which these details are collected, organized, and dealt with. The designer's mind, and hopefully his notes, record the disposition of those details. But when this strategy breaks down, the scope of the problem and the mass of detail quickly combine to numb the mind's ability to cut through the jungle of relationships. Both designers and their supervisors must be able to deal sensitively with this saturation effect, acting both to prevent it and to repair it. It is the prime cause of failure to achieve a logical design in a reasonable period.

## A STRATEGIC PRINCIPLE FOR LOGICAL DESIGN

The best way to cope with complex tangles—be they tangled ideas or tangles of twine—is to spread them out. Pulling and tugging separates the twine, loosening it up so that "subtangles" can be worked on. This is a delicate process, and one must be respectful of the medium. Pulling too vigorously will aggravate the central "subtangle." If one

approaches logical data base design with this imagery, a strategy based on separating*
things out has a certain appeal.

The only way to solve certain differential equations is to use a technique called "separating the variables." An equation of the form

$$M(dx) + N(dy) = 0$$

is separable if the expressions $M$ and $N$ meet certain conditions that allow us to inte-
grate both sides

$$Mx + Ny = C$$

This moves us out of the realm of differential equations and paves the way for solving
the problem by conventional algebra. For this reason, problems in differential equations
are "pulled and tugged" through all kinds of manipulations in an effort to place them
in "separable" form.

In logical data base design, the strategy of separating things out is manifest most
clearly in the way one deals with objects. The proper choice of objects is particularly
important because the data base will store all the information it contains in the form of
assertions about the objects that are selected. In order to find the right combination of
objects to choose, it is both necessary and commonplace to separate most familiar
object-concepts in a variety of ways. To begin, the object itself is almost always separated from its name. That is, the object itself (a person, say) is one thing and the name
(be it text, an ID number, or whatever) is another thing. Further "pulling and tugging"
often creates a small constellation of different objects out of the concept (person) that
initially seemed indivisible. Sometimes each role of a person (as lawyer, as owner of a
farm, as selectman) deserves to be a separate object. Sometimes the person (or even a
role of a person) is separated into a set of "snapshots" over time, and each snapshot is
an object. This way of thinking is absolutely crucial to the development of a logical data
base design. It is through this process that "The man submitted a claim" is more precisely interpreted as "The man in his capacity as owner of a farm during a particular
period in time (during which his crop is insured) filed a claim."

A particularly detailed example of the subdivision of objects was illustrated in the
Chapter 2 example. To meet the needs of the New Plants Division, there were several
ways in which the concept of an item in the plant was reinterpreted. The result was a
variety of different objects at different levels of abstraction that were recognized by the
data base:

- The item as a resource (see RESOURCE)
- The item as a general class containing many identical parts with the same form
  and function (see CONTRACT ITEM TAG)
- A specific individual member of such a class that is actually installed in the plant
  (see CONTRACT ITEM INSTANCE)

and several more.

The same strategy—separating the variables—is also applied to relationships, pri-

---

*Note that "separating" does not include cutting the tangle in four parts and handing the mini-tangles to
four team leaders.

marily with the aim of separating complex relationships into their component parts. Usually, it is rather easy to parse a complex relationship once the relationship has been clarified in depth. Naturally, such deep clarification of the relationship requires excellent insight into the objects which participate in the relationship. Accordingly, it is sometimes necessary to work out the objects as a prerequisite to analyzing relationships. In the process, a relation like "A, B, and C are related" is separated into "A is related to B," "B is related to B′ sometimes," and "B′ is related to C."

The result of approaching logical data base design with a top-down approach and this focus on separating the variables is a process that has two major phases. In the first phase, which we call *factoring* because of the way compound objects and relations are broken into components, the designer is studying the real world problem and sketching the outlines of a design. In the second phase, called *perfecting* because of the critical attention paid to details, the designer works primarily with the charts, making sure that all the details fit together into a coherent structure.

At this point, it is possible to give the reader a perspective on the process of factoring, and the rest of this chapter is devoted to explaining and walking through the general activities that take place during the effort. Perfecting is a process which requires total familiarity with both the notation and various questions of interpretation. This activity is one which we shall treat as an epilogue to achieving a design that seems to fit the problem. The operations involved in tightening up and polishing a logical design are thus deferred to Chapter 5.

## FACTORING

Factoring is the intellectual process in which the data base logical designer selects and defines the primary entities and relationships to be administered in the data base. During this process, the designer is analyzing the properties of various abstract and concrete objects in the real world and also sorting out the relationships that apparently hold among them. Some of these relationships can be extremely complex and need to be broken apart into simpler components. It is generally the case, however, that information about these objects and relationships in the real world is reported to the designer in an uncontrolled way. Even when a considerable effort has already been invested by analysts to define the data processing problem, the information is still in unfactored form—principally because such understanding is heavily process-oriented rather than data-oriented. Beginning with an information base that is rarely certain, the designer works toward the goal of discovering the basic organizing principles of the data base. In the process, objects and relationships are defined and included as elements of the logical data base design.

Ordinarily, the process of factoring is executed smoothly and expeditiously—provided the aggravations noted earlier are avoided. These aggravations concerned limitations of the designer, the presence of unusually many relationships, open-ended management objectives, and the need to cross organizational lines to gain agreements. Except in these circumstances, the factoring process is straightforward enough to be flowcharted—very crudely—in the pattern shown in Figure 3-1. An informal narrative of the process is as follows:

  A  After some initial learning about the problem, the designer proceeds—in no particular order—to dissect "relationship clusters" which have come to his

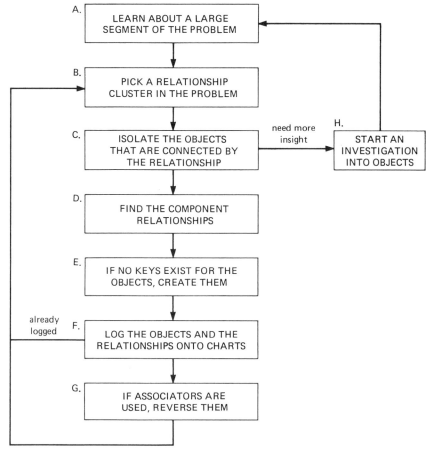

Figure 3-1. Usual flow of steps in the factoring process.

attention in the problem. These "relationship clusters" are the analogs of the "subtangles" in the ball of twine analogy, and each cluster typically provides 3–6 relationships among 5–10 objects.

B  Here is a representative "relationship cluster" drawn from the problem statement in Chapter 2:

"The client company enters into a contract with the New Plants Division to design and build a carefully specified plant at a stated place. The New Plants Division contracts to design and then deliver a plant in working order on a targeted date for an appropriate fee."

C  As such a cluster if factored, the designer immediately sees some "easy" data objects:

- targeted date
- appropriate fee
- stated place
- contract

as well as some potentially "hard" ones:

- client company
- plant

    — carefully specified
    — in working order

D  Certain simple relationships among these objects can now be established. For example, the designer investigates whether "targeted date" is a property of the plant or of the contract; it is determined to be a property of the contract.

E–G  Accordingly, the results attained so far are written on the charts—tentatively—as follows:

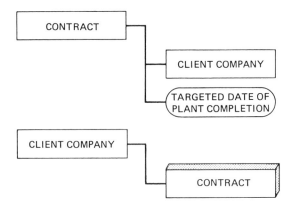

Observe that the drawing shows the decisions that were actually made and omits some decisions that are pending. It shows the two keys that were created to represent tentative objects, a relationship between them, and the contract-date relationship that was investigated and established during Step D. In accordance with the conventions of this notational scheme, note that the associator that connects the two keys has been correctly reversed.

H  In Step C, several objects were identified which were too imperfectly understood to be included confidently on the charts. To gain the needed insight, investigations are now launched to understand:

- plant
- carefully specified PROMISED plant
- in working order DELIVERED plant

It is vital to learn if these are the same object or three different objects. Naturally, such investigations take time. Rather than wait for the outcome, the designer returns to Step B. The next relationship cluster chosen is one which is independent of the questions (What is a plant?) under investigation, and the process continues as before.

Throughout factoring, the charts that hold the designer's notes are constantly extended. New keys are added—quite frequently at first, then more slowly. Nearly every cycle through the routine presented in Figure 3-1 adds some new elements and relationships to the charts. The effect is that the pages of information under any given key begins to fill up, resembling handwritten replicas of the charts at the end of Chapter 2. Naturally, each time an element is added under a key, the designer checks previous assumptions as revealed by elements added previously—to the best of his ability. But it is hard to think of a key like "plant" or "person" comprehensively when you have just approached it with another problem (say "vendor") in mind. As a consequence, only the most glaring inconsistencies and misconceptions in the definition of objects are detected early on. The rest have to be found by sweeping through the keys, one at a time, considering their meaning and behavior in respect to the entire data base.

## THE FACTORING OF OBJECTS

Almost all of the energy devoted to factoring objects is devoted to sorting out alternatives—often by grappling with issues of considerable philosophical depth. One such issue that recurs with some regularity concerns an object that is "seen" several times. The question which arises is whether the *same* object has in fact returned.

To serve as an illustration of this question, consider a scenario in which people walk up to a counter and are serviced by the attendants, during which time data about their visit is placed in the data base, and then walk out. Clearly, each of these people is an object—a PERSON—that needs to be dealt with in the data structure. It certainly appears that the same person can return on a subsequent day, so that a person has several "visits." But a logical designer needs more evidence before concluding that the *same* person returned. How do we know it is the same person? Even with perfect identification (like comparing signatures to prove it is the same human being), there is no assurance that this person has returned unchanged. Suppose the person has been divorced, inherited a fortune, or been convicted of a crime between visits. There are systems (tax, welfare, employment) where one would question if this is the "same" person. Under these circumstances, the data base designers will and *must* set up a new object, INSTANCE OF PERSON, if there is any real doubt about how this is going to work out.

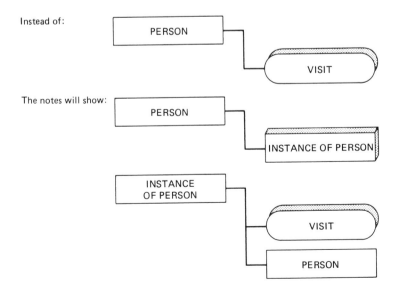

This is a clear case of separating a variable PERSON into two variables, PERSON and INSTANCE OF PERSON. Doing so provides a standing reminder of the question that was raised. Every data element and relation encountered hereafter needs to be considered to see if it belongs with PERSON or the INSTANCE OF PERSON. Fixed data like DATE OF BIRTH, for instance, would tend to attach to the first key, while all data that affect the organization's behavior toward the person would be attached to the second key. Even relationships borne to other people go in different places; parents attach to the PERSON, but children are properties of the INSTANCE OF PERSON. People can have children between visits, but their parentage is immutable. This, however, is done only if we exclude adopted parents, step-parents, etc., from the definition of parent.

The point we wish to stress using this example is the existence of a dualism in the definition of an object. On the one hand, there is the external world definition of a person. But after the structure has been developed, there is also an internal data base definition of a person. Much later in the design process, when a page or so of elements have been attached to these keys, the question can be reconsidered; if all the data and relations are under PERSON, then the other key is probably superfluous. It can be deleted from the charts with negligible effort, and the only penalty paid for having considered it as a possible key arises in making those independent decisions for each data element that is hooked onto the PERSON key. Because those are good questions to consider, the effort is not wasted, even when the hypothesis is disproved.

Thus, the factoring of objects in the early stages of data base design places heavy emphasis on separating initial object concepts into narrower, more well-defined objects. This forces the kind of critical analysis about what the object (and its properties) really is. Sometimes, it turns out that two or more initial object concepts should be combined. This combining process is discussed in a later chapter; it is not so important in the early stages because combining can always be done later on. But separating out involves the recognition of subtle distinctions and needs to be done early on.

## THE FACTORING OF RELATIONSHIPS

In addition to untangling the structure of objects, the process of factoring concerns itself with identifying and characterizing data relationships. Put simply, factoring translates facts about objects into data structures which are capable of representing or reflecting those facts. In practice, however, the problem becomes difficult when the facts are complex and interrelated—the data base designer must probe each supposed fact to determine precisely what relationships are established and what their meaning and implications are.

One of the most frequent sources of error in logical data base design is a misinterpretation of the relationship dependencies embodied in the facts presented. Relationship dependencies reflect in a precise way how each data item is related to others. Given a fact, what are the relationship dependencies involved? This question is addressed during the factoring stage of data base design. Consider, for example, the following fact:

Vendors always deliver parts to the same place.

Our initial factoring of this seemingly simple fact would reveal three kinds of objects of interest: VENDORS, PARTS, and DELIVERY LOCATIONS. If we interpret the given fact to mean that each VENDOR delivers all PARTS to the same place no matter who the VENDOR, or what the PART, then we do not seem to have a relationship between DELIVERY LOCATION and PARTS or VENDORS; DELIVERY LOCATION is independent of PARTS and VENDORS. Further probing of the situation may reveal that DELIVERY LOCATION doesn't depend on anything at all (i.e., not only is it the same for all PARTS and VENDORS, but is is the same for all CONTRACTS, for all PLANT SITES, for all time). This condition suggests that DELIVERY LOCATION is not a variable at all but more of a constant. Its value could be coded into application programs, or stored once and for all in a reference file where similar constants are kept. Let's depict such a reference file as follows:

There is one place to which everyone delivers everything.

Alternatively, we could easily have interpreted the same given fact to mean that each VENDOR always delivers PARTS to the same place, but not necessarily the same place as another VENDOR. Thus the DELIVERY LOCATION has a relationship dependency on VENDOR:

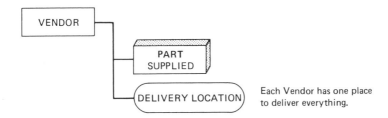

Each Vendor has one place to deliver everything.

Then, of course, there is the possibility that all deliveries of Part 1 go to Location A, all deliveries of Part 2 go to location B, etc. In other words, the DELIVERY LOCATION is dependent on the particular PART, and not at all on VENDOR:

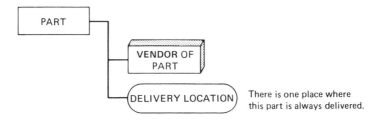

There is one place where this part is always delivered.

We can also interpret the same fact to mean that the DELIVERY LOCATION is dependent on both the VENDOR and the PART:

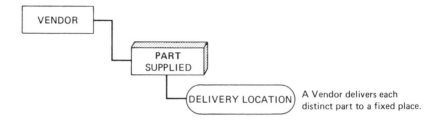

A Vendor delivers each distinct part to a fixed place.

Finally, we can do some additional probing of the real meaning and determine that not only does DELIVERY LOCATION depend on VENDOR and PART, but it depends on the CONTRACT in question, and may change over time ("always" meaning that it stays about the same for long periods of time, but can be altered.) These revelations would cause us to factor the example as follows:

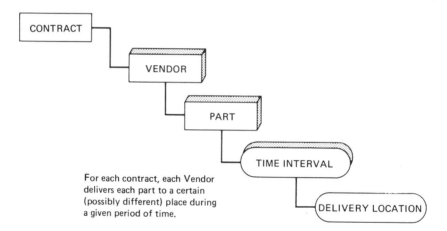

For each contract, each Vendor delivers each part to a certain (possibly different) place during a given period of time.

Note carefully that each different interpretation is a very realistic possibility given the vagaries of the initial "fact." Also, observe that in each case, the logical design notation was able to represent the interpretation clearly. The notational system is geared to force the designer to decide on the proper interpretation; no vagueness should remain once the design option has been selected.

Obviously, the logical data base designer must be suspicious of seemingly simple facts. In the process of factoring, he must constantly ask what depends on what and explore the nature of the relationships which the data base must faithfully reproduce. In factoring relationships, one often finds that this process uncovers objects which were not previously recognized, just because some other object is dependent on them. Thus, the factoring of objects and relations is highly interdependent.

## A FACTORING EXAMPLE

In order to examine the process of factoring, it is necessary to proceed methodically to reconstruct the facts about the problem and the reasoning about those facts that yield a coherent and relevant data structure. Toward this end, let us assume we have interviewed the chief engineer of the New Plants Division in an attempt to gain an understanding of current practice as a basis for how the data base should handle part numbers. The sum and substance of this interview might be noted in the following way:

> Plants are made up of parts, some of which are common with other plants and some of which are not. When we recognize that a part has been or could be common, we enter it into our Standard Part Book and give it a Standard Part Number for later reference. Sometimes however we don't recall that a particular part is already in the book (probably because we changed vendors) and we enter it again. Later on, we may discover the duplicate, so we write the new number in red next to the old one; or of course, we may never discover it. Parts are produced and installed by tasks called Work Packages, which may in turn require other standard type parts in order to be accomplished, such as the special bolts necessary to mount our centrifugal fan unit. For parts which are custom designed for a specific contract, one of my Job Engineers assigns a number which is unique to that contract; so for example all the parts we designed for the Acme Pulp Mill begin with the prefix ACME-PM, like ACME-PM-1278-A09-C, which happens to be the number of that fan unit I mentioned. This works out well because we can tell exactly what plant a part number like this is for. Some of our customers want all the parts in their plants numbered like this, even the standard ones, but we can't do it for them because it's too complicated. Parts are also made up of other parts in what we call our parts tree, and after they are purchased or built, are installed in the plant at a certain location specified on the drawing.

Now in real practice of course we would be unlikely to obtain such a succinct statement from a single person. More likely, we would need to talk with several persons before such a statement could be written down; in the process, several real or apparent differences in viewpoint may have had to be resolved. However, for illustrative purposes, we can proceed from this point.

Notice that while the statement is succinct, it is still quite involved—a reasonably appropriate way to reflect the conditions expressed in terms of data elements and relationships is not immediately obvious. So we proceed to factor the statement, separating out the key facts, and building up and revising the design as we go along.

*Fact 1:* Plants are made up of parts, some of which are common with other plants and some of which are not. When we recognize that a part has been or could be common, we enter it into our Standard Part Book and give it a Standard Part Number for later reference.

This fact suggests the following (three key) data structure:

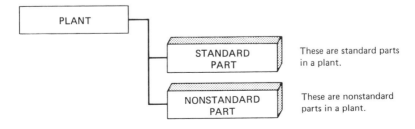

These are standard parts in a plant.

These are nonstandard parts in a plant.

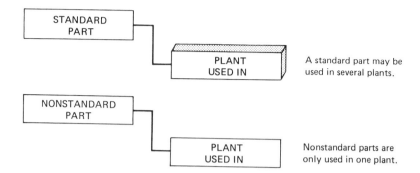

Fact 2: Sometimes however we don't recall that a particular part is already in the book (probably because we changed vendors) and we enter it again. Later on we may discover the duplicate, so we write the new number in red next to the old one; or of course we may never discover it.

This additional fact reveals that standard parts are subject to duplicate numberings. We can handle this in the data base by assigning an internal name—call it STANDARD ITEM TAG. We can now depict the situation like this:

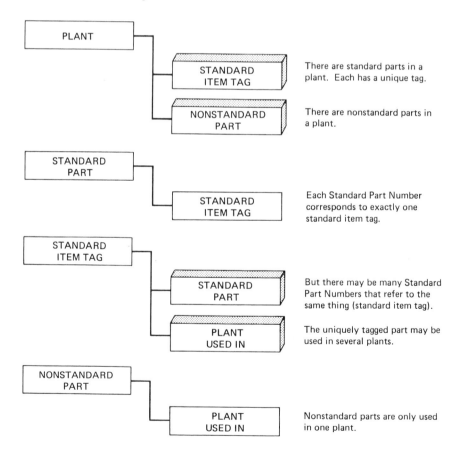

This structure permits us to continue to deal with multiple external identifiers for a standard part, and yet recognize that each refers in fact to the same part.

*Fact 3:* Parts are produced and installed by tasks called WORK PACKAGES, which may in turn require other standard type parts in order to be accomplished, such as the special bolts necessary to mount our centrifugal fan unit.

We are now prepared to embellish the design showing:

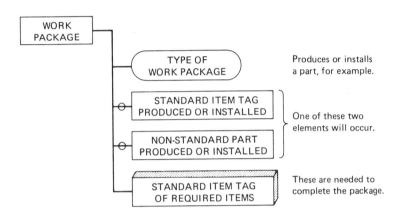

Notice that without further information, we have assumed that a WORK PACKAGE can either produce or install one standard part or one nonstandard part, but not both. Further questioning of the precise meaning of this fact is probably in order.

*Fact 4:* For parts which are custom designed for a specific contract, one of my Job Engineers assigns a number which is unique to that contract; so for example all the parts we designed for the Acme Pulp Mill begin with the prefix ACME-PM, like ACME-PM-1278-A09-C, which happens to be the number of that fan unit just mentioned. This works out well because we can tell exactly what plant a part number like this is for. Some of our customers want all the parts in their plants numbered like this, even the standard ones, but we can't do it for them because it's too complicated.

First, it appears reasonable to assume that parts which are custom designed for a particular contract are the same as parts which are not common across plants (from Fact 1), i.e., are nonstandard parts. We now know that these are identified by what we shall call JOB ENGINEER'S ITEM NUMBERS, but let us also assume that multiple such numbers can be assigned to the same item, and thus we need to relate these to a unique CONTRACT ITEM TAG. Finally, we try to accommodate the desire to assign JOB ENGINEER'S ITEM NUMBERS to standard parts as well. This we can do if we generalize the notion of a CONTRACT ITEM TAG to be either a custom designed part (possibly assigned several JOB ENGINEER'S ITEM NUMBERS) or a standard part as used on this particular contract (also possibly assigned several JOB ENGINEER'S ITEM NUMBERS).

This thinking yields:

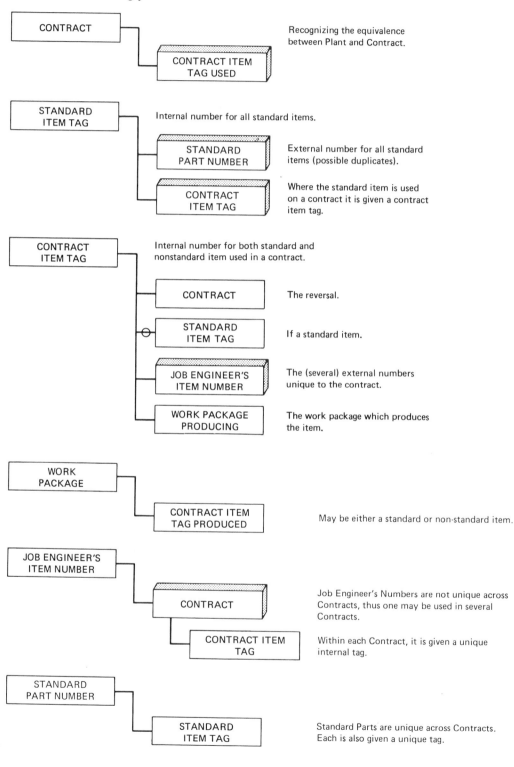

CONTRACT
CONTRACT ITEM TAG USED

Recognizing the equivalence between Plant and Contract.

STANDARD ITEM TAG

Internal number for all standard items.

STANDARD PART NUMBER

External number for all standard items (possible duplicates).

CONTRACT ITEM TAG

Where the standard item is used on a contract it is given a contract item tag.

CONTRACT ITEM TAG

Internal number for both standard and nonstandard item used in a contract.

CONTRACT

The reversal.

STANDARD ITEM TAG

If a standard item.

JOB ENGINEER'S ITEM NUMBER

The (several) external numbers unique to the contract.

WORK PACKAGE PRODUCING

The work package which produces the item.

WORK PACKAGE

CONTRACT ITEM TAG PRODUCED

May be either a standard or non-standard item.

JOB ENGINEER'S ITEM NUMBER

CONTRACT

Job Engineer's Numbers are not unique across Contracts, thus one may be used in several Contracts.

CONTRACT ITEM TAG

Within each Contract, it is given a unique internal tag.

STANDARD PART NUMBER

STANDARD ITEM TAG

Standard Parts are unique across Contracts. Each is also given a unique tag.

This example so far has shown a case in which an entity can be viewed in two perspectives: sometimes the distinction between standard parts and nonstandard ones is important, sometimes not. We handled this by providing for data elements which emphasized the distinction (STANDARD ITEM TAG, STANDARD PART NUMBER, JOB ENGINEER'S ITEM NUMBER), and for ones which did not (CONTRACT ITEM TAG), and then cross-referencing the two. Within this framework, there is no reason why standard parts cannot also be assigned JOB ENGINEER'S ITEM NUMBERS within a particular contract, as the desire was expressed. To do this, we merely allow CONTRACT ITEM TAGS to refer to *both* STANDARD ITEM TAG and JOB ENGINEER'S ITEM NUMBER.

The flexibility of this scheme can best be seen by examination of the following instances:

CONTRACT = Acme
            CONTRACT ITEM TAG = 1234 (bolt)
            CONTRACT ITEM TAG = 1235 (fan)

STANDARD ITEM TAG = STD-987 (bolt)
            STANDARD PART NUMBER = Western #4X3A
            STANDARD PART NUMBER = Ajax #4X9B
            CONTRACT ITEM TAG = 1234         (the Acme contract)
            CONTRACT ITEM TAG = 5678         (another contract)

CONTRACT ITEM TAG = 1234 (bolt)
            CONTRACT = Acme         (the reversal)
            STANDARD ITEM TAG = STD-987         (the reversal)
            JOB ENGINEER'S ITEM NUMBER = ACME-PM-1278-312-B

CONTRACT ITEM TAG = 1235 (fan)
            CONTRACT = Acme
            JOB ENGINEER'S ITEM NUMBER = ACME-PM-1278-A09-C

JOB ENGINEER'S ITEM NUMBER = ACME-PM-1278-312-B (bolt)
            CONTRACT = Acme
            CONTRACT ITEM TAG = 1234

JOB ENGINEER'S ITEM NUMBER = ACME-PM-1278-A09-C (fan)
            CONTRACT = Acme
            CONTRACT ITEM TAG = 1235

STANDARD PART NUMBER = Western #4X3A (bolt)
            STANDARD ITEM TAG = STD-987         Western and Ajax

STANDARD PART NUMBER = Ajax #4X9B (bolt)         have different
            STANDARD ITEM TAG = STD-987         numbers for the same
                                                             thing (STD-987).

In this example, note that:

- For the Acme contract, two CONTRACT ITEM TAGS have been defined. One of these, the bolt, is a standard item, the other item, a fan, is not a standard item.
- The bolt, being a standard item, has been assigned a STANDARD ITEM TAG (STD-987), as well as distinct CONTRACT ITEM TAGS for each of the contracts on which it is used. Additionally, there are two external STANDARD PART NUMBERS which have been assigned to this item.

- The fan, being a contract item, has been assigned a CONTRACT ITEM TAG for the Acme contract.
- Both the fan and the bolt have been assigned JOB ENGINEER'S ITEM NUMBERS which permit him to utilize his own numbering scheme for both standard and nonstandard items.

When the distinction between standard and nonstandard items is not important, the data structure references CONTRACT ITEM TAG. This is the case when we reference an item as a RESOURCE, or when we relate an item to the WORK PACKAGE which assembles it. Purchasing data, however, would more than likely reference STANDARD ITEM TAGS as only standard items may be purchased.

This chapter has provided the reader with an introductory feel toward the kinds of thinking and activities which take place during the early stages of logical data base design. The emphasis has been on attitudes. Beware of details—they will surely overwhelm you. Be prepared to break entities apart. Always treat a thing and its name as two distinct (yet closely related) objects. Beware of truths: "Vendors always deliver parts to the same place." And remember that factoring is needed because real data relationships are rarely obvious. These attitudes fall short of guidelines or rules for designing data bases, as these must await development of additional formalism. We begin that development in the next chapter.

## REFERENCES

1. Kahn, Beverly. "A Method for Describing Information Required by the Database Design Process," in *Proceedings of the SIGMOD Conference,* Washington, D.C., 1976.

   This paper describes one of a number of straightforward approaches toward data base design which do not involve a deep understanding of the semantics of the data. Such design methodologies are extensions of traditional approaches suitably modified for the use of data bases, and thus treat the logical design as a step toward the physical design rather than an end in itself. This method suggests a separation of the Information Structure Perspective, which depicts the natural and conceptual relationships in the information, and the Usage Perspective, which defines the system's processing requirements. The data which the designer might collect about each of these perspectives is discussed and a formalism introduced for recording it. The formalism has been designed to serve as input to the Problem Statement Language (PSL) which is part of the ISDOS project for automating systems design activities being pursued at the University of Michigan.

2. Bubenko, J. A., *et al.* "From Information Requirements to DBTG-Data Structures," in *Proceedings of Conference on Data: Abstraction, Definition, and Structure,* 1976.

   The authors present a method of analyzing a data problem and developing design alternatives for a CODASYL data base management system. The method places heavy emphasis on the "usage perspective," with estimated data occurrences and transaction volumes being collected (in this respect, the method differs greatly from that presented in this book). The authors develop a relatively detailed example in which different design alternatives are shown to favor inquiry processing over update, and vice versa.

3. Buchmann, A. P., and Dale, A. G. "Evaluation Criteria for Logical Database Design Methodologies," *Computer-Aided Design,* **11**:3, May, 1979.

   A general comparison of the different approaches to logical data base design is made, and then three specific methods are briefly reviewed. The reader will want to contrast these methods with the approach taken in this book. With respect to the material presented in this chapter, the paper contains the relevant statement:

   "If a requirements first logical database design methodology is advocated, it is necessary to ensure that a good requirement gathering analyzing procedure is part of the selected methodology. The need for this is recognized by most authors but is carried through only by a few. Frequently emphasis is put into the development of requirement specification languages and automated analysis procedures, which are helpful only when the physical reality has been correctly perceived. The problems which are most difficult to eliminate arise from false perceptions of reality, resulting from a natural language barrier between the 'database naive' user and the 'application naive' database designer and the lack of appropriate tools for communication between them."

4. Yao, S. B., Navathe, S. B., and Weldon, J. "An Integrated Approach to Logical Database Design," *NYU Symposium on Database Design,* New York University, 1978.

The authors include the following important steps in logical data base design:

- Requirements Analysis: Analyzing the real world and identifying the content of the data base and processing requirements
- View Modelling: Developing abstract views of the data identified above which serve each user
- View Integration: Combining the various user views into a global view capable of supporting each user view

The paper reviews the principles of ten different approaches to design which have been proposed by others, with emphasis on the View Integration step.

5. Gane, C., and Sarson, T. *Structured Systems Analysis: Tools and Techniques,* Englewood Cliffs, N.J.: Prentice-Hall, Inc., 1979.

Structured analysis methods such as the one described in this popular methodology emphasize the flow of data in an organization. Successive levels of refinement are used to depict the inputs, processes, outputs, and "data stores" which are required. While such methods analyze data flows in a top-down fashion, the data and data structures are developed bottom-up—i.e., working from the most detailed requirements. A high level, application-independent conceptual view of an organization's data is not considered.

# 4

# Data Elements

## INTRODUCTION

This chapter builds a rigorous definition of a data element in terms of two primary concepts: domain and assertion. In the process, a deeper understanding of the nature of a data element and its role as the building block of data bases is developed. First, we present a brief overview of the major points to be made, and then delve into the nature of domains, assertions, and data elements more closely.

The external world, that is, the world outside the data base, contains objects that need to be represented inside the data base. These external objects must be represented by symbols because the data base can only work with symbols and contains nothing but symbols. Therefore we must assign selected symbols to represent external world objects. There are also some less tangible objects that are sometimes created *inside* a data base. These also need to be represented by the assignment of selected symbols.

When the assignment of a symbol has taken place, the identified external world object is called an *entity*. The associated symbol is its *entity identifier*. Similarly, an identified internal object is called a *construct* and the associated symbol is a *construct identifier*.

We take the perspective in these pages that every symbol in a populated data base is interpretable as an entity identifier or as a construct identifier. The interpretation requires adjectives like "red" to be interpreted as nouns like "redness," with corresponding adjustments to the verbs. The result of this discipline is to lay bare, in stark simplicity, what a populated data base is. It is a conglomeration of symbols, all of which are substantives.

Since the data base contains only "nouns" and, in particular, only the entity identifiers and construct identifiers defined above, it is orderly and useful to assume that an entity inventory is recorded. This is a list showing which symbols have been assigned to which objects. Separate inventories can be maintained for entities and constructs.

Both inventories grow and change with time, of course. But at a chosen instant, a populated data base will consist entirely of symbols drawn from these inventories if the foregoing formulation is adopted.

The entity inventory* is divided into classes. Each class has a name and a defining condition so that it will be decidable whether or not some new object is a member of the class. Some symbols are reserved to serve as entity identifiers for these future members.

---

*Constructs will be dealt with later as secondary structures built upon the more basic entities in the data base. We omit them from further discussion in this introduction.

Notice carefully that each class contains:

— entity identifiers assigned to objects
— entity identifiers reserved for future use
— entities (objects) that have been identified

It excludes objects that are not entities.

The set of all entity identifiers in a class (those assigned plus those reserved) is called the extension of the ⟨class-name⟩.

An indeterminate is a *named symbol* (strictly, a *meta-symbol*), associated with a specified set, which may take on (as its value) any member of that set and only a member of that set. Only one set member at a time may be so substituted for an indeterminate. The indeterminate is said to be "defined over" the associated set, and the associated set is called the domain of the indeterminate "defined over" it.

Every data element in a data base is such an indeterminate defined over a specified set of entity identifiers. As a rule, a data element's domain is a subset of the entity identifiers in a single class. While most domains are further restricted to entity identifiers that have already been assigned to objects, there are data elements in every data base whose domain includes the *entire* extension of a class; these domains include entity identifiers not yet assigned.

## DOMAINS

One of the objectives of the data base described in Chapter 2 is to reflect the actual real world conditions as they pertain to the New Plants Division. In fact, the representation of things in the real world (meaning outside of the data base) is a primary concern of *any* data base investigation. In the process of designing a data base, there is a great choice of both how to represent things and what things to represent, greater in fact than most data base methodologies account for, or in practice than most designers consider. And, as we shall show, the choice of the representation can have profound consequences on the capabilities and limitations of the resulting data base.

There is a temptation to look about the real world, observe how people represent or identify objects (in verbal discourse or in written documents, for example) and to adopt these naming or numbering mechanisms directly. Similarly, if no convenient identifier exists for an object or class of objects we wish to represent, we invent one with little thought and proceed to other matters. We wish to depart from this temptation rather dramatically.

Since the data base only contains symbols, there is only one way for the data base to acknowledge that an object (or anything) exists. That is done by reserving a symbol (or an interpretation of a symbol) for this identification purpose. The act of identifying a thing by assigning it an identifying symbol occurs every day in court as objects are duly marked "Exhibit A" for purposes of identification. Since computers and data bases work with a limited number of discrete symbols (ultimately the binary pair 0,1), it is necessary to acknowledge that the identifying symbols are strings of discrete symbols, not just single letters like "A." Still, everything the data base is capable of identifying is and must be assigned such a symbol string. We shall call a thing (be it a real object, or an abstract thing in the real world), that has actually been assigned an identifying symbol an *entity*.

It is extremely useful to imagine that the data base has available an inventory of entities, even when the data base is implemented in a way that makes it difficult to find a record of such an inventory. Our use of the inventory is to understand, to describe, and to help design the data base. This does not imply that the entity inventory is necessary as such when *operating* a data base.

Visualize the inventory as a long list of pairs, where the left-hand member is the identification symbol and the right-hand member is some wholly distinctive manifestation of the thing identified. The purpose of the right-hand side is to define the thing named, and we can record whatever is needed. For people, we can use signatures, fingerprints, and photographs. For parts, we can use blueprints, material lists, etc. For abstract things, definitions and illustrative diagrams may be needed. Since we have difficulty representing an idealization of an entity on these pages (a photograph would be useful for certain entities), we will use double quotes instead. Be sure not to confuse ""Phil Smith"" with a person's name ("Phil Smith" is the person's name—think of ""Phil Smith"" as the person himself). A sample of the entity inventory might be as follows:

| Entity Identifier | Real World Entity |
|---|---|
| A%B12X | ""NPD contract with xyz client"" |
| 143-27-8099 | ""Phil Smith"" |
| N5MA46JL | ""The pump for the steel plant now sitting on the receiving dock"" |
| Blue | ""The color blue"" |

Naturally, entities may be added to this inventory whenever they are identified via the symbol-assignment process; deletion of entities is not so free, however, since we want to keep an entity in the inventory so long as there is any reference to it in the data base.

In this process of assigning *entity identifiers* to represent real world entities, several kinds of correspondences can emerge. The correspondence can be one-to-one so that for each distinct real world entity there is one and only one distinct identifier. Or the correspondence can be one-to-many, many-to-one, or many-to-many. These last three types of correspondence are troublesome. For if we observe '1234' as the value of an entity identifier assigned to a contract item in the data base, we would like to have some assurance that it represents a particular contract item, and not many different contract items. Questions and problems which arise from other than one-to-one correspondence types are very important, because they do in fact occur in many existing data bases. We shall be returning to this topic later.

Clearly, it is insufficient for the inventory to be limited only to entities which have been assigned identifiers in the past. A data base is a generalized facility, and must provide for a mechanism which allows for entities not yet identified. We do this by visualizing an extended entity inventory of "dummy" pairs added for future growth. In addition, it will be necessary to classify the entities and hence their identifiers into subsets, for reasons to follow. The concept of a class of entity identifiers, combined with the extended inventory forms a key concept in logical data base design—that of a *domain*. Several domains are exhibited in Figure 4-1.

While it is possible to imagine a data base in which only one or several entity classes are defined, most data bases contain quite a few. The need to classify the entities of

Domain of People

| Identifier (Social Security Number) | Entity |
|---|---|
| 123-56-8976 | ""Phil Smith"" |
| 543-47-6693 | ""Gloria Jones"" |
| . | . |
| . | . |
| . | . |

Domain of Colors

| Identifier (Color Name) | Entity |
|---|---|
| Blue | ""Blue"" |
| Red | ""Red"" |
| . | . |
| . | . |
| . | . |

Domain of Contract Items

| Identifier (Contract Item Tag) | Entity |
|---|---|
| 8346-87B | ""a certain valve"" |
| 7768-33N | ""that gear"" |
| . | . |
| . | . |
| . | . |

Domain of Days of the Week

| Identifier (Day Code) | Entity |
|---|---|
| 1 | ""Sunday"" |
| 2 | ""Monday"" |
| . | . |
| . | . |
| . | . |

Figure 4-1. Examples of domains.

interest arises for a number of reasons. A major one stems from the desire to restrict occurrences of entity identifiers in specific portions of the data base to a "certain" class. For example, in that portion of the data base which conveys information about the phone numbers of vendors, we would like to restrict the entity identifiers to those which, in fact, identify legitimate parts and phone numbers. This will help avoid the pitfalls of dealing with the phone numbers of a part, or the time required to "heat treat" a phone number.

Other reasons for classifying entity identifiers into domains can be found. On a very practical level, it provides for reuse of the symbol strings used as entity identifiers across domains, without upsetting the nature of the mapping within a domain. Thus the string "1234" may identify a contract item (using the ITEM NUMBER) in the item domain, and a vendor (using DUNS NUMBER) in the vendor domain, because the rules for interpretation can always specify the domain of an identifier appearing in a certain portion of the data base.

Beyond these validation and editing uses, the domain concept permits ready comparisons of data elements which are defined over the same domain. Thus, if we have two assertions represented as follows:

and both REGISTRATION NUMBER OF CAR OWNED and CAR are defined over the same domain, then we know that we can derive assertion instances about the color of particular person's cars by matching the assertion occurrences on the entity identifiers which share a common domain. This enables us to answer questions like "Which persons have yellow cars?". Notice that merely matching on symbol strings does not provide the same result; if the symbol strings are from distinct domains, then the derived assertions will not hold logically.

Readers familiar with the relational model will recognize this as a join operation. While in the relational model, join operations are generally defined *only* where there is a common domain, there may be cases where it is meaningful to drop this restriction. For certainly we can perform the join type operation on entity identifiers which are not drawn from a common domain—for example, to answer the question "Which people have last names which are the same as the color of their cars?".

Mr. Brown and Mrs. Green might be such persons. But notice this kind of match is on a different level than the one involving matching vehicle numbers to determine the color of a person's car. We don't mean to say "find a person (or a person's name) which *is* the color of his car" as this would be meaningless. What we mean is "find instances where the entity identifier for a person's name is the same as the entity identifier for the color of his car." In other words, the *representations* are equal, not the real world objects themselves. The differences can be readily appreciated if we transform the data base into Spanish; the answer to the first question would be the same, but the second would yield Sr. Rojo and Sra. Blanco.

In addition, it is useful to assign identifiers to entities within each domain according to a set of rules. Most often, these rules define a set of possible valid symbol strings (for the extended inventory) which is greater than the number of objects in the real world which are in that domain (or are of potential interest). For example, if we utilize the set of all nine-digit symbol strings as entity identifiers for the domain of oceans, then very, very few of the possible identifiers will ever be actually used (as there are only about seven oceans). This phenomenon builds redundancy into the identification scheme, because at any time we are very unlikely to make a transcription error of some sort on an assigned symbol string and get another *assigned* string.

In other cases, the rules for entity identifier formation for a class of entities can specify certain symbol string syntax. For example, contract item identifiers will be of the form "AXXX-BXX" where X can be any digit. So if we see a symbol string purporting to be an entity identifier in the domain of contract items, and it begins with "Q," we know there is an error.

How should the entities of interest to a data base be classified into domains? This is a most important question which receives too little attention in many data base design efforts. There are choices and the choices have important consequences. We could certainly find various people or functions within an organization who view the entities of interest from different perspectives, and who would classify or partition them in different ways. For some purposes ⟨people⟩* should be distinguished from ⟨corporations⟩ but for others ⟨people, corporations, and trusts⟩ should be a single set of ⟨legal entities⟩.

Again, consider our plant construction company which deals with purchased contract items and manufactured contract items. We wish to record various kinds of information about both kinds of items in our data base, sometimes the same information about both kinds. Thus, sometimes the distinction is important, sometimes not. Information about purchase orders, vendors, and transportation costs apply only to purchased items. Information about manufacturing processes, labor hours, and machine setups apply only to manufactured items. And information about inventory, quality controls, and next assembly requirements apply to both kinds. It will be shown in Chapter 6 that the impact of a choice between two domains such as ⟨manufactured contract items⟩ and ⟨purchased contract items⟩ and a single domain ⟨contract item⟩ can be significant. For now, we are content in showing that reasonable choices exist.

Now let us recapitulate the discussion so far, and provide a more rigorous definition for domain.

- There exist things, concrete or abstract, in the real world. These are called *real world objects.*
- Each such object in the real world which is of interest to the data base is called an *entity,* and will be identified with a label called an entity identifier consisting of a string of symbols. We distinguish an entity identifier name which names a class of symbol strings (such as Social Security number) and instances of an entity identifier (such as 143-59-9844).
- A *domain* is a set of ordered pairs which define the correspondence of entity identifiers and real world entities for a subset of real world entities having a common, stated property.

Thus, we can define the domain of ⟨contract item⟩ which consists of the subset of real world entities which are, or could be, used as parts or components in a plant, and their associated entity identifiers (e.g., item tags). Such a domain was shown in Figure 4-1.

## ASSERTIONS

The previous section described a mechanism by which things inside a data base (entity identifiers) can refer to things outside a data base. To reflect reality, a data base must be capable of conveying information about these things. The basic mechanism which accomplishes this is the assertion.

A *data base assertion* is the representation of a relationship or mapping between entities in two domains (or between entities in the same domain). The mapping for a simple relationship maps each entity identifier in one domain to none, one, or more than one entity identifier in another domain (or the same domain). We distinguish between the *assertion type* which provides the template for the mapping, and an *assertion occurrence* (instance) in which actual entity identifiers are related.

*We shall use this notation to refer to a class of entities and their identifiers (a domain) from this point on.

An assertion type or template is composed of a key or subject and one or more targets. The subject and each target are defined over the entity identifiers in one of the domains between which the mapping holds. Thus, consider the assertion type and occurrences exhibited in Figure 4-2. In this assertion:

- The key or subject has the domain of ⟨vendor⟩ whose entity identifiers are vendor names.
- The target has the domain of ⟨standard items⟩ whose entity identifiers are standard item tags.
- The mapping is from the vendors to the standard items which they supply.

By definition, the key of an assertion forms its primary subject—i.e., represents the entity which the assertion is about. In contrast, the target(s) of an assertion form the object of the mapping.

Assertion Type or Template: Standard Item which is supplied by Vendor

| Assertion Occurrences: | *Vendor* | *Standard Item* |
|---|---|---|
| | Acme Co. | A124 |
| | Brown Inc. | C312 |
| | . | . |
| | . | . |
| | . | . |
| | United Co. | L771 |

Figure 4-2. Assertion type and occurrences.

Thus, if we wish to express the owning relationship between the domain of ⟨people⟩ and the domain of ⟨vehicles⟩, we construct an assertion type which will have people as the key and vehicles as the target. The entity identifier for the domain of ⟨people⟩ might be Social Security number and the entity identifier for the domain of ⟨vehicles⟩ might be registration number. The complete assertion can be depicted in our notational system. Note that the relationship itself is expressed as part of the target. In this case, the

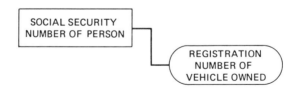

relationship is one of being owned and is expressed by the target REGISTRATION NUMBER OF VEHICLE OWNED.

One of the reasons for expressing the relationship as part of the target is to enable us to build up compound simple assertions. Compound simple assertions are ones with multiple targets. Each target can express a different relation in a compound simple assertion, all with the same subject (key). This is not so if the key carries the expression of the relation. So a compound simple assertion is of the form:

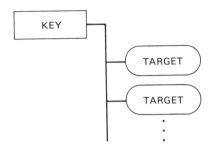

and an example might be

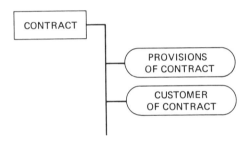

Remember that the targets can be defined over the same domain as the key, representing relationships which map a domain onto itself. For instance,

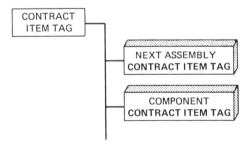

A logical data base can be thought of as containing a set of assertion templates. And the process of logical data base design is largely one of constructing and defining proper assertion templates and their constituents (entity identifiers, domains, data elements, and relationships). A data base assertion template can be likened to the concept of logical record type.

Nonsimple assertions involve "cascades" of targets in which a target is dependent on (varies by) the combination of targets and key above and to the left of it; thus in this cascade:

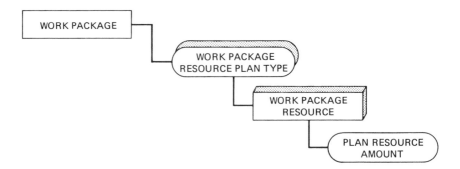

The value of the target PLAN RESOURCE AMOUNT depends on the combination of WORK PACKAGE, WORK PACKAGE RESOURCE PLAN TYPE, and WORK PACKAGE RESOURCE. Finally, compound cascades can be built up as shown throughout the NPD sample data base. The semantics or meaning of an assertion template is outlined in Figure 4-3. The key of the assertion is its subject, and reflects the entity which the assertion is about. The key enters into relationships with each target at the next level. The combination of key-target can itself form a secondary subject which enters into a relationship with a target at the next lower level. The resulting key-target-target can then form another subject.

Each of these subjects bears one or more relationships to variables at the next lower level. Notice that in all assertion templates, each vertical line reflects a distinct subject. The subject is defined by the cascade above and to the left of the vertical line. Each

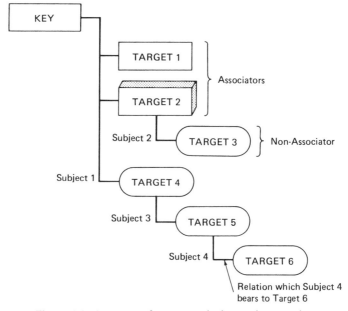

Figure 4-3. Anatomy of a prototypical assertion template.

such subject bears one or more relationships; each such relationship is borne to the target on the next lower level.

This is important: the relationship is *not* borne to all targets nested below the target at the next level nor to "the whole cluster of targets" below a certain point. The relationships proceed one step at a time, relating the entire accumulated subject to *one* target at the next lower level. Strict adherence to this practice has the tangible advantage that a new target can be coordinated to any existing subject in the structure without requiring (or implying) a redefinition of existing relationships. As always, this requires diligence in the analysis of the candidate subject to make sure it exactly matches the subject of the relationship to be added.

## DATA ELEMENTS

We are now in a position to define what is meant by a data element:

A data element is a key or a target, suitably defined over a domain, in a data base assertion template.

(There are many names for the same data element. One name is the text that appears inside the box or oval in the assertion template chart. Other names include the "COBOL name" and similar shortened forms that are used for various purposes inside computer systems and by external users.)

Note in particular the distinction being made between data elements and entity identifier names, as exhibited in Figure 4-4. Employee Number per se is not to be considered a data element; rather each place in an assertion template where Employee Number is the entity identifier of the underlying domain constitutes a separate and unique data element. This distinction between data element and entity identifier is crucial in logical data base design. For example, Employee Number may be used many places within a data base design:

EMPLOYEE NUMBER OF APPLICANT
EMPLOYEE NUMBER OF DEPARTMENT MANAGER
EMPLOYEE NUMBER OF RELATED EMPLOYEE

We cannot merely define "employee number" as an identifying number assigned to each employee and be done with it. This is not the definition of any data element!

Before embarking on a more thorough discussion of the proper way to define data elements, consider the issue of how to name them. This issue causes considerable problems in many data base projects, and is partially solved by having a meaningful idea of what a data element is, such as has been provided here. Yet there are still some choices to be made. For instance, it is not at all necessary to specify the name of the entity identifier in the name of the data element. Thus we might have

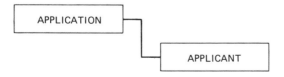

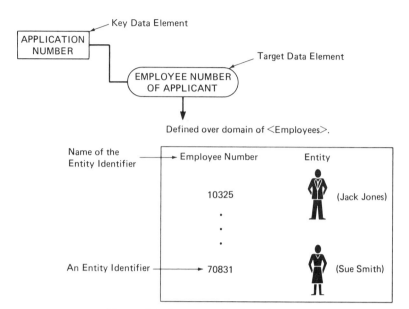

Figure 4-4. Anatomy of a data element.

provided, of course, that the identification of the underlying domains were clearly spec-ified and recognized. Alternatively, we can insist that all data element names begin with the entity identifier name of its domain followed by "of" (or other suitable preposition):

EMPLOYEE NUMBER OF APPLICANT
EMPLOYEE NUMBER OF DEPARTMENT MANAGER
DEPARTMENT NUMBER OF EMPLOYEE
STANDARD ITEM TAG WHICH IS SUPPLIED BY VENDOR

In general, a data element name could include such prepositional qualifiers as "of" for each level in the cascade which forms its subject. This convention yields long qual-ified data element names such as

PART NUMBER OF LINE ITEM OF REVISION OF PURCHASE ORDER

Whatever data element naming rules are applied in a logical data base design, they should

a. be consistently applied
b. provide each element with a unique meaningful name
c. suggest the nature of the relationship with the subject, if the data element is a target

This last rule is important if we wish the name of the element to be at least suggestive of its meaning, since the meaning of an element is bound up in the relationship it bears with the key. In fact, to a large extent the meaning of an element is more dependent on this relationship than on the domain over which it is defined. In the APPLICATION-APPLI-

CANT example, no domain is specified (whether applicants are identified by Social Security Number or Employee Number, or Name is not known). But we do have a good idea of the meaning conveyed by APPLICANT. In this respect, the preposition "of" provides very little indication of the meaning of the relationship, as in

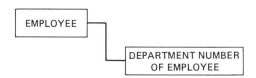

DOES DEPARTMENT NUMBER OF EMPLOYEE mean his assigned department, the department for which he is responsible, or the department in which he is currently physically located? The word "of" is quite vague. If there is to be only one relationship among employees and departments, then this issue is less critical. If there can be more than one such relationship, then the names of the different elements must be distinct and reflect the meaning of the specific relationship embodied in each element. Since we generally cannot guarantee that additional relationships will not be added to the design at a later point, using the most descriptive name from the start constitutes a good practice.

In the New Plants Division sample data base, we use data element names which are complete enough to distinguish one element from another, yet are not fully qualified using the "of" rule above. Moreover, for associators, we include the name of the entity identifier in the element name (and underline it in the templates). We strive for names which are meaningful yet not awkward—sometimes this causes us to put the identifier name first (e.g., CONTRACT ITEM INSTANCE OF WORK PACKAGE RESULT) and sometimes not (e.g., NEXT ASSEMBLY CONTRACT ITEM TAG).

Data elements form the basic building blocks of a data base design. Providing clear, meaningful, and unambiguous definitions for all the data elements in all of the assertion templates of the design is one of the most important activities of the data base designer. Complete documentation of each data element (perhaps in an automated data dictionary) will be required; further discussion of data element documentation is contained in Chapter 6. The definition of the data element is only a part of the complete documentation, although an important part. Note that the annotations which may appear to the right of each element in an assertion template, such as those in the NPD example, are not intended to provide complete definitions of the data elements.

In a moderately sized data base design, involving many hundreds of data elements, it is likely that many data elements will be defined over common domains. Thus it becomes natural to define the domains separately from the elements, rather than repeat their definitions as part of each element. These domain definitions can be provided in a glossary to the data base design.

Here we provide a few guidelines on what to include in a domain definition:

1. The description of a domain should emphasize the nature of the entity identifier involved—namely, that its purpose is to identify a set of real world objects. The definition should clearly specify what those objects are and any rules for determining whether or not an object is to be included in the domain.

For example:

> Domain is ⟨Factory⟩. A Factory is a contiguous physical location which is capable of producing any of the company products. Factory Number identifies each such location. Locations which are on opposite sides of town, for example, receive separate Factory Numbers. Locations which repair products but do not produce them are not regarded as Factories.

2. The nature of the correspondence between the entity identifier and the real world object in the domain should be specified, including rules for reassigning identifiers, and in general highlighting cases where other than a one-to-one correspondence is in effect.

For example:

> Factory Number is intended to identify uniquely each producing location, from the time the Factory is first operational until five years after it has been inoperative, at which time the Factory Number may be reassigned. However, in South America, Factories in different countries occasionally have the same Factory Number assigned to them.

3. Reference should be made to the authority for assigning the entity identifiers to the entities.

For example:

> Factory Numbers are assigned by the Corporate Production Scheduling Department and are published in Section B-3 of the company's Procedures Manual.

4. Be sure to include any exceptions or special cases not covered by the normal definition.

For example:

> Factory Number 000 is reserved for use when no factory is involved in production of the product—for instance, when a service but not a product is being referenced. Factory Number 999 is used when the product is produced at a field site and not at a production factory.

Given that the underlying domains have been adequately described, definitions of data elements can be prepared. These should emphasize the meaning of the appearance of an entity identifier in the assertion template. Some guidelines for the development of data element definitions are:

1. The primary focus of the data element definition is on the *function* of the element in the assertion. Thus the definition of the data element

FACTORY ASSIGNED TO CUSTOMER ORDER

should emphasize what it means for a factory to be assigned to a customer order; it should be less concerned with what a factory or customer order is—these will be defined elsewhere as part of other data element or domain definitions.

For example:

> Indicates the factory which the production scheduling department initially expects to produce all the products on the customer order. It may or may not be the factory which actually produces the products for the order.

In order to encourage emphasis on the function of the data element, it is helpful to begin the definition with verbs.

For example:

> specifies
> identifies
> indicates
> provides
> represents
> quantifies
> qualifies

2. For a key data element, the definition is meant to identify the primary subject of the entire assertion. Thus an occurrence of this element corresponds to an occurrence of the assertion and the definition should specify which occurrences are expected in the data base. Thus the key CUSTOMER ORDER might have included in its definition a statement that all regular customer orders will be in the data base from order entry time until three months after shipment, but special orders will remain on the data base for nine months after shipment.
3. For optional data elements, a clear description of the conditions under which it will appear or not appear is required.
4. Nonkey data elements reflect a relationship between a subject and target (the data element being defined). It is important to define the conditions under which the relationship holds, the time period for which it holds, or when the observation reporting the relationship took place. Thus, CREDIT RATING OF CUSTOMER OF ORDER refers to the customer's credit rating at the time the order was placed, and not the current credit rating.
5. Data elements which are quantities need to have the unit of measure specified, unless it is given by another data element.

It is important to note that in the development of the notion of a data element, no distinction between entities and attributes has been made. Some methods for data base design make a distinction between objects and their attributes (or characteristics) at the outset. We do not. The nature of colors, for example, can be no different from that of persons. Color can be an entity, which itself has attributes (e.g., consider a paint factory data base where color is the key of a file, and has attributes like inventory values, degree of pleasantness to the eye, covering ability, etc.). Similarly, people can be used as an attribute (e.g., in a file of cartoon characters, we describe the voice of the character as similar to that of a certain person). It seems more prudent to have only one kind of object. So we do not make the separation between things and properties. This point of view will allow us to use the noun form for properties, even though they often appear as adjectives: redness for red, greenness for green, sturdiness for sturdy, and so on. This convention is consistent with the point made earlier that data base assertions are always about symbols that stand for objects.

## A TAXONOMY OF DATA ELEMENTS

The data base designer will find that in a typically large design problem, the vast majority of data elements can be dealt with quite easily, given the definitions and guidelines provided earlier in this chapter. There will remain, however, a few situations which are perplexing and not easily molded into this scheme. It is thus helpful to have a taxonomy of types of data elements to which the designer can refer and to which a new perplexing element can be compared. We have included such a taxonomy below. In it, we discuss several of the more common types of data elements in some detail, both to provide an account of how the framework described above can encompass each situation, and equally important, to provide examples of the conduct of inquiries into the semantics of data. For no matter how complete this or any taxonomy is, the designer will always encounter new and varied data problems to be thought through with each design.

The taxonomy presented here is a partial one which the designer will want to flesh out with emphasis on the kinds of elements likely to be encountered in each design situation. The taxonomy provides for the classification according to the scheme shown in Figure 4-5. There are three basic element types: referents, constructs, and symbol strings. Referents can be further classified according to the domain type—whether the entity identifier is external, internal, or fuzzy. Any of these types can be used to identify either of the two entity types—concrete and abstract. Other bases for classification can, of course, be found (such as one based on the nature of the relationship between the target and key), but we have found this one to be useful.

### I. Referents

By far, the vast majority of data elements are referents which refer to or stand for entities in the real world. The major breakdown of such referents in the taxonomy is according to the manner in which the entity is identified.

| Element Type | Domain Type | Entity Type |
|---|---|---|
| I. Referents | A. External Identifier<br>B. Internal Identifier<br>C. Fuzzy Identifier | 1. Concrete<br>2. Abstract |
| II. Constructs | | |
| III. Symbol Strings | | |

Figure 4-5. A taxonomy of data elements.

A. External Identifiers. This major class of data elements are those which refer to enti-ties with identifiers which are assigned in the external world. This implies that the data base system has little if any control over the identifier symbol assignment process. Thus the relationship between the entity identifiers and the entities can be one-to-many, many-to-one, or many-to-many in addition to the more desirable case of one-to-one.

Often, external identifiers are designed to help people associate certain properties of entities with the identifier. These "meaningful" numbering schemes are to be avoided in any data base because they will surely lead to problems. The identifying properties of the entity, thought to be invariant, turn out to change over time, forcing a change in the identifier.

There are generally two varieties of meaningful identifiers. In one, the properties of the entity form part of its identifier. For example, some manufacturing firms identify parts with a classification code in which the first part of the code identifies the basic function of the part (cam, gear, axle, bolt, etc.), the second part identifies its material (steel, tin, brass, etc.), and so on. In the second variety, a portion of the identifier would not uniquely identify each entity and so has to be combined with another identifier to obtain uniqueness. For example, suppose Salesman Number were assigned indepen-dently within Sales Division. The unique Salesman identifier would be the Division-Salesman Number concatenated. Even though the Division Numbers and Salesman Numbers are not in themselves meaningful, the combination is: we can determine the Division to which a Salesman is assigned by examining his Salesman identifier. And obvious problems result if a Salesman changes Divisions.

B. Internal Identifiers. Internal identifiers are assigned by the data base system itself; they are obviously meaningless and guaranteed to be in no worse than a many-to-one correspondence with actual entities. We have used the suffix "tag" as in STANDARD ITEM TAG, rather than "number" to signify use of an internal identifier.

Internal identifiers are not meant to replace external identifiers because people will continue to use the external identifiers. Instead, they supplement the external identifiers and are recommended for use in situations where duplicate external identifiers could be assigned, where the same external identifier could be assigned to two entities at the same time, or where it is important to track an entity over a historical period during which its external identifier could be reassigned.

C. Fuzzy Identifiers. Consider the following: we twice print out the symbol string in the data base for an entity identifier in the ⟨Area Code⟩ domain and once observe

$$011\ 001\ 101$$

and next observe

$$3\ 1\ 5$$

Are these different entity identifiers? Do they represent different entities? In general we would say no, they are the same identifiers representing the same Area Code. This seems to be because there exists a well-defined translation rule for transforming one symbol string into an equivalent one.

Now try these two:

Harris, Dr. J.

and

Dr. J. Harris

Here we are considering the symbol string to identify a person's name, not a person; so we have no problem with the correspondence between name and people. Rather, we are asking if two *names* shown are equivalent. Certainly, we can construct a rigorous set of rules to translate one form of the name shown to the other. This would suggest that the names are equivalent, and that these two entity identifiers are thus equivalent even if the symbol strings aren't exactly.

We often find this case of fuzzy identifiers when *textlike domains* are involved. We say textlike because text data items are classified by themselves and differ from the fuzzy identifier category. Fuzzy identifiers are meant to refer to some entity (someone's name in the above example)—thus they are referents. The textlike property is present because "textual" data items have a great deal of redundancy built into them. Consider the two data elements

SOCIAL SECURITY NO. OF EMPLOYEE

and

ADDRESS OF EMPLOYEE (as one single string)

If we make a slight alteration in the first element, say

134-07-2103

to

134-08-2103,

then these are clearly two different Social Security numbers. But the same kind of alteration in the second has little effect, e.g.,

Three twenty seven first street

Boston, Mass.

to

Three Twenty Seven First Street

Boston, Mass.

In fact, the following address on a letter would probably be properly delivered:

Tree Twnty Sven First St.

Beantown Mass.

Notice that in all of the examples above, the correspondences are many-to-one. That is we may have many identifiers for the same entity. As discussed above, this case is not nearly as bad as when we have one string which identifies many different entities. For one reason, as we have seen here, there is always the possibility of translating (e.g., via automatic spelling correction) one identifier string into an equivalent one, thereby discovering the entities are the same. In fact, being an external identifier (even though we gave it a separate category), there is *benefit* to the many-to-one mapping: people don't have to remember the exact symbol string in order to identify the entity. There appears to be no benefit to a one-to-many mapping; while we can determine if two entities are the same, there is no hope of discovering or identifying the proper one if they are different but assigned the same identifier.

*1. Concrete Entities.* External or internal identifiers can be used to identify either concrete or abstract entities. Concrete entities are those entities which have a direct physical manifestation. Definitions of data elements which are referents to concrete entities are relatively easy to construct in most cases. However, the mistake most often made is one of considering an abstract entity to be a concrete entity.

For example, a Person is a concrete entity while an Employee is not; a Building is a concrete entity while a Company is not. Part Serial Number refers to a concrete entity; Part Number does not. In general, if the data element refers to a class of things or a condition or property of things rather than directly to a "single" thing, it is not a concrete referent.

A typical concrete entity is a person. Most commercially-oriented data bases appear to have something to do with persons. However, a little thought will show that what most data bases contain is really a reference to a person in a particular role, such as student, stockholder, beneficiary, employee, etc., and not to the person per se. Thus an insurance data base may contain data about policyholders and agents, but have no capability to determine if an agent is a policyholder. Conversely, if the data base knew about which persons were policyholders and which persons were agents, then the question could be answered; in such a data base, the reference is to the person as well as the role. If the data base uses AGENT NO. as an identifier, then it is identifying agents (an abstract entity) and not persons. It's almost like saying the data is about AGENT NO. 3770, whichever person that happens to be.

Certainly the trend in modern integrated data bases is to track a person in the various roles he/she may play with respect to the organization, and over substantial time periods. These roles include employment candidate, employee, director, consultant, stockholder, pensioner, and so on. Use of the ubiquitous "employee number" often causes problems when employees transfer to other divisions, leave and return, or become of interest wholesale by acquisition of other companies.

All of this is not to say that identifying such roles is bad, but the designer should not suggest that the data base knows much about persons, and should be aware of the consequences as described above.

Data bases need to reference various types of inanimate objects which relate to the organization's business, such as parts, machines, documents, vehicles, classrooms, and so on. External identifiers are most often in existence to reference these objects, and frequently they are used directly as entity identifiers by the data base.

Again, sometimes reference is being made to a class of objects instead of to individual concrete objects. This is the case with "part number," which usually refers to the class of physical objects which share a common design. Reference to the physical object itself must be done with some kind of serial number. The importance of such "serial numbers" has risen recently in response to requirements for product safety and recall.

*2. Abstract Entities.* Abstract entities do not have physical manifestations. Sometimes abstract entities are idealized or generalized versions of individual concrete entities, such as part number, and this causes some confusion. But a little analysis will reveal the true nature of an entity.

Abstract entities tend to be more difficult to define because, being abstract, they are the products of our minds. We cannot point to a "design change level" or to a "date" in the physical world. Rather, we must all agree on what is meant by these concepts, and most often the organizational conflicts resulting from uniformity efforts revolve around the definitions of abstract entities.

*Dates.* The concept of date has a number of interesting aspects. These will be used to exemplify a rather complete analysis of the semantics of data elements built upon this concept.

At first blush, a date is such a familiar and commonplace data item that its properties seem obvious and trivial. One simply stamps "January 20, 1980" on a document in the "expiration date" position and everyone knows what that means. Yet there are many implications hidden behind calling something a date.

Very large computer networks of national and transoceanic scope span many time zones. Clearly, the system clock in New York still indicates it is January 19 when it is midnight in London and January 20 further to the east. The time period called "January 20, 1980" is distinct for every time zone. In systems of such scope, one needs to know where (geographically) the date is being observed in order to know precisely which of 24 possible time intervals is meant by the reference to January 20, 1980. The standard solution is to record time and hence dates at a standard reference place. The Greenwich time zone is often used for this purpose.

Even when the date is referred to a standard time zone, ambivalence clouds the moment of midnight. Shall it be the last moment in yesterday or the first moment of today? There are at this writing two official standards on this question: we must choose one or another before expressing confidence that we have fully defined what is denoted by the entity identifier "January 20, 1980." Many data bases, of course, are forever destined to be concerned with highly localized data (e.g., the municipal power plant) and it is the rare system that cares how midnight is defined. Yet the designer should be alert to the possibility that in time, a system may grow in scope or precision of measurement and run up against a poorly chosen definition of what a date refers to.

Having presumably decided what this abstract object is to which "date" refers, let us call it a "calendar day." Each day is a set of moments, an agreed-upon interval in absolute time. The *day* is an external world object; the *date* is a carefully controlled and standardized external *identifier* for that object. Given this one-to-one correspondence between a date and a day, two events that allegedly happen on January 20, 1980 (Greenwich) can be imputed to occur in the same 24-hour period. Contrast the other case where local time is used in defining dates. One event on January 20, 1980 (Greenwich) is compared with another event on January 20, 1980 (New York). Assume five hours difference. Did the two events take place in the same 24-hour period? Perhaps yes, perhaps no. A diagram of the overlap period suggests several possibilities.

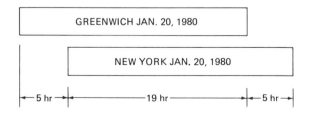

There are five hours where the answer is "No, they did not occur in the same 24-hour period. There are 19 hours where they surely did occur in the same 24-hour period. We are reduced to saying something probabilistic: "If we assume that the two events took place in the same 24-hour period, we will be right (on the average) in 19 out of 24 cases; we will be wrong (on the average) in 5 out of 24 cases where we make this assumption."

Data bases rarely operate on the probabilistic basis just suggested. They operate on a logical basis, and what happens in the case where multiple time zones use the same name (date) for different time intervals (days) is quite interesting. Refer again to the same drawing of two days, the Greenwich day and the New York day. Observe that the total time span covered by the figure is 29 hours. Given two events that occur on January 20, 1980 we are *certain* they fall within 29 hours of each other. If the scope of the system is larger, the area of certainty is extended to 36 hours or more. When one asks the data base whether two events happened on the same date, the meaning of this data element called *date* in the query is adjusted as necessary. The answer is given: "Yes, both events happened on the same date, January 20, 1980." Observably, both events are so marked, but the "date" in the answer assertion, unlike other dates, refers to a time interval greater than 24 hours. To phrase the same point differently, there is a definition of the *date* January 20, 1980 floating around in the system that treats it as a 29- or 36-hour day.

Consider the representation of dates that have the following familiar structure:

$$\text{Month/Day-of-Month/Year/Zone}$$

A well-formed date, like "January 20, 1980 Greenwich" refers to a specific 24-hour period in time. An ill-formed date, like "January 66, 1980 (Greenwich)" does not refer to any 24-hour period.

We shall also, for comparison, introduce the *Julian calendar*. In the Julian calendar, a reference date (say January 1, 1800) is chosen, and assigned the number 1. Subsequent dates are numbered by counting forward. A useful property of the Julian count* is that the interval between two events, in days, is easily established by subtracting the Julian counts.

Consult a calendar and list the dates from January 1, 1800 to January 1, 2000 inclusive. Since the Greenwich time zone is always understood, the suffix can be omitted. This list is the domain of ⟨date⟩; each entry refers one-to-one to a well-defined day in a well-defined set of days. Each entry is an entity identifier.

Since the calendar seems so well-behaved, it is natural to inspect the constituent parts (MONTH, DAY-OF-MONTH, YEAR) and to inquire if they are entity identifiers. Choose YEAR first. What is a YEAR? The two possible definitions of interest are:

(a) A YEAR is a set of days at Greenwich between one called January 1 and the next December 31, inclusive.
(b) A YEAR is a set of ⟨Date⟩ that have the same number after the DAY-OF-MONTH.

Clearly, the second definition (b) is making the definition of a YEAR dependent on the definition of another domain ⟨Date⟩. Recall that we listed the ⟨Dates⟩ from January

---

*We avoid calling it the Julian date in this section, though that is the common term, reserving "date" for calendar date identifiers in MONTH, DAY-OF-MONTH, YEAR, ZONE format.

1, 1800 through January 1, 2000, adopting the Greenwich definition. As a consequence, it follows that only the *years* from 1800 to 2000 inclusive are defined, that only Greenwich years are defined, and 2000 is a year consisting of a single date: January 1, 2000.

This last, bizarre property could easily be repaired by extending the definition of the ⟨Date⟩ domain through December 31, 2000. It could also be repaired by curtailing the list so it stops at December 31, 1999. If this is not done, then the system's definition of a YEAR departs unacceptably from common usage; it allows years to contain any number of dates (from 1 to 366), depending on how the ⟨Date⟩ domain is defined.

A similar contrasting pair of definitions can be developed for MONTH, but here an extra ingredient is added. There are two kinds of MONTH that need to be distinguished. One is an instance of a PARTICULAR MONTH, like January 1970; another is the GENERIC MONTH, like April, which has seasonal properties regardless of the year. As before, we can define a PARTICULAR MONTH as:

(a) The set of all Greenwich days between a specified first-of-month day and the next first-of-month day.
(b) The set of dates such that the month name is fixed and the year number is also fixed.

The GENERIC MONTH is a set of PARTICULAR MONTHS under either definition. The consequences of using definition (b) should be apparent, since the same problems arise when defining MONTHS in terms of dates as they occur when defining YEARS in terms of dates.

The third ingredient of the date is the DAY-OF-MONTH number. As usual, it can be defined in terms of days or of dates. the DAY-OF-MONTH is:

a. A set of days at Greenwich such that each one begins the same number of days after the nearest preceding first of the month.
b. A set of entries in the domain of dates such that each has the same symbol between the MONTH and the YEAR.

In this case, the second definition (b) in terms of dates is even more defective than usual; it fails to acknowledge the noteworthy fact that the fourth day of the month always follows the third day of the month. This is not entirely surprising, for the series of (b) definitions (using dates) is considerably more permissive than the (a) set. The (b) set allows us to exclude weekends from the set of dates, omits the concept of time intervals, and allows months and years that consist of a single date.

A way out of the difficulties raised by the (b) definitions is shown in Figure 4-6. It is based on setting up the Julian count as the basic, unique identifier for a Greenwich *day* and building all the other constructs (MONTH, YEAR, etc.) on this foundation. Because the Julian count is defined over a countable interval, it is possible to define MONTHS, etc., as intervals. This preserves the properties of sequence that were lost in the (b) series of definitions above.

The figure shows that YEAR, DAY-OF-MONTH, and PARTICULAR MONTH are declared for each JULIAN COUNT and that the sequence of JULIAN COUNTS is implied. The YEAR and the PARTICULAR MONTH are defined as intervals of JULIAN COUNTS. The DAY-OF-MONTH is, however, a set containing all the JULIAN COUNTS that fall on the 24th of the month, for example. Finally, the GENERIC MONTH (e.g., April) is a set of PARTICULAR MONTHS; it is not a single time interval.

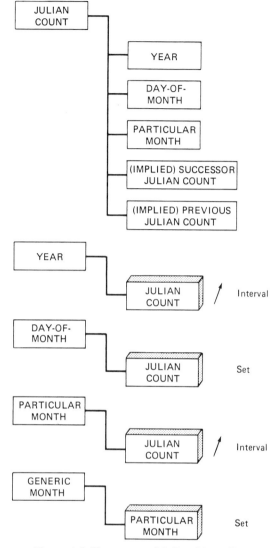

Figure 4-6. Treatment of Julian "dates."

Notice that the date construct has completely disappeared. Given a JULIAN COUNT, the date can be assembled from the PARTICULAR MONTH, DAY-OF-MONTH, YEAR data, but it is not explicitly acknowledged on the chart. There is, for example, no domain over which a date may range. There are domains for the constituent elements. In order to obtain the JULIAN COUNT for some given date, it is necessary to break it into its components.

$$\text{MONTH} = \text{January}$$
$$\text{DAY-OF-MONTH} = 24$$
$$\text{YEAR} = 1985$$

These components can now be used to obtain the JULIAN COUNT, as follows: Access YEAR to get an interval of JULIAN COUNTS. Since January is a GENERIC MONTH, access

GENERIC MONTH to get a set of PARTICULAR MONTHS. Now access these PARTICULAR MONTHS looking for one which falls inside the YEAR'S span of JULIAN COUNTS. Finally, access the DAY-OF-MONTH and pick the JULIAN COUNT which falls inside the span of the PARTICULAR MONTH. Naturally, some designers will elect to supplement Figure 4-6 with shortcuts to avoid this intricate procedure. The most effective supplement is, of course:

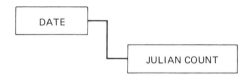

which needs to be reversed under JULIAN COUNT.

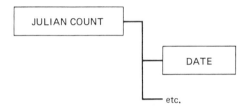

when the dates are unique. Naturally, there are also cases where we wish to assign multiple names to the same day (JULIAN COUNT). For example, the holiday names like "Christmas" and "Easter" could be considered "dates." In such cases, the reversal would be drawn:

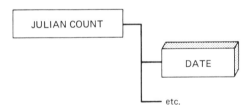

The point we wish to stress is that the structure in Figure 4-6 is invariant to these shortcuts and supplements. The alternate access path using "date" can express the date in any convention (e.g., year first) and any language (e.g., German) of the designer's choosing. Each choice produces a slightly different domain for the "date" that appears in the supplemental figure.

*Measures.* Measures are data elements which reflect a quantifiable relationship between the subject of the measurement, i.e., the key of an assertion, and either another key or some quality or characteristic (which must itself be an *object* according to our scheme of things). Consider the following assertion, likely to be found in many data bases:

If we were to examine an occurrence of this assertion, we might find the string "70" as the value of the target data element. Now, we must ask, to what entity does the entity identifier "70" refer?

As a unifying principle, the following convention will be imposed:

All numeric quantities will always be considered counts of a basic unit of measure.

Thus, the above assertion will be regarded as a shorthand for the full form:

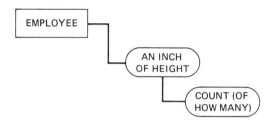

In other words, the employee in question (subject) bears a certain relationship (height) to an inch. And the count (70) modifies this relationship. One of the consequences of this perspective is that all quantities are each's—i.e., counts (not necessarily integral, of course).

Units of measure are convertible into other units according to certain relationships; these may be implicit, or explicit through assertions in the data base. Thus, for *any* data base containing the domains ⟨INCH⟩ and ⟨CENTIMETER⟩, the following assertion occurrence is implicitly assumed (if not explicitly contained in the data base):

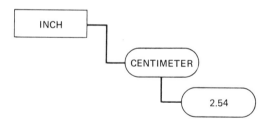

Notice also that the measure MILES-PER-HOUR is different from MILES or HOURS.

As mentioned above, the actual number in the measure is considered dimensionless—it is merely a count of some unit of measure. This count is defined over the domain of cardinal numbers—it is in essence the *cardinality* of the unit of measure in question. And so, both the unit of measure (inch) and the count (70) are identifiers for (abstract) *objects*. Nevertheless, certain well-defined operations can be performed on counts. What results must always be a count as well, but perhaps modifying a different unit of measure. Sometimes the rules are external to the data base (e.g., in the programs), or sometimes they are internal as in the assertion above. Notice that any computation involving measures never results in the identification of a new object. All we have to deal with is one or more units of measure, and a domain (whose extended inventory is infinite) called *counts*.

Often, the unit of measure for some measurement is in fact not fixed, but rather variable and specified by another data element called UNIT OF MEASURE. The two data elements always go together, as

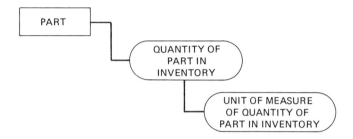

In this example, the domain of QUANTITY OF PART IN INVENTORY is again merely ⟨Count⟩, while the domain of UNIT OF MEASURE is the list of possible ⟨Units⟩ (gallons, tons, eaches, dozens, etc.).

## II. Constructs

In the introduction to this chapter, we referred to objects which were inside the data base as constructs, and the identifiers of these as data base construct identifiers. We now return to this notion, which has been eliminated from the recent discussion.

Precisely what distinction are we making between objects in the external world and those inside the data base? Consider, for instance, the following assertion:

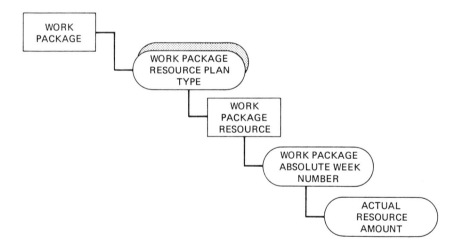

In this example, the data element, ACTUAL RESOURCE AMOUNT, is reflecting a count of a number of Resource Units which have been observed in the real world; thus it is a referent.

Contrast this with the following case. A program is written which proceeds through the data base and tallies one each time it finds an assertion instance in which ACTUAL

RESOURCE AMOUNT is greater than PLAN RESOURCE AMOUNT. And then suppose the program stores this value in the data base in an assertion something like this:

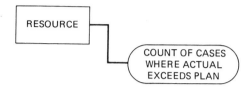

Now we ask, to what object is this new data element referring? Certainly not Resources because Resources do not *exist* in the data base, so how could we count them? Clearly, we counted something *inside* the data base. The result of that count is a data base construct.

Data base constructs can be of two kinds. In one kind, we count, average, compare or otherwise process many entity identifiers, and "compute" the value of a data element which becomes a data base construct. To give an extreme example, suppose we added together two zip codes. The resulting data element would not be a zip code (addition is not defined for zip codes). What we get is a data base construct.

In the other kind, we subdivide or dissect an entity identifier to get a portion of the symbol string. FIRST DIGIT OF ZIP CODE is not a zip code, nor does it refer to any object in the real world; it is a data base construct. But it can also clearly form the domain of a data element. This is why any definition of data element which includes something about the smallest meaningful unit of data is not a useful definition. We can usually invest some meaningfulness in just about any piece of an external entity identifier.

Notice that data base construct instances don't necessarily have to be identified themselves with entity identifiers. This is because they exist within the data base and can be observed or computed directly—we don't need surrogates for them, as we have the real thing. Of course, there are many constructs which are not stored in the data base—like those printed on output reports. These are data elements in their own right (each report could be thought of as a set of report assertions and so on). Whether stored in the data base or not, construct type data elements need to be carefully defined in terms of the other data elements from which they are computed or otherwise derived.

Construct data items are generally limited at the present time to the results of arithmetic computations. However, as the theoretical foundations of data management are expanded, they will be used to store the results of logical or even probabilistic inferences, such as found in decision support systems. One can think of referents being empirical, while constructs are analytical. The distinction can be quite important. Consider, for example, an air traffic control data base which reports that two airplanes were on a collision course at 7:15 p.m. on January 3. Now, was this assertion entered as empirical data directly into the data base, or was it constructed from a set of many different assertions? These are two distinct possibilities with different implications.

### III. Symbol Strings

Note that data base constructs are still referents of a kind; they refer to things inside the data base rather than in the real world. A symbol string type of data element does not refer to anything—rather, it *is* actually that thing (more precisely, its value is that thing). Thus if we picture the domain of a symbol string (or text) data element, each side of the symbol string-object correspondence list is identical. The string identifies itself.

The text data element DESCRIPTION OF PLANT might contain the symbol string: "NUCLEAR FUEL REPROCESSING," for example. In a real sense, names are symbol strings rather than referents. Even though in the real world we think of say a person's name as his or her identifier, most data bases do not use names per se as identifiers as we have defined them. Instead, the name data element appears in an assertion whose key is some other more controlled data element which identifies the person. As such, a relationship is depicted between the object identified by the key (the person) and the object identified by the name (the symbol string itself).

**Codes.** A code is a short symbol string that takes the place of a more lengthy and constant symbol structure. Ordinarily, there are hundreds of different coding systems used in storing, inputting, and displaying the contents of a data base. Many of these systems exist only to condense the number of symbols that need to be processed. These pure string abbreviations (e.g., two-letter codes like MA used instead of state names like Massachusetts) are of little or no interest in logical data base design. However, they are bona fide codes, and this discussion pertains to the string abbreviations in full, as it does to the more subtle and complex cases introduced below.

The relationship of interest between a code and the encoded material is unidirectional. We are interested in proceeding *from* the code *to* an expansion of the code. For example, "delivery instructions code 27" means "please telephone addressee to schedule a convenient delivery time." There are occasions when it is valuable to print the text, though in most operations the code "27" is sufficient. It is also important to establish that there is no interest in proceeding in the reverse direction, from the single place where the "please call" message is stored to all places where code 27 is used. The distinctive feature of a code is the absence of a logical need to record the reverse, or where-used, relationship. Obviously, a prime requirement is that there is no foreseen need to change the value of the code in some of its usages: the code needs to be constant, stable, and reasonably permanent for this requirement to hold.

The result is an assertion template whose key is a code and which has *no* associator stored under it, like this:

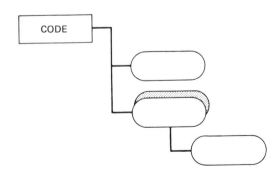

There are only circles on the right side since the code does not need where-used associators and is not an entity identifier that bears relationships.

Classifications are extremely interesting cases that may appear to be codes but really are not. Consider a set of catalog items associated with a positional coding system:

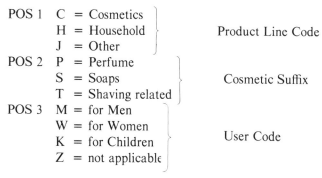

POS 1   C  = Cosmetics ⎫
        H  = Household  ⎬   Product Line Code
        J  = Other      ⎭
POS 2   P  = Perfume         ⎫
        S  = Soaps           ⎬   Cosmetic Suffix
        T  = Shaving related ⎭
POS 3   M  = for Men         ⎫
        W  = for Women       ⎬   User Code
        K  = for Children    ⎪
        Z  = not applicable  ⎭

In this system, an item marked CTM (cosmetic, related to shaving for men) might be an after-shave lotion, while one marked HK (household item for children) might be a stuffed toy animal. These classification "codes" are *not* codes by our definition even though they generally are called codes. The letters are short-form names of sets (each letter above—when used in the proper position—stands for a set, e.g., P = the set of catalog items that are perfumes); assigning the letter to a catalog item establishes the item as a member of the designated set. The relation "is a member of" is not the same as the relation "is an abbreviation for" that was shown to exist from "MA" to "Massachusetts." The structure of this example needs to be represented by:

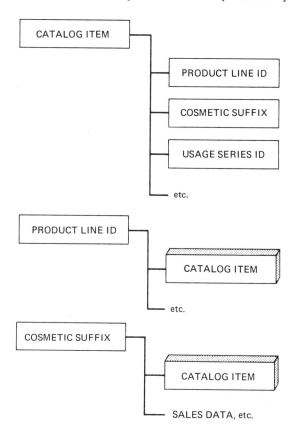

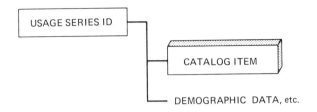

## CONCLUSION

An entity is a distinct external world object that has been (or can readily be) identified by assigning an identifier to it. An inventory of such entities is, in principle, available, and the inventory is subdivided into classes. A domain is the set of entity identifiers in one such class, including a few entity identifiers reserved for future use. Indeterminiates can be defined which take on values from domains. An indeterminate that takes on one value at a time from one domain is a data element. In the notation used in Chapter 2, all the shapes on the charts are data elements except those in dashed outlines and those which contain a LABEL or a REL attached to another shape.

Domains need to be defined carefully, especially those that are shared by many data elements. Focus on the membership condition or the nature of the correspondence between the entities and their identifiers. Data elements should be *named* carefully, and attention should focus on clarifying the function of the data element, not on "defining" it. One should avoid saying too much about the domain over which it is defined, since that is presumably said elsewhere.

Data elements are endlessly diverse. However, a taxonomy of frequently occurring element types (referents, constructs, symbols), domain types (external, internal, and fuzzy identifiers), and entity types (concrete, abstract) leads to a convenient classification of the kinds of elements most often encountered. Within this framework, attention was directed at the properties of fuzzy identifiers (address on an envelope), and the structure of a *date* was analyzed to illustrate the depth of analysis that is needed in critical cases. Quantities, units of measure, arbitrary constructs, and the qualities of codes were defined and examined.

While the philosophical intricacies are substantial when *explaining* what is or is not a domain, or a data element, users of the notation have little or no trouble in practice. If one is able to draw an assertion template (avoiding the two advanced shorthands mentioned), then the data elements are exhibited. Each shape is a different data element. The words inside the shape provide the basis for constructing an acceptable *name* for the data element. And the domain over which the named shape (thought of as an indeterminate or "variable") is defined is usually obvious. Thus, while domains and data elements are difficult ideas in the absence of an assertion template, they are very easy ideas when one of the charts is available for reference.

## REFERENCES

1. Senko, M. E., *et al.* "Data Structures and Accessing in the Data Base Systems-II Information Organization," *IBM Systems Journal,* No. 1, 1973.

   The "Entity-Set" model for information structuring is introduced; this model is the basis for the highest level of representation within the Data Independent Accessing Model (DIAM) developed by the authors.

A data base system consists of name representations of facts about real world things, which are called entities. No distinction is made between entities and properties or attributes. Entity names are used to represent entities in the data base; there could be several representations of the same name (Arabic and Roman numerals, e.g.), and one entity can have more than one unique or nonunique name.

In the Entity-Set model, entities are grouped into Entity Sets. The sets of names for these entities are called Entity Name Sets, and these are given Entity Name Set Names. Associations are relationships among entities, and are represented in the data base by relating entity names. Simple binary associations are rejected in favor of the Entity-Set model which calls for an Entity Description for each entity consisting of a *set* of triples:

- The Entity Name Set Name of an entity associated with the entity being described
- A Role name, identifying the role the Entity plays in describing the associated Entity
- An Entity name drawn from the name set above

The Entity description of a particular part might contain the following triples:

| Entity Name Set Name | Role | Entity Name |
|---|---|---|
| Part Name | Names the Part | Gear |
| Part Number | Numbers the Part | 7 |
| Weight | Indicates Weight | 17 |
| Color | Indicates Color | Blue |

One or more entity names may uniquely identify the entity; these are called Identifiers. Role names must be distinct across the entity description.

Three kinds of associations are introduced. Associations among the various triplets and the Entity being described are one kind. Associations among Entity Descriptions within the same Entity Description Set form the second kind. And Associations among the entity descriptions (of the same or different type) on the basis of common entity names form the third type (e.g., associating parts with the purchase orders they appear on).

Rules are provided in the Entity-Set model to reduce redundancy. Note that a many-to-many association must be represented by a third entity to stand for the association itself, even if there is no intersection data.

2. Smith, John, and Smith, Diane. "Principles of Database Conceptual Design," in *NYU Symposium on Database Design*, New York University, 1978.

In this and other articles, the Smiths propose a framework for conceptual data base design based on the fundamental principle of abstraction. Two specific kinds of abstractions are introduced: *aggregation* and *generalization*. Aggregation is a process which forms a new abstract object as a relationship among several other objects. Generalization is a process which forms a new abstract object from a class of other objects. In either case, an underlying premise is that the "objects" are clearly defined and well-understood by the designer.

The object DRAWING is, for example, considered to be an aggregation of the objects DRAWING NUMBER, DRAWING SIZE, and DRAWING DATE. Similarly, the object MATERIAL is an aggregation of the objects MATERIAL ID, MATERIAL NAME, and MATERIAL QUALITY. Constituents of an aggregation are called components. Instances of objects are made up of the *names* of instances of other objects. This is represented as follows:

| | Object: DRAWING | | | Object: MATERIAL | | |
|---|---|---|---|---|---|---|
| Components | DRAWING NO. | DRAWING SIZE | DRAWING DATE | MATERIAL ID | MATERIAL NAME | MATERIAL QUALITY |
| Instances | X1 | A | 1/79 | A23 | Cement | OK |
| | X2 | B | 2/79 | A25 | Brick | OK |
| | X3 | A | 1/79 | A27 | Steel | X |

|  | Object: DRAWING SIZE | | |
|---|---|---|---|
| Components | DRAWING SIZE ID | Length | Width |
| Instances | A | 8 | 11 |
|  | B | 11 | 17 |
|  | C | 30 | 40 |

Generalization forms a more generic object from a class of other objects; constituents of a generalization are called *categories:*

|  | Object: RESOURCE | | |
|---|---|---|---|
|  | Components | | Categories |
| Resource ID | | When Required | Type of Resource |
| X1 | | 3/79 | Drawing |
| A23 | | 8/80 | Material |
| X2 | | 5/79 | Drawing |

Notice in this example an object is a product of both aggregation and generalization. Also note that the name of an object—DRAWING—has become a category value in another object (resource). This is an example of the principle of object relativity, which basically states that relationships, objects, attributes, and types and instances of each are merely interpretations of the same abstract objects.

As the Smiths point out, the process of aggregation is regularly used in data base designs, but generalization is not. An understanding of the approaches involved in forming a generalization hierarchy will help the designer sharpen and clarify the objects in the design.

3. Kent, W. "Entities and Relationships in Information" in Nijssen, G. (ed.), *Architecture and Models in Data Base Management Systems,* Elsevier North-Holland Publishing Company, 1977.

   Some of the important problems which arise when we try to define entities and the relationships among them are treated in this paper. For example, collective nouns can cause particular problems (e.g., use of the term "Part" to mean "Part Type"), as can the issue of changes to entities over time (e.g., is it the same company after the owners and its location change)? Deciding what an entity is by the categories to which it belongs is also discussed (e.g., do employees of subsidiary companies, retirees, part-time employees, those on military leave, or someone who signed a contract but has not yet reported to work qualify as "employees")? As for relationships, the paper covers the following characteristics: complexity, category constraints, self-relations, and optionality.

4. McLeod, Dennis. "High Level Domain Definition in a Relational Data Base System," in *Proceedings of Conference on Data: Abstraction Definition and Structure,* Salt Lake City, 1976.

   The author of this paper proposes a system in which domains may be defined independently of each usage in columns of a relational data base. By verifying that each data value of a column was in fact a proper member of the domain, the semantic integrity of the data base will be upheld.

5. Kent, W. "The Entity Join" in *Proceedings of the 5th Very Large Data Base Conference,* 1979.

   In this article, the author elaborates on issues of matching (e.g., in a join operation) at the entity level and the representation level (recall the example dealing with the colors of cars and peoples names). In most cases, we wish to count a match if and only if the *entities* to which two symbols strings refer are equivalent. The article discusses this objective when the entity–symbol string correspondence is other than one-to-one.

6. Date, C. *An Introduction to Database Systems* (second edition), Reading, MA: Addison-Wesley Publishing Co., 1977.

The relationship between a target element and its subject (the cascade above and to the left of the target) in an assertion is such that the value of the target depends on the value of the subject. The nature of this dependency or "functional dependency" and its role in relational data bases is nicely explained in Chapter 9 of this book.

# 5

# Advanced Notation and Design Principles

## INTRODUCTION

This chapter is devoted to a complete exposition of the notation for logical data base design that was introduced in Chapter 1. The basic signs and patterns remain unchanged, and only a few new conventions are added. However, the full notational system is reviewed for completeness.

The first chapter's brief explanations were designed to permit someone to read a logical data structure; this chapter extends the concepts to the level needed to compose logical data structures. The acquisition of a "writing knowledge" requires mastery of a number of rules and principles which are stated, defined, and justified in this chapter. Admittedly, these rules and guidelines are incomplete, for they are empirical observations which have proved helpful to others in the past and promise to be helpful to others in the future. They are recorded in that spirit. At the present state-of-the-art of logical data base design, it is neither rules (nor notation) that lead to successful problem structuring. Everything rests on the designer's perceptiveness, creativity and skills.

As the design process unfolds, there are subtle changes in the usage of the notational elements. Initially, as discussed in Chapter 3, the designer's effort is concentrated on studying the fine grain of the problem, and objects and relationships are factored into primitive forms. Later on, when the whole problem has been thoroughly analyzed, emphasis turns toward recombining elements that may have been subdivided too finely. Increasing attention is paid to precision as the charts and their contents are transformed into a logical data base *design*. A casual observer might be hard pressed to detect changes in the use of the notation that take place as a design is achieved. But new standards of quality, of accuracy, and of precision become applicable as the transition is made. Standards which applied only informally during the earlier phases (when the charts show "sketches" and "working drawings") are applied more seriously in the last stages of design, where the notation provides a well-disciplined formalism.

It goes without saying that a logical data base design must capture the structure and organize the details of the real world problem. But there are also many other goals (some of which were touched on in Chapter 1) which the logical design must endeavor to meet whenever possible.

*Long-term Adaptability*

- The design should be capable of accommodating to routine changes in the environment of the enterprise without requiring radical redesign.
- The logical data base design should support several alternative pathways for evolution of the data base.

- Major problems of change-over that are foreseen should be provided for explicitly. For example, the switchover to metric units of measure may require retention of both units during the switchover period and invention of a way to reconcile the historical records for reporting purposes.

*Short-term Flexibility*

- It should be easy to define alternate plans for phased implementation of the data base in the short term.

*Completeness*

- Every entity type about which an assertion is to be stored should be represented as the key of an assertion template.
- Every construct about which we wish to store an assertion should be defined as a subject in an assertion template, and the elements comprising that assertion should be defined in the logical data structure.
- All interesting and useful relationships among entities should be explicitly recognized and fully described in the logical data base design.

*Parsimony*

- There should be no redundancy in the logical data base design. (This goal can be satisfied by marking intentionally redundant elements "probably useful" if they can be derived from more basic data. It is then understood that the logical data structure excludes these elements.)
- The logical data base design should avoid making provisions for managing uninteresting relationships.

*History*

- The logical data base design needs to be explicit concerning the disposition of the previous value of any element that is changed.
- If a historical record needs to be kept, the logical data base design needs to express a method for tracing that history in its entirety. A plausible method for relegating "inactive" records to less expensive media may need to be provided. We consider it a problem of logical data base design to set up the design to permit access to a six-year old record in the face of intervening changes. Sometimes the logic of what is attempted is dominated by such a requirement.

*Local Properties*

- It should be possible to change any one element value without affecting the stored values of more than a few (e.g., two or three) other stored values. Stated in opposite terms, a logical data base design is ill-constructed if a change to one value propagates over more than "a few" related elements.
- The logical data base design should be so constructed that it is always in a consistent state (provided certain changes are made simultaneously in two or more places in the data structure).

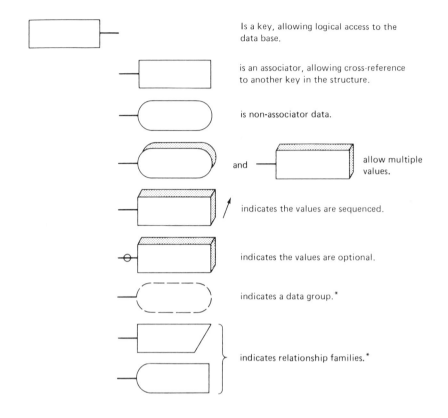

Is a key, allowing logical access to the data base.

is an associator, allowing cross-reference to another key in the structure.

is non-associator data.

and          allow multiple values.

indicates the values are sequenced.

indicates the values are optional.

indicates a data group.*

indicates relationship families.*

*Introduced in this chapter.

Figure 5-1. Elements of the complete notation.

*Comparability*

- Planned and actual values should be readily comparable.
- Related data in different time frames should be comparable.

These are challenging goals, and they impose exacting standards on the design effort. The purpose of the notation, the guidelines, and the rules is to free the designer's mind so it can attempt to meet such goals.

With this aim, the notation is reviewed and extended in Notational Conventions. Rules and guidelines for using the notation are discussed in Using the Notation. Advanced design techniques are then considered in Fundamental Rules of Logical Data Base Design.

## NOTATIONAL CONVENTIONS

### Summary of the Basic Notation

The basic notation which was introduced and discussed in Chapter 1 is summarized in this section for completeness. Three additional notational elements are introduced which permit the designer to express some important distinctions in a shorthand form.

**Inventory of the Notational Elements.** The elements of the complete notation, including the elements to be introduced in this chapter, are shown in Figure 5-1. These notational elements are combined to form assertion templates that prescribe the logical structure and the contents of data bases. Figure 5-2 shows three such assertion templates. The one at the top shows the detailed anatomy of an assertion template. This drawing will prove useful in reviewing the definitions of all the notational elements and the way in which they are used. The two assertion templates at the foot of the figure are included to illustrate the associator reversal rule.

- *Data Element.* A data element is the name of an indeterminate (variable) that appears in an assertion template, and which takes on values from a specified domain. While any distinctive symbol (e.g., "x" or "g") can be a data element, in practice it is useful to use memorable and understandable words and phrases as data elements. (Remember that the data element includes the actual *name of the*

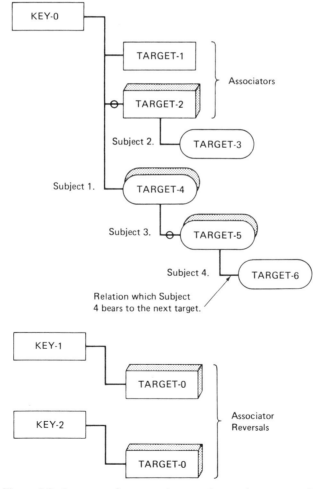

Figure 5-2. Anatomy of an assertion template and two reversals.

*variable:* the text. Once the text has been placed inside a box or oval on the charts, the whole shape becomes a data element. A variable is not a data element until (a) it has been placed inside a shape and (b) the whole shape has been connected correctly to another element in an assertion template.)

- *Key.* Each assertion template has exactly one key. The key is a simple data element written in a box on the left-hand side of the page, e.g., KEY-0 in Figure 5-2. A given data element appears no more than once in the key position in a logical design. The key plus the entire data structure depicted to its right form one assertion template.

- *Target.* All other elements in the assertion template are referred to as targets.

- *Associator.* A target data element in a box at the right is an associator (e.g., TARGET-1 at the top of Figure 5-2). It is always a reference to exactly one key located on the charts. (i.e., KEY-1 as a key at the bottom of the figure). Any data element used as an associator will almost always appear somewhere in the charts as a key. Each associator signifies the designer's intent to provide a logical access from the assertion template that contains the associator *to* the assertion template indicated by the cited key.*

- *Data.* Data elements which appear in ovals do not cite keys. The ovals may be thought of as containers for "ordinary" data values. Examples are TARGETS 3-6 in the figure. These data elements do not ordinarily appear as keys at the head of any assertion template. In the exceedingly rare occasions when the name in the oval does match a key, the oval signifies the designer's intent *not* to provide a logical access to the other key.**

- *Sets.* Solid figures are used to indicate that more than one value of a data element may appear. Examples are TARGET-2, -4 and -5. Unless explicit provisions are made, all such sets are assumed to be unordered, and they never contain duplicate values. In these respects, the given collection of data values is treated in accordance with the mathematical definition of a set; needless to say, all sets are finite in data base work.

- *Mandatory/Optional.* A small circle that stands for "optional" may be placed on the horizontal line that connects a shape to the remainder of the data structure above it. This "O" indicates that values of the data element so marked may be omitted. TARGETS 2 and 5 in the figure are optional.

- *Primitive Assertion Templates.* A primitive assertion template is a relationship between a key and a single data element at the next lower level. The relationships between the key and TARGETS 1, 2, and 4 in the figure are examples of primitive assertion templates.

- *Compound Assertion Templates.* To form *compound* assertion templates, other data elements may be attached to the vertical part of any connecting line, without limit.

*Notice that this definition requires that the domain of the associator must match the domain of the data element that appears in the cited key. Moreover, in general, the domain of the associator will be a subset of the key's domain since the key must cover potential members of the data base (the "extended inventory"), while the associator would never cite a value that is not already loaded in the data base.

**Consider a data base that contains a tickler file whose key is "date." Consider some material unrelated to the tickler file: a person, an event, or any other key. There can be dates associated with these other entities. Such dates may or may not be linked to the date that keys the tickler file. Dates that do connect are declared as associators (boxes); dates that do not connect are placed in ovals.

- *Cascades.* A data element may be subsumed under any "higher" data element to form a cascade:

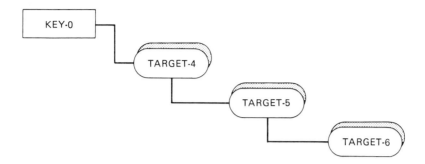

The cascaded templates and the compound templates can be used together to form elaborate tree structures under the key.

- *Subjects and Targets.* In all assertion templates, the vertical portions of the connecting lines mark the boundary between subjects and targets. The cascade above and to the left of the vertical line is the subject. It bears one or more relationships. Each such relationship is borne to a single data element on the next lower level, which is the target of the relationship. In Figure 5-2, Subject 3 is made up of the cascade formed by combining the key and the data element named TARGET 4. The target of this subject's relationship is the element named TARGET-5. The target element (TARGET-5) continues to be the target of the given relationship even if a whole structure of additional elements were to be subsumed below it.

- *Associator Reversal Rule.* If an associator B appears in a template whose key is A, then a corresponding associator A must also appear in the template whose key is B, in such a fashion that the existence of the first relationship is expressed in inverse form by the second relationship (and vice versa) for all values of A and B that are so related. Associators for TARGETS 1 and 2 in Figure 5-2 are reversed at the bottom of the figure.

When associators appear in cascades, reverse the relationship from the target to the entire subject. For example, Figure 5-3 shows the required reversal of the three-level cascade A-B-C. Further discussion of cascade reversals are discussed in Using the Notation.

Five distinctive features which have been introduced and explained in earlier chapters, are of fundamental importance to this discussion:

- The key of an assertion template is required to consist of a *single* entity identifier.
- Every subject is a cascade.
- The subject bears a distinct relationship to each data element on the next level immediately below it and only to that next element. We call this second element the *target* of the relationship.
- Elements that appear on levels below the target, in a continuation of the cascade, do not affect nor participate in the relationship between the subject and the target.
- If A "points to" B then B "points to" A.

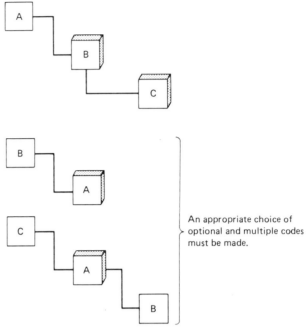

Figure 5-3. Required reversals of the three-level cascade.

These premises lead to a point of view toward data that has the following consequences:

1. All data elements (all named shapes on the diagrams) are either *keys* or they are *targets*. All elements at the first level below the key are targets of the key, all elements at the second level are targets of two-element cascades, and so on.
2. All target data elements either refer to keys (these are the associators) or they refer to something else. (The latter are the oval shapes in the diagrams.)
3. The subjects of all relationships are cascades which begin with a key and proceed down the assertion template through *n* successive levels. At the ($n + 1$)st level is the second member of the relationship, the target.

It follows from these observations that all the relationships in the current approach fall into three classes or types:

1. *Internal:* cases where the subject bears a relationship to a nonkey target.

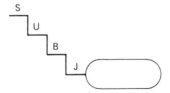

2. *Self-Referent:* cases where the subject bears a relationship to a target which cites the key of the *same* assertion template.

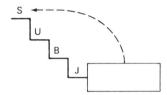

3. *Cross-Reference:* cases where the subject bears a relationship to a target which cites the key of another assertion template.

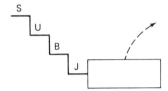

No matter how elaborate or extensive a logical data base design becomes, each elementary relationship can always be analyzed in terms of these three cases. Imagine a large collection of assertion templates similar to the design in Chapter 2. Pick any non-key data element at random from the charts for inspection. Notice how much is known about that element as a consequence of the discipline being advocated.

- It is known that the chosen element is connected to exactly one "next higher" element and that this parent is either the key or connected to the key.
- It is known how to ascertain the cascade that forms the subject of the chosen element, simply by concatenating the various elements above it.
- It is known that the subject so constructed bears a single well-defined relationship to the data element that was picked.
- It is known that the complete relationship (subject and verb and target) is independent of any other elements, including those directly connected below the one picked.
- Then, by inspection of the shape of the chosen element, we can tell if the element should be treated as party to a class I (internal) relation, a class II (self-referent) relation, or a class III (cross-reference) relation. The class implies how much context is needed for a full understanding to the relationship. If it is an internal relation, the entire data base except for the given relationship (subject and verb and target) can be disregarded. If it is a self-referent relation, then the rest of the data base except for the given assertion template can be disregarded. If the element we picked is an associator that references another key, then we only need to examine and consider the cited assertion template in conjunction with the subject and target at hand.
- Finally, it is known whether the subject can bear the relationship to only one or to multiple target values—and it is also known if the subject can exist without a target (i.e., the target is optional).

In summary, the point of view towards data which is developed further in this chapter endeavors to limit the number of other elements that need to be interpreted in order to reach complete knowledge about any given one. The rules and conventions that are presented in this chapter generally encourage the construction of logical data structures that stress "interpretive independence."

## Extensions to the Basic Notation

A few additional notational elements are added to the basic notation in this section. The new notational elements are never essential in the development of a logical data structure. However, they provide valuable "shorthand" expressions that make the design process simpler and the result more precise.

**Sequenced Sets.** It is standard practice to assume that the values of a data element are stored in random order. The basic premise, which treats all values as mathematical sets, applies both to multiple associators (in boxes) and multiple occurrences of ordinary data values (in ovals). Sometimes the sequence of the values has real significance, and the designer needs to regard the values as stored in a prescribed order. This is indicated by drawing an arrow* next to the solid shape on the charts:

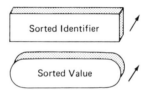

The arrow is a very crude shorthand. It indicates, as an exceptional condition, that the stored values are kept in some sorted sequence, without specifying the sequencing rule. The arrow alone is not sufficient to make the design fully precise. Sometimes the arrow means the entire set of values is in ascending or descending order (on some unspecified sort key). Sometimes there is no sort key. Rather, the most recent value is placed first or last—again without definition of "first" or "last" or "most recent." Sometimes there is some other function which isolates the "largest" or the "most frequently accessed" element. In such cases, the sequencing is really meant as a flag which marks the fact that one selected item is exceptional: the ordering of the remaining items, provided the highlighted one is first, is unspecified. It generally surprises people to realize how much information needs to be given to make the design specific when sequence is used.

In a logical design, the use of sequence should be avoided. Where possible, leave the sequence unspecified. When the logical design does assume that data values are sequenced, it is very important to mark these cases by using the arrow. The arrow indicates that sequence is significant. More subtly, it signals the presence of an implied data element. Indeed, the arrow is considered to be a bona fide data element which (for simplicity of presentation) has been omitted from the chart. Formally, a data structure that contains a sequenced set can always be portrayed like this:

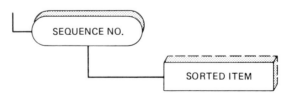

*This is also illustrated in the New Plants Division data base (Chapter 2). See LINE SEQUENCE NUMBER (11.5).

where the integers 1, 2, 3, etc., serve as the domain of the SEQUENCE NO. data element. The arrow which is attached to the sorted items can be shown to be roughly equivalent to the data element SEQUENCE NO. that is used to group the sorted items. No arrow needs to be shown opposite SEQUENCE NO. since the set of integers is inherently well-ordered. Specifically, by choosing the values 1, 2, 3, etc., a program can retrieve all the values in sequence through this procedure. Obviously, it can find the smallest or the largest sorted item as necessary. Thus the use of the arrow is formally equivalent to leaving out a SEQUENCE NO. data element.

Use of either the sequence number or the arrow is a reminder of the need to specify:

- The sort key (which governs the assignment of SORTED ITEMS to sequence number positions)
- The treatment of duplicates* (allowed? not allowed?)
- What to do when one of the data values in the sort key is changed

It is evident, looking at these points, that control over the sequence of values ought to be left to the physical design stage. It will be clearer then whether data should be kept sorted or sorted "on the fly." And it will be clear, after a DBMS is chosen, whether it provides adequate facilities for sequence management or whether this capability needs to be custom designed.

Nevertheless, the primary reason to avoid sequence assumptions in logical design is to avoid unnecessary complexity. The little arrow (or the SEQUENCE NO.) implies that "there exists a known procedure by which the data can be sequenced in an indicated way." It is sobering to see how easily this claim can be falsified. Three tests will illustrate the point.

- Suppose that the data base is in recovery. Explain how the sequence is preserved.
- Suppose that users have decided to examine the state of the data base as of two months ago. Show that the sequence of the values is correctly reconstructed (set back in time) to reflect the conditions of two months ago.
- Suppose that as of January 1, a different rule is to be used for sequence management. Show how to do this, keeping history using the old sequence rule.

These tests and others like them will generally point out that "sequence" is a hiding place for profound dependency on procedures. Such dependency cannot be ruled out completely, particularly in complex data bases. But sequence should be introduced into a *logical* design only after careful deliberation. Use of more than three or four arrows in a medium-sized design (e.g., Chapter 2) should be a cause for reconsideration.

Relationship Families. Every data base is likely to include a few relationships which are best handled as a family. For examples of these patterns which are capable of being treated as a family, see Figure 5-4.

In each case, the subject is repeatedly related to target elements from the *same domain*. In the notation of Chapter 1, no provision was made for such family groups, and each individual relationship would have to be listed separately as illustrated. Usually it is wasteful to treat each of the different relationships separately. Indeed, it is preferable to generalize the family so that new relationships of the same form can be

*Notice that a sequenced set (i.e., a data element marked with an arrow) does not contain repeated or duplicated values. None of the sets in the notation, be they ordered or unordered, contains duplicate values.

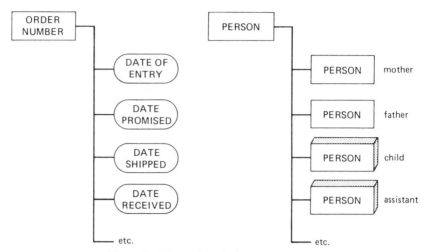

Figure 5-4. Potential relationship families.

added as necessary. For these reasons, it is useful to treat the family of relationships as a single unit.

The shorthand notation for relationship families is easily visualized: imagine that each of the dates in the above example (each value of a date that might be stored in a physical record) is prefixed with a short code that explains what kind of date it is. This imaginary set of prefixes is a great convenience in dealing with relationship families since it permits each instance of one of the relationships to be treated as a pair: LABEL-DATE. This left-hand example* can then be collapsed to read:

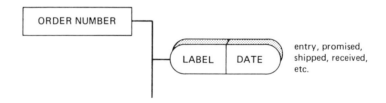

It makes no difference whether LABEL is prefixed or suffixed. What does matter is:

- The notation is a shorthand for multiple relationships between ORDER NUMBER and DATE.
- Though it may appear that two data elements have been concatenated and stored as pairs, LABEL is really not a data element.**
- Every occurrence of the target data element (DATE, in this case) has the label attached.
- The pair LABEL-DATE is a set and contains no duplicates. However, the same DATE

*Other examples appear in the New Plants Division data base (Chapter 2). See elements 2.21, 2.23, 5.3, 7.3, 8.10, 9.9, and 11.6.

**The shorthand under discussion is never in conflict with other guidelines and comments about data elements. To prove this, expand the relationship family back to the original exhaustive list. This process will make the label disappear and restore the assertion template to the format introduced in Chapter 1. The new shapes which cover relationship families neither extend nor alter the basic properties of the notation. (But see Using the Notation in which real extensions are developed.)

| VEHICLE | | PERSON | |
|---|---|---|---|
| PERSON | owned by | VEHICLE | owns |
| PERSON | leased by | VEHICLE | leases |
| PERSON | operated by | VEHICLE | operates |
| PERSON | repaired by | VEHICLE | repairs |

Figure 5-5. Relationship family involving reversed associators.

may appear with different LABELS (i.e., in different relationships), and the same LABEL may have different DATES attached (a "multiple" relationship).

- If any one of the relationships in the family is mandatory, the pair is marked mandatory.

When relationship families apply to associators, the relationship needs to be reversed along with the associator. Figure 5-5 shows a relationship family of associators before it is expressed in shorthand form.

In this case, the label encompasses codes both for a set of "forward" relationships and for a set of "converse" relationships in the reverse direction:

$$owns - is\ owned\ by$$
$$leases - is\ leased\ by$$
$$operates - is\ operated\ by$$
$$repairs - is\ repaired\ by$$
$$etc.$$

A special symbol $\boxed{REL/}$ is used to highlight the fact that the relationships appear in pairs. Figure 5-6 shows the family in Figure 5-5 in shorthand form.

This angular shape signifies the reversal of the relationship indicator. The reversal is

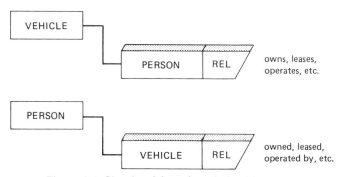

Figure 5-6. Shorthand form for relationship reversal.

very strict: if a vehicle is owned and operated by the same person, we expect to find *two* references to the same person under vehicle, one labeled for owning, the other for operating.

In summary, $\boxed{REL\diagup}$ is used with associators to indicate very strict reversal of each relationship in the relationship family. Ordinarily, a relation family from a key to itself will use the stricter case $\boxed{REL\diagup}$ .

Since families of relationships that apply to nonassociator elements use the prefix LABEL and families of associators use $\boxed{REL\diagup}$ , the two different cases are:

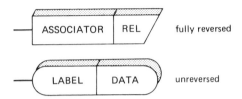

Under Fundamental Rules of Logical Data Base Design, there is a discussion of "generalization" in which consolidation of elements with different domains is permitted so that people, partnerships and corporations are treated as similar things called "legal entities" instead of three distinct classes of objects. Generalization of that kind produces a different logical design, reflecting a different level of perception. While it can be argued that there is a minor amount of perceptive creativity in discovering a relationship family and that it therefore represents a kind of "generalization," we prefer to treat these families as notational shortcuts unworthy of being treated as real generalizations. After all, a computer program could examine the raw assertion templates, recognize the same repetitive patterns we found in Figures 5-4 and 5-5 and coalesce them into relationship families. It is for this reason that we do not attach great conceptual significance to the use of this shorthand, even though it does imply that the relationship family can be easily extended. In the sense that new relationships of like kind can be added to and are covered by the relationship family, it presents an elementary form of the kind of "generalization" treated under Fundamental Rules of Logical Data Base Design.

**Data Groups.** At the lowest level of data description, there will usually be found a number of very commonplace, well-established data units which do not demand the intensive analysis and documentation effort devoted to "more important" data items. A good example, in many applications, is NAME AND ADDRESS. This data group, in fact, is not at all trivial to define accurately, and there are applications where it must be examined in detail. For example, if the NAME is part of a directory (to establish who the person is) or if the ADDRESS contributes to deciding what agency (or what distributed data base) has cognizance, then the NAME AND ADDRESS requires full-scale analysis. But often a group of data like this does not have such impact. If so, the entire collection of elements that make up the NAME AND ADDRESS can be treated as a single unit called a data group. In the New Plants Division data base (Chapter 2), CUSTOMER ADDRESS (1.2) is a data group.

A data group is recorded on the charts by placing the name* of the data group inside a dashed or dotted oval:

---

*The significance of the name of the data group is discussed further at the end of this section.

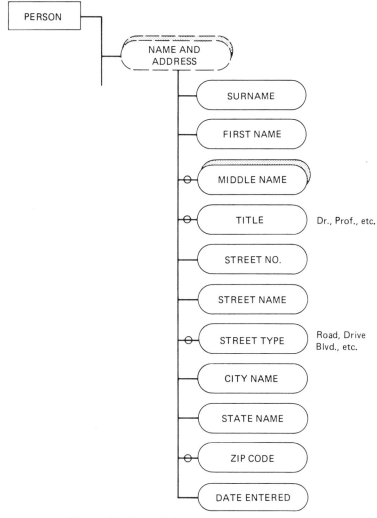

The data group stands for a bunch of data elements which can, temporarily, be thought of as a unit.

It is permissible to list some or all of the data elements in the data group if that is useful for clarity of presentation. The preferred procedure, however, is to list all the elements on a separate worksheet and to place none of them on the chart. Figure 5-7 shows how the NAME AND ADDRESS data group might appear if listed on the charts.

The contents of the data group are "ordinary" and "routine." Even so, the list of constituent elements is important since it reveals useful insights. In this design, since

Figure 5-7. Expanded portrayal of a data group.

NAME is combined with ADDRESS, a person with an alias would have two NAME AND ADDRESS entries, with the same ADDRESS repeated. Similarly, this list does not allow for foreign addresses, rural addresses, company addresses, and so forth. The serious danger in using data groups is that one neglects to inspect the inventory of constituent elements and assumes the group is something it is not.

Notice that the data group *does* contain optional elements and it *does* contain multiple elements. It may not under any circumstances contain associators. It may contain cascades (of ovals) but data groups with this level of complexity should be approached with caution and perhaps treated with more formality.

When a data group is recorded on the charts as part of an assertion template, it is always a reminder that some data definition work has been omitted. Usually it is the definition of the constituent elements of the group that is omitted; sometimes the inventory is not even completed. A situation like this is "ill-formed" when compared with the standards employed elsewhere in the notation, but it has practical value since an approach that requires 100% treatment of every detail can be overwhelmingly expensive.

Users of the notation should be careful to perceive the difference between a data group and other notational elements that have been employed. Notice, for example, that the name of the data group is placed in a dashed outline to highlight the fact that it is not a data element. It has no domain. NAME AND ADDRESS is nothing but a reminder the designer wrote down to indicate that something not yet defined (in logical data base terms) belongs here. The purpose of the dashed outline is to signal intentional incompleteness and an excursion outside the established notational pattern.

It is remarkably easy to fold a data group "back in" once the definitional work has been done, if circumstances permit the use of a tag. Let us sketch the process in three stages:

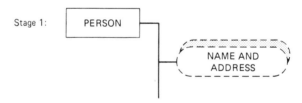

In Stage 1, the designer uses a data group, with only a vague idea what the full inventory of elements entails.

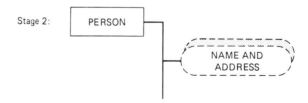

A separate sheet or Data Dictionary entry is added which states: "NAME AND ADDRESS contains Surname, First Name, several Middle Names, Titles, Street Numbers, etc." as drawn in Figure 5-7.

In Stage 2, the definition work has been done, but it is still informal and outside the notational framework.

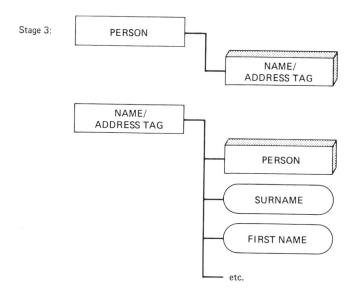

Stage 3:

PERSON

NAME/
ADDRESS TAG

NAME/
ADDRESS TAG

PERSON

SURNAME

FIRST NAME

etc.

In Stage 3, the process is completed and the logical data structure is fully defined in terms of assertion templates. Notice that a new data element called "NAME/ADDRESS TAG" has been created whose domain is some system for uniquely identifying the names and addresses that are being used. Notice also that the reversal from NAME/ADDRESS TAG to PERSON shows that several different people can have the same name and address.* Deciding whether this is so is one of the steps in the process of "folding in" the data group. Other methods which do not use tags can be used to "fold in" the data groups once they are sufficiently defined. Because it is easy to fold in the data groups when desired and does very little harm to omit them when they do not contain problems (like hidden associators, complex substructures, etc.), the designer should use data groups freely. For safety's sake, however, always perform a final check: walk through the process which "folds in" each data group that is allowed to remain in the logical data structure, to verify that there are no hidden surprises.

## USING THE NOTATION

### Definitions Relating to Populated Data Bases

For ease of reference, various basic definitions introduced earlier (particularly in Chapter 4) are repeated here because they bear on the more formal definition of the way an assertion template is populated. The definitions which establish the relationship between an assertion template and its populated analogs (assertion trees and assertions) are listed without further explanation.

- *External Object.* An external object is an object or a class of objects that is capable of being identified in the real world.
- *Construct.* A construct is an object or a class of objects which depends on the data base for its existence.

---

*This is a rare condition which arises, for example, when a mother and daughter, both named Mary Hix Johnson, both live in the same home.

- *Domain.* A domain is a finite set of symbols to which a unique domain name has been assigned, and which is in some correspondence to a set of objects.
- *Entity Identifier.* An entity identifier is an ordered pair consisting of a domain name and a symbol drawn from that domain.
- *Entity.* An entity is an external object or a construct, to which at least one entity identifier has been assigned.
- *Tree Structure (on a set T).* The members of a set $T$ are said to be organized in a tree structure if:

  — A set of nodes (of the tree structure) is exhibited
  — Each node except one (the topmost) is connected upward to exactly one node
  — The topmost node is connected upward to no other node
  — Each member of $T$ is assigned to exactly one node

- *Assertion Template.* An assertion template is a set of domain names organized in a tree structure. Furthermore, each node of this tree structure except the topmost node may be marked:

  — 'M' to indicate *multiple;* nodes not 'M' are *single*
  — 'O' to indicate *optional;* nodes not 'O' are *mandatory*
  — 'A' to indicate *associator;* nodes not 'A' are *nonassociator*

- *Data Element.* Each node of an assertion template is a data element if it consists of:

  — An appropriate node identifier that distinguishes this node from other nodes
  — Identifier of the parent node, if any
  — The domain associated with this node
  — The markings 'M,' 'O,' 'A' associated with this node (or the absence of these markings)

  A data element name must be assigned to each data element.
- *Key (of an Assertion Template).* The topmost data element in an assertion template (i.e., the one data element that has no parent node) is the key of the assertion template.
- *Assertion Tree.* An assertion tree is the result of populating an assertion template. An assertion template is populated by substituting, for each node of an assertion template, $n$ (= one or zero or more) symbols (values) chosen from the domain of the node, obeying the following restrictions:

  — For the key, $n = 1$
  — For any node marked 'O' (optional) and only for such nodes, $n$ may be zero.
  — For any node marked 'M' (multiple) and only for such nodes, $n$ may be greater than 1.

  Furthermore, this substitution must be made top-down—beginning with the key—and any unpopulated portion of the assertion template that was under a node being replaced by $n > 0$ values is to be "copied" under *each* of $n$ values. (See Figure 5-8). This process, which is completed when values have been substituted for all the nodes in the assertion template, produces a tree of values whose interpretation is meant to be obvious from consulting the original assertion template.

- *Assertion.* An assertion (the analog of a cascade) is a sequence of values obtained by proceeding down the assertion tree for some distance, starting with the key of course. In Figure 5-8, the pair "January 23–Atlanta" is an assertion; so is the triple "January 23–Atlanta–9:27 p.m."

### The Interpretation of Assertion Templates

**Populating an Assertion Template.** Each assertion template expresses a syntactic form. This form establishes the permissible pattern that must be followed by each combination of data values that is stored when the data base is populated.

Thus, the assertion template illustrated in Figure 5-9 provides for one or more names, exactly one date of birth, and at most one place of birth under each Social Security number. This assertion template could legitimately be populated by the following combinations of data values:

```
    123-45-6789   Rogers, J.   370615  Alberta, Canada
    123-45-6789   Rogers, J.   370615
    123-45-6789   Rogers, J.;  Smith J. 370615
and 123-45-6789   Rogers, J.;  Smith J. 370615 Alberta, Canada
```

Each of these representative ways of populating the assertion template illustrates a distinct allowable formation. The examples all have a Social Security number and at least one name, as is required by the assertion template. In the first case, the place of birth is also given. In the second case, the place of birth is omitted, which is legal since the place of birth is an optional element. In the third case, two names are listed since the assertion template allows for aliases (or married names). The fourth case shows the place of birth as well as multiple names.

These are the only kinds of alternatives allowed by the given assertion template (if it is understood that any number of person names is allowed by the template). Any other combination of data values is not allowed by the assertion template syntax. For instance:

```
    123-45-6789   Price, K.   Lancaster, PA
```

is not allowed because a mandatory value (date of birth) has been omitted. Similarly:

```
    123-45-6789   Price, K.   491216; 501216 Lancaster, PA
```

is not allowed because the syntax calls for exactly one, not two, dates of birth in year-month-day form. Equally invalid are:

```
    123-45-6789   XVI 501216
    123-45-6789   Price, K. LMN
and 1L2-JK-P123   Price, K. 501216
```

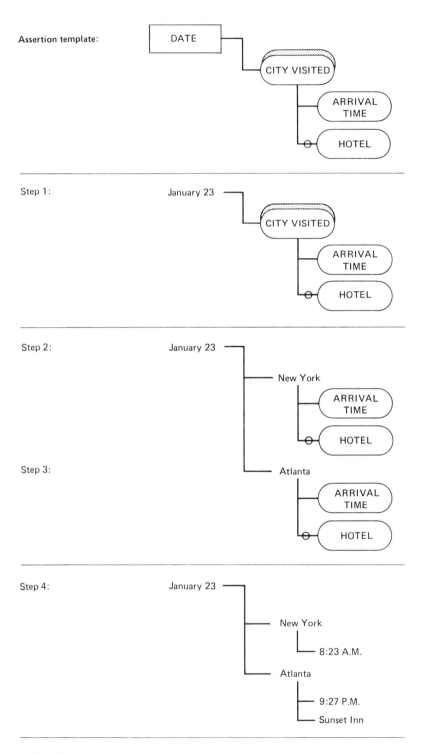

Figure 5-8. The process of populating an assertion template to produce an assertion tree.

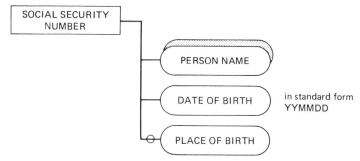

Figure 5-9. Illustrative assertion template.

because "XVI" is not in the right form to be a standardized person name (omitting the comma and the first initial); "LMN" is not in the right form to be a date (not numeric, not YYMMDD); and "1L2-JK-P123" is not a Social Security number (not numeric). Also not allowed, because they violate the syntax, are:

        123-45-6789   Price, K.   (needs date of birth)
        123-45-6789   370615      (needs person name)
        123-45-6789               (needs both date and name)

Only certain prescribed combinations of data values meet the requirements laid down by an assertion template. Not only must each value be drawn from the right domain (so that a date looks like a date and a person name looks like a person's name) but also the patterns of dependency, multiplicity, and optionality must always be obeyed.

Each assertion template forbids combinations of data that are not explicitly provided for. The example keyed by Social Security number, just above, does *not* provide for an address. If we wished to store the address of a person whose SSN was known, it would not be possible to store the address under SSN in this template. While there may be a provision for addresses elsewhere in the logical data base design, there is no way to store an address under Social Security number using the assertion template that was given. The assertion template declares the possibility of storing specified data values in specified ways; data not explicitly provided for are, by implication, forbidden.

Each assertion template, when it is populated, results in a set of assertions: one assertion for each distinct combination of values. Though all of the assertions in such a set conform to the same mold (given by the assertion template), each assertion can have a slightly different structure from all the others. For example, when multiple names are allowed, as in the SSN example above, the first assertion can have one person name, the second assertion two names, and the $n$th assertion can have $n$ names. All the assertions are thus observably different in form, yet they obey the same syntactic rule given by the assertion template that was presented at the outset. Even a single assertion, one which is initially stored with six values of the "name" element, may be changed. A name can be added, or a name can be subtracted, and the result will still obey the given syntactic rule, provided that one name remains. The individual assertions adhere to the assertion template at all times.

Within a given assertion, which is a populated instance of an assertion template, the values are invariably arranged as a tree structure. The single value of the key is at the

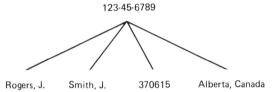

Figure 5-10. Assertion tree for the SSN template in Figure 5-9.

"top" of the tree, and values that conform to other data elements are easily perceived as nodes below it. Using the SSN example in Figure 5-9 once again, Figure 5-10 shows a tree structure representation of one of the assertions.

Notice that each value in the assertion is a node in the tree. When all the optional elements are filled in, the number of levels in the tree is equal to the number of levels in the corresponding assertion template. This is easy to check by populating a cascade that has multiple levels, as is done in Figure 5-11.

There are four levels apparent in the assertion template; these levels are clearly reproduced in the assertion for U.S. that is shown. Naturally, it is understood that another assertion for another value of COUNTRY will also obey the same assertion template. Thus for COUNTRY = Guatemala, it is understood that there would be provinces (Oriente, Verapaz, Los Altos, etc.) that a province like Oriente would be subdivided into departments (Jutiapa, Santa Rosa) and that a department like Santa Rosa would contain

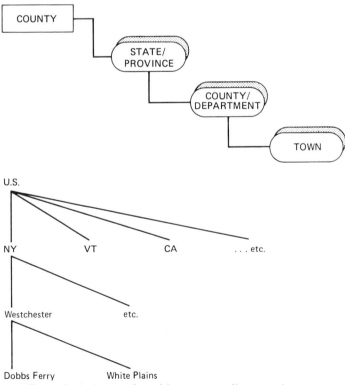

Figure 5-11. A cascade and its corresponding assertion tree.

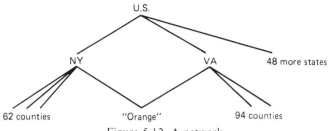

Figure 5-12. A network.

various towns. Both the U.S. and Guatemala would yield similar tree structures when the assertions are examined side by side.

The important fact about a tree structure is that every node except the top one has exactly one parent. The tree structures which result from substituting values for data elements in assertion templates meet the requirement faithfully. Under U.S. there can be as many as 50 nodes, one for each state.* Under NY there are up to 63 counties, one for each county in NY. Observe carefully that there are also 95 counties that can be listed under Virginia even though there is an Orange county in NY and also an Orange county in VA. (Indeed, Orange is a county in eight different states.)

Assertions are always trees. They are never networks like the case shown in Figure 5-12 where the node Orange has two parents.

The same value, Orange, will appear eight times in the U.S. assertion, as eight different nodes. It appears once under NY and it appears again under VA and the other six states. The set of values for COUNTY under NY contains no duplicates. The set under VA also contains no duplicates. But it is possible for the sets to appear to overlap—as they do when several states share the same county name.

Trees are more conveniently displayed by drawing them sideways in a format widely used in the representation of parts lists. The layout, called an *indented parts list,* is closely analogous to the form of the assertion template itself. An indented list representation of an assertion tree is shown in Figure 5-13.

Notice that the states, counties and towns are listed in no particular order, emphasizing the fact that this notation for assertion templates assigns no sequence to the sets

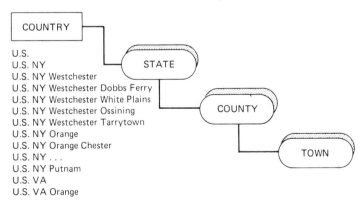

Figure 5-13. Indented list representation of an assertion tree.

*Depending on the detailed definition of STATE/PROVINCE, provision may be needed for more than 50 nodes to indicate the District of Columbia, Puerto Rico, and the Virgin Islands.

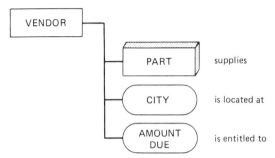

Figure 5-14. A compound primitive assertion template.

of values in an assertion. Notice also that the indented parts list provides an entry—a line—for each subject in the assertion. There is a line for U.S. alone, a line for NY and every other U.S.-STATE pair, and a line for each U.S.-STATE-COUNTY triple. All assertions, no matter how complex their structure, can be presented as indented parts lists.

**Interpreting Dependencies in Cascades.** Primitive assertions express a relationship between a single entity identifier as a subject, and a second entity identifier which is the target. When more than one relationship holds between the same subject and multiple targets, the result is a compound primitive assertion which is treated as a collection of binary relationships. Figure 5-14 shows a compound primitive assertion template in which the following binary relationships are considered to hold independently:

Each VENDOR supplies certain PARTS
Each VENDOR is located in a designated CITY
Each VENDOR is entitled to an AMOUNT DUE

These are *n*-ary relationships where $n = 2$. In other circumstances there are more than two data elements involved in *one* relationship. All *n*-ary relationships are shown as cascades in this notation.

There is a big difference between the primitive assertions arranged this way:

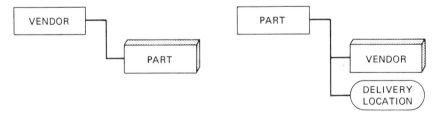

and the following arrangement which includes a three-level cascade;

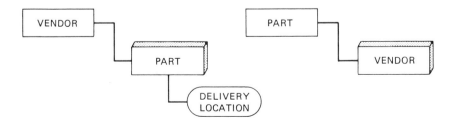

In the first case, it is clear that a part has one and only one delivery location, a location which is independent of vendor. No matter who sells the part, it is a property of the part that it is to be delivered "in Augusta." (This property could apply to special-purpose items like parts for one-of-a-kind radio telescopes or similar equipment). In the second case, a part may have more than one delivery location. The first vendor may deliver it at X, the second vendor may deliver it at Y. This second circumstance is far more common: the delivery location depends both on the vendor as well as on what part it is.

Even a three-level cascade admits a great many possible relationships. Figure 5-15 is an inventory of the different cases generated by different choices of "optional" and "multiple" designations on the component elements.

Each of these eight variations expresses a distinct relationship among vendor, part, and location. The different "readings" reflect the different limits that are placed on what is permissible, and it is important to take the notations (optional, mandatory, sin-

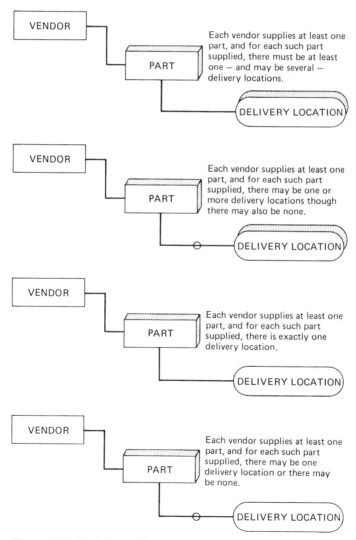

Figure 5-15. Variations of interpretation for a three-level cascade.

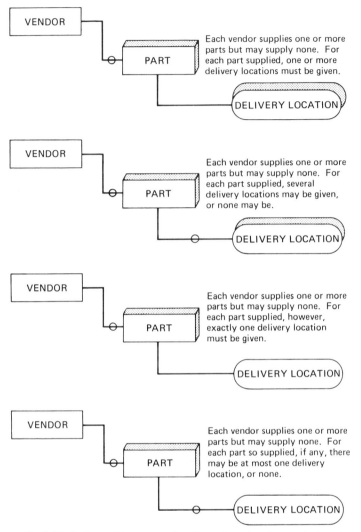

Figure 5-15. Variations of interpretation for a three-level cascade (continued).

gular, multiple) into account when interpreting the intent of a cascade. Note also that the eight examples, formed from three elements, consist of two relationships each. The first always holds between the key (VENDOR) and the next level element (PART). The other relationship holds between the pair subject VENDOR-PART and DELIVERY LOCATION. The language describing each variation first characterizes the VENDOR-PART relation and then goes on to talk about "each such part" or "each part so supplied." The subjects of relationships are always cascades that start with the key; the relationships are borne to the next lower element—the target. The placement of elements in the cascade is a matter of considerable importance, for it shows what the dependencies are. In these variations, delivery has always been dependent on both vendor and part. Contrast the earlier example where delivery location depended only on part and all vendors delivered the same part to the same place.

## Logical Access and Logical Change Transactions

**Accessing the Populated Data Base.** There is only one way to access an assertion in a populated data base. To perform the access, it is necessary to specify

— which key (i.e., which assertion template) is of interest,
— a value (which will be interpreted as an element in the domain of the key). This value of the key is the *access argument.*

Thus it would be appropriate to supply EMPLOYEE NO. = 12345 or BIRTH DATE = 621030 in an effort to access the populated data base which had these elements as keys.

The result is that a logical access takes place: an abstract device "reaches into" the populated data base and attempts to find a match between the key values that are stored and the value supplied as the access argument. If the access argument exactly matches one of the key values stored, the *entire* assertion tree for that key value is furnished to the requester, who will disregard any portions that are not of interest. The logical access is always a direct access to the key value. No searching, nor retrieval of "near misses" is allowed. The logical access either results in a direct hit on a given key value or it results in a total miss. When the access argument which triggers a logical access is "not found" in the data base, a "not on file" report is returned to the requester, and the empty set is retrieved.

The logical access is thus an intentionally primitive kind of access: it either succeeds (in which case everything stored under the key value is delivered to the requester) or it fails (in which case nothing is delivered).

Significantly, the only time an access can fail is when the requester supplies a search argument obtained from the external world. Accessing the data base with a PART NUM-BER, an EMPLOYEE NUMBER, or a SOCIAL SECURITY NUMBER might easily lead to a "not on file" report since there are PART NUMBERS, etc., which the data base has "never heard of." But once a successful access had been made, and new arguments are built from associators that were found in the data base, all subsequent accesses that use these associator values as follow-on search arguments are guaranteed to succeed. In short, after some mild difficulties are surmounted on the first access, the requester is enabled to follow the associator linkages throughout the data base without further obstacles. This facility for threading assertions together in a rich variety of ways is one of the most important characteristics of a data base.

Whenever an assertion tree is retrieved, its contents may be modified and the assertion may be rewritten, provided these actions conform to the framework specified by the governing assertion template. For example, it is always legal to add* another value to a set of values when the data element is outlined by a solid oval since the solid shape admits multiple values without limit. But it is not legal to add a duplicate of a value already present in the set, and it is not legal to add the new value alone when the assertion template prescribes one or more mandatory subordinates: values of these mandatory subordinates must also be added before the addition "conforms" to the governing assertion template. The rules for adding values to assertions are reasonably straightforward if the reader recognizes that the process always adds an assertion subtree which is prefabricated in the user's workspace in conformity with the assertion template.

---

*It is also legal to delete certain values, but the rules for deletion are sufficiently complicated that they deserve separate treatment (in the next section). In general, it is best to treat revision as a logical delete followed by a logical addition of the new combination of values.

While data governed by ovals may be added to the assertion tree wherever provisions have been made to allow it, the addition of an assertion subtree that contains associators is slightly more complex. If a new associator value is to be added, it is necessary to add the reverse member of the pair at the same time. But before we can add the reverse member of the pair, we need to establish where it belongs, which is usually under some other key elsewhere in the data base. This step—locating the place for the reverse associator link—is never regarded as interesting in a logical design: we assume the system knows which associator pairs "go together." It is, however, a worthy challenge for a physical data management system to translate this logical requirement into a practical procedure. However, done, we face the delicate step of adding the new subtree and the reverse associator at the same time, for clearly the data base would be inconsistent (momentarily) if we only add half the associator pair. More generally, if the subtree to be added contains $n$ associators, then $n + 1$ subtrees need to be added to the data base simultaneously. Let us not forget, finally, that each of these derivative transactions that insert reverse associators must also conform to the assertion templates that govern those remote parts of the data base. Thus, we might find ourselves trying to add a second value to an associator set that is limited to one member (i.e., outlined by a planar rectangle). This would force the transaction to be rejected. Similarly, the reverse associator may itself have a mandatory element or (more generally) a mandatory subtree which must be constructed in advance. Only when all this prefabrication and checking is complete can the complex of data be added, via $n + 1$ simultaneous "write" operations.

In summary, then, each logical access to the populated data base involves retrieval of the (at most) one assertion that matches the access argument. The entire assertion is retrieved (or a "not on file" report is given), and the entire assertion is placed in the requester's workspace. The assertion may be modified in conformity with the syntax of the governing assertion template. If these changes result in adding associators, then corresponding changes need to be made in the other assertions that would carry their reversals. In general, new assertion subtrees are constructed which are to be added in $n + 1$ places ($n$ = number of new associators), and these subtrees are added to the data base in a simultaneous (parallel) "write" operation. The transaction which permits new subtrees to be added to existing assertions also is used to add complete assertions that include the key. In the logical data base, the same transaction is used to "load" the data base originally and to add the assertion subtrees that are needed as the data base grows.

## Deletion

***Purpose.*** Values are deleted from a populated data base to reflect changes in the real world which the data base is meant to track. In a later section, the art of designing a data base with history will be investigated; that art, in its purest form, leads to history-preserving data bases from which nothing is ever deleted. But in most data bases, there are assertions which attempt only to record a current snapshot of the present world. What went before is not of interest, and so those older records which no longer hold current truth are deleted. This section is devoted to an exposition of the deletion rules that are postulated by the present notation for logical design.

For reasons that are not entirely clear, deletion appears to be the transaction which most stringently challenges a data base design. It is relatively easy to create a data structure that organizes a collection of data for retrieval and occasional updates, but arranging the structure so it stays intact in the presence of deletion is much harder. Part of the challenge comes from having another restraint (deletion) to consider, part because a data base must be perceived as completely dynamic when deletion is permitted. Just as architects can "see" (in their mind's eye) people living in the buildings on their blueprints, and inventors can "see" the workings of machines that have never been built, so experienced data base designers can "see" their data bases operating under dynamic conditions. The rules for deletion provide an important step towards understanding data structures from this more advanced point of view. It will be shown that some data values can be deleted with impunity, that others are protected by the logical data structure, that there are inherent sequences (so that elements a, b, c must be deleted in c, b, a order), and that certain groups of elements must be deleted together.

In the present notation, there is only one "user-generated" delete* transaction. It may be applied to any element in a populated data base to cause previously stored values to vanish. Our delete transaction is irrevocable: once the indicated values have been deleted, they are "gone forever." This is in contrast to some deletion procedures that flag deleted items without erasing them and sometimes permit one to peer at previous values (by ignoring the delete flag). We do *not* do this: deleted material is meant to vanish without a trace. The user-generated transaction always specifies a particular value of a data element. If the data element is populated by several values, the delete transaction must single out one of them for erasure. The selected value is the *argument* of the delete transaction.

In executing the delete, there is first a test to see if this data value is protected by the logical data structure. If the data value is the last value of the data element, and the data element is mandatory, then the delete transaction is invalid. It is illegal to delete the last value of a mandatory element since the logical data structure stipulates that at least one value must be present. But if the value may be deleted—as it is when the data element is marked "optional," for instance—then the whole subtree below that value will also be deleted.

An easy way to visualize deletion is to recall the fact that assertions are always trees and to "see" deletion as a pruning of the tree. The user-generated delete transaction selects a given value (node) in the assertion tree, and the tree is snipped at that point. Observe carefully that what "falls off" the assertion tree is a subtree of values: the deletion argument plus the remainder of the assertion below the cut point. In a well designed data structure, this consists of all those and only those values that are *dependent* on the deleted value.

Complications arise when the subtree to be deleted contains one or more associators. The same broad problem is faced whether the associator is the argument of the delete transaction or an element within the subtree. The associator gives notice that the data structure contains (elsewhere) a body of data that is linked to this subtree in some way. Ordinarily, there is no harm in severing both units of the bidirectional associator pair, and the reader need not approach such cases hesitantly. But certain situations do arise in which subtrees are heavily linked into the data base. Clearly, such highly linked substructures must either be deleted rarely, or they must be given added design to make the deletion process easier.

In any case, deletion of associators always involves the (automatic) issuance of a

---

*It would be possible to derive three user-generated delete transactions, each intended for a specific type of data element: delete key, delete associator, delete nonassociator, but we prefer to use the single all-purpose transaction.

separate "system-generated" delete transaction that finds the other half of the associator pair.

Other "system-generated" delete transactions are also triggered to delete the elements in a dependent subtree. As the rules below explain, these "system-generated" delete transactions have certain privileges not allowed to user-generated ones.

On occasion, multiple "system-generated" delete transactions need to be executed simultaneously. Though this feat is possible in an abstract (logical) system, it may not be feasible in physical data management environments. There is, of course, no reason why simultaneous action cannot be supported in principle—devices can be built with this objective in mind, or all the deletes can be implemented by time-stamping all the affected records so the deletion takes place at the same (future) time. Usually, in today's technology, the requirement for simultaneous action is accommodated by locking out the data base until the necessary operations have been run to completion. All of these techniques are valid ways of realizing the logical requirement for data base consistency.

***Rules.*** As previously noted, there is only one user-generated deletion transaction. It applies to values of all kinds of data elements, be they keys, associators, multiple, singular, mandatory or optional. Each user-generated delete transaction may trigger zero or more "system-generated" deletes that act as helpers. The result of these actions is to cause the deletion argument and the subtree below it in the assertion to vanish from the data base without a trace. This is accomplished, in detail, by adhering to the following rules which are summarized for reference in Figure 5-16.

*Rule 1: Deletion of Mandatory-Single Elements*
The transaction that attempts to delete a value of a mandatory-single element is invariably rejected as illegal.

Mandatory-single elements include the following shapes:

In these cases, the subject's relationship to the target (i.e., the instance being deleted) is such that one and only one target value must be present. This is why the data element bears the mandatory designation. Deletion of an instance "inside" the mandatory-single element* implies deletion of the last such element. Because this will violate the logical data structure, the attempt at deletion is forbidden, and the user-generated delete transaction is rejected.

*Rule 1S: "System-Generated" Delete*
A "system-generated" delete is a secondary delete transaction which acts as a helper in executing a user-generated delete. Its rules are identical to those which govern a user-generated delete in all respects save three. Trivially, it must be generated as a by-product of a prior user-generated delete: it has no way of being invoked independently. Sec-

---

*As noted later, there are situations where a mandatory-*multiple* data element contains but a single value (though it could, if circumstances were different, contain more). Deletion of the last remaining instance in a multiple-mandatory set is reducible to Rule 1, and it is also forbidden and rejected if attempted by a user-generated delete transaction.

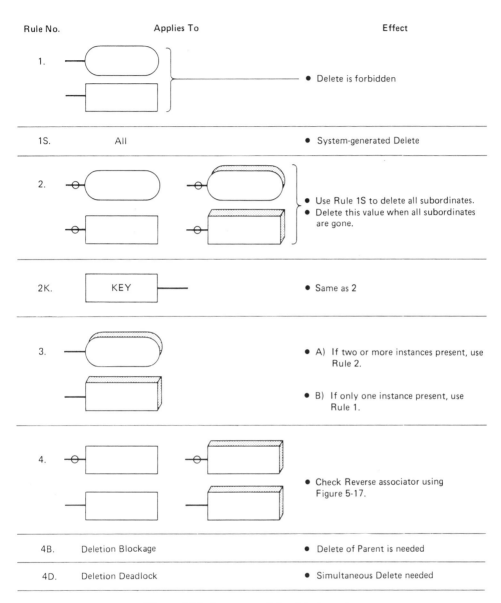

Figure 5-16. Summary of the deletion rules.

ond, a "system-generated" delete can trigger the issuance of other "system-generated" deletes. Third, and most significantly, the "system-generated" delete *does* have the power to overcome the mandatory-single condition that, in Rule 1, causes rejection of the user-generated delete: It is empowered to delete a mandatory child if its parent is about to be deleted.

The "system-generated" delete transaction is only used to delete the subtree of values which is subordinate to the value which is about to be deleted. Because we plan to delete the parent itself, the "system-generated" delete has no need to hesitate when it encounters the various mandatory-single cases.

The "system-generated" delete does, however, obey the requirements introduced by Rule 4 if associators are involved.

*Rule 2: Deletion of Optional Elements*
There are four different shapes, all marked by O, that represent optional elements. Rule 2 applies when the instance to be deleted is "inside" one of the following shapes:

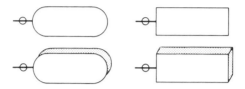

Because each of these elements is optional; the logical data structure stipulates that the subject (i.e., the cascade above it) bears a relationship that does not require a target. Because of this important property of the relationship, these instances can be deleted with impunity if they do not have subordinate elements below. The procedure is, therefore, as follows:

   *Action:*   1. Issue "system-generated" deletes to all subordinate instances.
                  2. Delete this instance if (when) it has no subordinate instances.

Naturally, the "system-generated" deletes in the first step are subject to restrictions on deleting associators presented in Rule 4.

*Rule 2K: Deletion of Keys*
For purposes of deletion, treat instances of keys as optional elements and apply Rule 2 to them. That is, issue "system-generated" deletes to all the subordinate instances, and delete the key value only when it is the only data item that remains in the assertion.

*Rule 3: Deletion of Mandatory-Multiple Elements*
Mandatory-multiple elements include the following shapes:

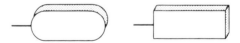

By definition, one value must be present to preserve the logical data structure. When many elements are present, deletion of one of them is relatively straightforward, but deletion of the last remaining value requires special attention. Thus there are two cases.

   Case A.   There are two or more values present, so that the set will not be empty after one value is deleted.
   *Action:*   Treat the deletion according to Rule 2, as if the shape were optional. Since at least one instance will remain after the deletion takes place, the provisions of a mandatory element will not be violated.
   Case B.   There is only one instance present, and therefore the last instance is about to be deleted.

*Action:*   Treat the deletion according to Rule 1, above, as if the shape were mandatory-single. (The delete transaction will therefore be rejected.)

*Rule 4: Deletion of Associators*
Because associators appear in pairs, deletion of one instance of an associator always
requires a companion operation that deletes its partner. A "system-generated" delete is
therefore triggered which finds the particular instance of the associator that "points
back to here," usually under another key, and deletes it.

While the reverse associator can generally be deleted by a "system-generated" delete,
note carefully that Rule 1S does not give unlimited power to the secondary transaction.
When we issue a user-generated delete to a particular B in

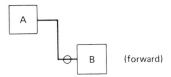

(forward)

it does not follow that the "system-generated" delete will automatically work on

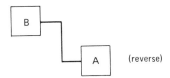

(reverse)

The reverse associator instance cannot be deleted if it is the last surviving instance of
a mandatory element.

This is true even when a "system-generated" delete is used, for we have not marked
the parent (B in the reversed assertion) in any way for deletion when we propose to
delete associator B in the first relation. Because of this, "deletion blockage" (Rule 4B)
can occur, making the deletion of associators a highly sequential process.

To study the deletion of associators, assume it has been established that the forward
associator instance A–B can be deleted. There are four cases that can be encountered
when the reverse associator B–A is analyzed for "system-generated" deletion, as shown
in Figure 5-17.

Except when deletion is blocked by the provisions of Rule 4B, deletion proceeds normally after the reverse associator has been deleted. (Naturally, there may be other
associators in the subtree *under* the reverse associator A that could block its deletion
and thus stop the whole transaction, but that complication is best overlooked for now.)

*Rule 4B: Deletion Blockage*
Deletion blockage is said to occur when the reverse associator B–A cannot be deleted
by the "system-generated" delete that endeavors to remove the reverse relationship.
This always happens when the reverse associator B–A is mandatory-single, and it also
occurs when it contains the last member of a mandatory set.

These mandatory associators are remarkably tenacious. For example, it might appear
that the correct procedure in such cases would be to execute the deletion in the opposite

Forward (Deletable) Pair          Reverse Associator                              Action

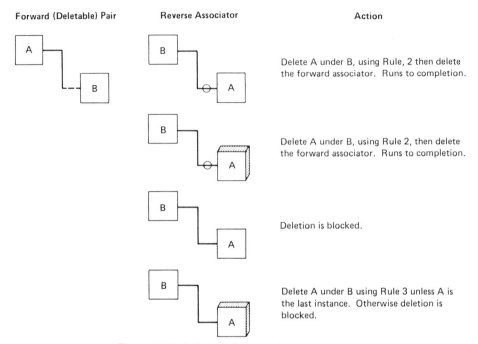

Delete A under B, using Rule, 2 then delete
the forward associator.  Runs to completion.

Delete A under B, using Rule 2, then delete
the forward associator.  Runs to completion.

Deletion is blocked.

Delete A under B using Rule 3 unless A is
the last instance.  Otherwise deletion is
blocked.

Figure 5-17. Deletion of reversed associator pairs.

order. This would entail issuing the user-generated delete against the reverse relationship B–A, instead of starting with A–B. But to no avail: the mandatory B–A relation
cannot be deleted (Rule 1) by a user-generated delete transaction. The only way to
delete it is to delete the parent (B as key in these drawings)—an outcome which under-
scores the seriousness of the "mandatory" label. The mandatory B–A relation says that
B *cannot exist* without A. The attempt to delete the associator A in B–A is blocked to
force recognition of this important stipulation of the logical data structure. Mandatory
associators can only be deleted by deleting their parents.

### Rule 4D: Deletion Deadlock
One consequence of the rules for deletion blockage is the occurrence of situations that
appear to cause deadlock. The last two cases in Figure 5-17 will cause deadlock if the
forward associator A–B is also mandatory. The deadlock cases shown in Figure 5-18
have the property that a user-generated delete will be rejected whether it is applied first
to A–B or first to B–A. In these cases, it is necessary to issue deletes to both the forward
and the reverse relationship simultaneously.

### Definitional Interdependency
The importance of the associator reversal convention is evident in any treatment of
deletion. Rule 4, which deals with associators, postulates an ability to locate the "back
pointer" that corresponds to a "forward pointer" whenever we try to delete one or the
other member of the pair. Admittedly, this is an administrative convenience: had we
omitted the reversal in the first place, there would be no need to go through the paired
deletion that the "double-entry bookkeeping" of associators requires. The real benefit
of reversed associator pairs occurs at the next higher level, especially when an effort is

made to delete a key that "points away" to many other places in the data base. Such a key is shown in Figure 5-19; observe that keys with a large number of associators are the rule in realistic logical data base designs, e.g., Chapter 2, though Figure 5-19 shows more than most assertion templates would normally have.

It is obvious by inspection of the large assertion template keyed by A that certain associator linkages to other keys can be deleted without affecting A. These are the optional elements, both those marked optional (D, E, I, J) and those that are optional by inference (L, M). On the other hand, there are some associators that cannot be deleted (or altered in any way) without affecting A drastically. These are the mandatory-single elements (B is the only example) and possibly C, if there is only one value stored. Notice, finally, that G (or the last value of H) cannot be deleted without also deleting a value of the nonassociator F; when removal of G or H affects the last value of F, deletion cannot take place without affecting A. Thus inspection of the forward associators in an assertion template reveals most of the constraints that permit or prevent ready deletion of the assertion as a whole.

Inspection of the reversed associators generally completes the picture. Consider, for example, the optional associators (D, E, I, J, L, M) under key A. If any one of the reversals D–A, E–A, through M–A is designated mandatory, particularly if it is mandatory-single, then it is not possible to delete the assertion for A without affecting the other key (suppose it is D) where this mandatory relationship is shown. Speaking more generally, the *entity* represented by A and the *entity* represented by D are very strongly related. The relationship, for purposes of illustration, might well be that between the insurable object A—a valuable gem, for instance—and an insurance policy D that covers the gem. A record concerning the gem A could easily stand alone without any need for D. The gem record could give data on the gem's weight, cut, and ownership, for

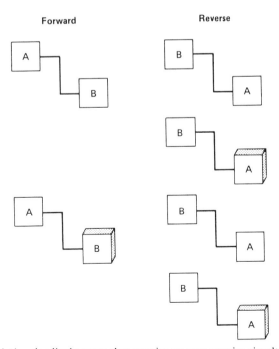

Forward     Reverse

Figure 5-18. Deletion deadlock: cases that require or may require simultaneous deletion.

instance. But an insurance policy is not an insurance policy unless it fully specifies and identifies the property at risk. Thus policy D depends on gem A for its existence. This leads to a definitional dependency (policy D is defined in terms of gem A). It also leads to an implied sequence of events in the data base in which one type of data (in this case, gem A) must be registered on the data base before the other (in this case, policy D) can be considered complete enough to be recorded.

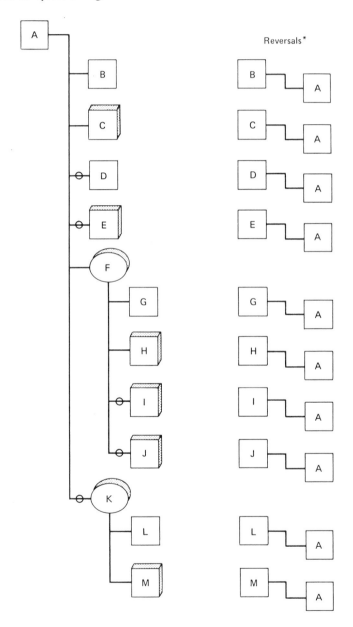

*Reversals may show any combination of mandatory/optional and single/multiple coding.

Figure 5-19. A key (A) with many associator linkages to other keys.

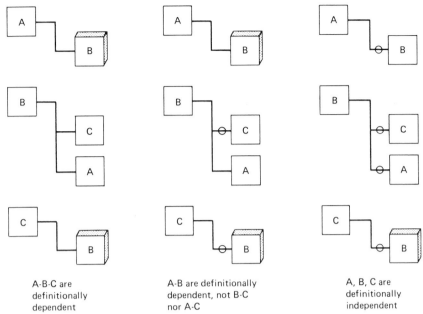

A-B-C are
definitionally
dependent

A-B are definitionally
dependent, not B-C
nor A-C

A, B, C are
definitionally
independent

Figure 5-20. Definitional dependence and independence.

Given this order of precedence—that gem A must be defined before policy D can be defined—which applies when the "records" are created, it is not at all surprising to learn that deletion also has a sequential rule. To delete a policy D, we merely disconnect it from the designated gem A, leaving the gem A on the data base "uninsured." But before we can delete an insured gem A, we must first delete the policy D which cannot exist if the gem A no longer exists. In general, the order of precedence for deletion is the exact opposite of the order in which the assertions need to be created. The priorities are controlled by the pattern of optional and single designators on the reversed pairs of associators.*

More generally, two keys are *definitionally dependent* if they are linked, directly or indirectly, by an associator chain that consists entirely of mandatory relationships. The dependence exists regardless of the direction (forward or back) of the mandatory chain. On the other hand, two keys are *definitionally independent* if there is no direct or indirect chain of mandatory relationships that links them. Figure 5-20 illustrates these cases.

## FUNDAMENTAL RULES OF LOGICAL DATA BASE DESIGN

There are certain conventions which the user of the notation needs to follow. Some of these conventions are so fundamental that they may seem obvious and axiomatic. These fundamental rules are developed in this section, and a modest effort is made to explain them (though many readers will regard these rules as self-evident). Other more elaborate design techniques are developed in the next section. These seemingly less funda-

---

*The relationship between these code patterns and the correspondences that must be preserved between pairs and keys is developed further in the section on correspondences in Chapter 6.

mental rules are given more detailed commentary, and the reader is given more latitude in deciding when and whether to follow the second group of "guidelines."

## Minimal Redundancy

Ideally, a logical data base design will contain no redundancy. An assertion, once entered in the data base, is not to be entered again in some other guise. The redundancy to be avoided is thus redundancy on the semantic level. Fortunately, nearly every logical design is successful in avoiding the error of storing the same assertions twice.

The fundamental reason for the prohibition of redundancy arises from considerations of consistency. It is a premise that the data base should be in a consistent state at all times, if possible. If it is permissible to enter the same assertion twice, and if it is permissible to execute changes against the data base, then it is possible to throw the data base into an inconsistent state by changing one record of the assertion before changing the other one. It would undermine one's confidence in the data base to learn that John is 6 feet tall one place in the data base and that John is 7 feet tall from another area of the data base. Such inconsistency will soon occur if changes are permitted and the two readings of the same assertion are stored independently. If changes are not permitted, or if the redundant assertions are "connected" so they can be changed together, then redundancy is permitted in a logical design.

Consider, for example, a subdata base that contains a collection of immutable facts. Assume that assertions, once entered in this subdata base, are never changed. It would be possible to enter the same assertion in many different guises without fear of causing a contradiction. To provide an elementary example—and one which is not likely to be changed—consider:

> Assertion 1: There are 4 quarts in a gallon.
> Assertion 2: There is 0.25 gallon in a quart.

The only harm that arises from storing the data redundantly (under the given assumption) is some modest duplication that uses up storage space. That extra space is easily justified by avoiding the re-computation of the inverse factor (0.25 vs. 4) when it is needed, so the "wasted" storage can easily turn into "savings" in computation. When steps are taken to forbid changes; this argument can be used to justify the storage of redundant assertions.

Assertions are redundant when one assertion can be derived from other assertions. In the general case, one assertion is derived from a larger number of other ones, rather than from its single "dual," as shown in the case of quarts and gallons. A routine example of such extended redundancy is provided by the total:

$$X_T = X_1 + X_2 + X_3 + \cdots\cdots + X_N$$

Were we to store all of these $X$ values, the total $X_T$ as well as the $N$ components, there would be redundancy. Storage of the total $X_T$ would be unnecessary since we could, if we wished, add up the $X_i$ "on the fly" to calculate it when needed. Nearly the same argument could be used to show that $X_1$ or $X_3$ is superfluous if we store $X_T$: The missing value can be calculated if the total and all the other $X_i$ are known. If we know (as before) that these values would not be allowed to change, there would be little harm in calculating the total once and for all and storing a known redundancy in the file.

These examples can be generalized even further. From an architectural point of view, visualize a derivative subdata base which is marked "inquiry only." It is prepared overnight, and it is not changed during the day. This data base contains "frozen food" answers—answers that have been prepackaged awaiting a probable inquiry during the day. By construction, *all* of these assertions are derivable from the master data base: the entire subdata base is redundant. But because there is no pretense that this subdata base will track the changes in the master data base, this architecture receives no criticism from the logical designer's point of view.

The criticism arises when redundancies like those illustrated creep into the design of the dynamic data base itself. When the same assertion is entered twice, and the data base "does not know that they are related" or "how," the design is obviously faulty—even a novice can throw the data base into an inconsistent state. The situation is more interesting when the designer takes pains to "tell the data base" that some assertions are closely related.

We call these relationships *Data Base Rules*. They read like mathematical equations. In the first example, a data base rule would state "the number of quarts per gallon in Assertion 1 is the reciprocal of the number of gallons per quart in Assertion 2, and conversely." In the second example, the equation $X_T = X_1 + X_2 \cdots + X_N$ tells the story. In a logical data base design, it is permissible to invoke a *procedure*. A Data Base Rule outlines a procedure for keeping data element values in some sort of relationship. Such a procedure would allow the designer to store $X_T$ as a value to be redundant—presumably because anticipated usage patterns would make it prohibitively expensive to add up the $X_i$ every time $X_T$ is needed. The Data Base Rule (i.e., procedure) would be executed each time one of the $X_i$ is changed, and the total $X_T$ would be recalculated as a consequence of the change. If the $X_i$ change once a day and the $X_T$ is used dozens of times, storage of $X_T$ as a "frozen food" item is probably defensible. If the $X_i$ change dozens of times per day and $X_T$ is needed once a day, then a frozen food approach is clearly wrong.

In this discussion, use of a limited amount of redundancy in a logical design has been permitted. The reasons for introducing the redundancy—on purpose—have all been physical, practical reasons, like the faster response attainable if the data is stored in prepackaged form. From a *pure* logical design point of view, no such redundancy would ever be permitted. But in practice it must be recognized that designers (and, more important, their audiences) are generally influenced by concerns that the data base will not prove to be practical. Because these concerns are so real—and, in many cases, they are valid—the logical designer must adapt his or her methods to address them. Introduction of a few (5 or 10) Data Base Rules is generally sufficient to illustrate very powerful techniques for blending fast response to predefined questions with the underlying flexibility which the data base offers. By prescribing a procedure (the Data Base Rule) or by freezing certain values as a snapshot of an earlier time, the designer can introduce useful redundancy without undermining logical design principles.

## No Searching of Files

In Accessing the Populated Data Bases, it was made clear that access to the data base is always a *direct* access which makes use of a given access argument that is believed to be a value of the key. Either the access argument is not found (not on file) or else it is found, and the entire assertion tree for that key value is placed in the user's workspace.

It is a violation of the rules of logical design to conduct a "search" that crosses assertions. For example, in a collection of assertions keyed by PERSON, it is illegal to pass the collection of PERSON assertions to select those which represent males or those which owe more than $10 or those which have any other property. The reason it violates the rules to do this is a further widening of the split between logical design and physical design.

Traditional storage media (tapes and disks) tend to arrange like records in some sort of physical proximity. Thus one is able to find a record by addressing via its key, and one is also able to proceed to the "next" record without knowledge of its key. It is this second step that is forbidden in a logical design: "next record" has no meaning until (at some later date) the physical arrangement is specified. Many people have grown up with the belief that they can always read the "next record." Were it not for this tradition, there would be no need to point out that file searching is impossible.

In a logical design, if there is reason to search a file, the remedy is simple. Merely chain the assertions together:

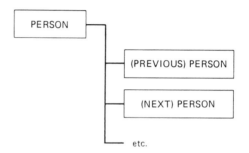

This arrangement makes the designer's intent clear, and the exhaustive search proceeds by a series of logical accesses to the "next" person. The arrangement also dramatizes what a wasteful procedure it is to search an entire "file" when it is not absolutely necessary.

The prohibition against searching does not apply *within* an assertion. Once the assertion tree is placed in the requester's workspace, it can be searched and scanned in its entirety with zero extra cost from a logical point of view. Naturally, it is understood that such "in-core" processing has a tangible physical cost in practice, and designers must be wary of wasting the processing resource by unnecessary use of this capability. Most logical designs make *no* use of searches that cross assertions and *negligible* use of searches inside a single assertion. The whole thrust of the logical design philosophy is to share data in such a way that all transactions can proceed forthrightly to the data. Searching and thrashing about is generally the mark of an ill-considered logical design approach.

Despite the force of the fundamental rule against processing entire files, such processing does take place in a physical system. In recovery, for example, it is routine to reconstruct an index like MARITAL STATUS by processing the PERSON "file" in its entirety.

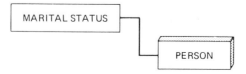

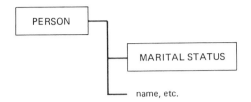

Reconstruction is accomplished by examining the MARITAL STATUS information in each PERSON record, in turn, and posting the result in the index. Alternatively, of course, one generates a file of PERSON-MARITAL STATUS pairs, sorts by MARITAL STATUS, and develops the index by wholesale rather than piecemeal methods. In any case, these procedures for specific recovery and reconstruction operations are outside the scope of logical design and are not affected by the prohibition against searching files.

In summary, the basic reason for forbidding file-search operations is to concentrate awareness on the fact that data bases are primarily random-access systems. The use of searching and implied record-sequence assumptions obscures the logic of the data relationships, hiding them behind a search procedure that is generally too complex to specify. If one allows any search procedure in a logical data base, like "Fetch all the Persons who are Male, Not Married, and owe $10 or more," it becomes extraordinarily difficult to restrain it. Why not allow a fetch of all Persons who, in addition, have Month-of-Birth larger than the number of their siblings—or any other search key for which there is data? There is no easy way to place limits on a search, and thus allowing freedom to search files is equivalent to permitting a runaway logical design in which all fields are inverted (or there is no need to invert any). To avoid this kind of frivolity, the present notation permits no searching across assertions in the data base. This fundamental rule has no exceptions, and the charts must always be interpreted in accordance with the direct access method which has been prescribed.

## Associators Cite Keys

In pictorial form, assertion templates can be viewed as trees with the key at the top. Then, as shown in the figure:

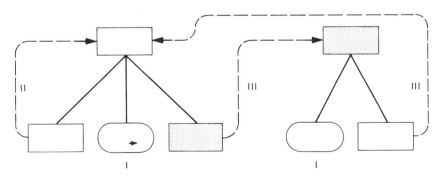

all the relationships are either internal (Type I) or they proceed *from* the inside of a tree structure to the top element (key) of a tree structure (Types II and III).

Notice that associators cite keys and that all the external relationships point to the tops of the trees. The current approach does not allow relationships which try to make reference "into the middle" of a tree structure. The citation shown in the following figure is completely prohibited by the notation:

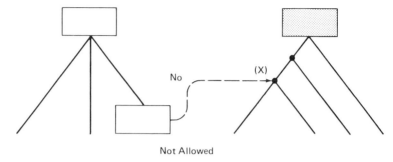

Not Allowed

While this might seem at first to be a major ommission of the current approach, it is important to understand exactly what is being prohibited. It is perfectly legitimate to reach the indicated node by traversing down from the key in a fashion which might be diagrammed like this:

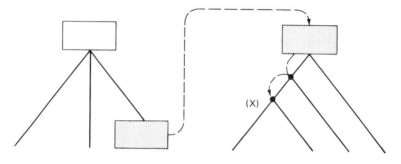

Allowed

The standard mechanism for accessing or referencing a node in the middle of a tree is to provide (inside the calling structure) the various elements needed to traverse the tree being cited, so that all the elements from the key down to the desired node are specified. For example:

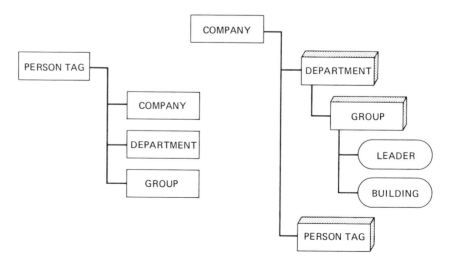

Observe that one can proceed from the PERSON TAG tree to the COMPANY tree, carrying along knowledge of the person's DEPARTMENT and GROUP. These values provide the basis for selection in the right-hand cascade and permit retrieval of data stored at the node marked (X) (like the leader of the group, the building where the group is housed, etc.). This arrangement violates none of the rules of the current approach; Indeed, it is quite routine to operate a logical data structure in this way. The step that is forbidden is to invent compound identifiers (like COMPANY/DEPT./GROUP) to jump into the middle of a tree, bypassing the regular access path via the key.

To fix the idea of the difference between what is allowed and what is not allowed, observe that one way to provide an "alternate" access path to the node marked (X) is (in diagrammatic form) to draw it as follows:

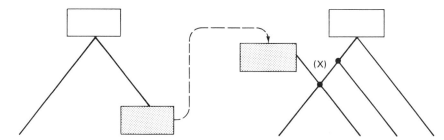

A new key has been invented, and now the associator at the bottom left makes access to this key with the objective of reaching node (X) more directly. Since the whole objective of the alternate path is to cite a specific node, this new key must be a unique identifier of the (X) node in question. Obviously, the (X) node is now accessible by two paths, and it is no longer the case that there is a tree structure for each key. (In a tree structure, as was noted earlier, every node except the top one has exactly one parent.) Node (X) now has two parents.

Is anything gained by discarding the tree structure property in favor of allowing this alternate path? It is easy to see there is no gain. If every (X) node has a unique identifier (the case we are assuming) then the previous diagram can be redrawn as follows:

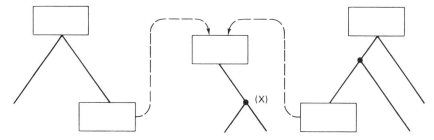

That is, the subtree headed by (X) is moved out to form a new tree structure which has the node identifier as key, and routine linkages via associators are established. Thus the attempt to make direct references "into the middle" of existing tree structures is readily accommodated without altering the simple conventions of the current approach.

Because the current approach disallows "alternate" paths of dependency, every node in an assertion is accessed via a path down from the key and via no other path. All the nonkey data elements in a logical data structure have exactly one access path, namely, down the cascade starting with the key. Only the keys have multiple entry points: they can be cited from any assertion template in the data structure.

Let's examine a complex case in more detail. Recall that in the New Plants Division data base, there appear to be a few associators which do not cite keys, e.g., those to CONTRACT AUTHORIZATION. As explained at the end of Chapter 1, the full design might have looked like this:

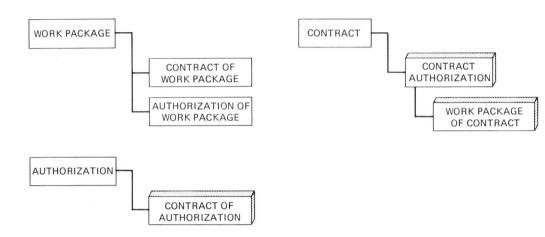

This design is well formed. However, the key AUTHORIZATION is not unique, nor is it meaningful independent of CONTRACT; no logical access by AUTHORIZATION alone need be provided and so this key was eventually omitted from the design. However, reference is made from other keys to AUTHORIZATION within CONTRACT, e.g., from WORK PACKAGE. So it is useful to maintain the status of AUTHORIZATION as an associator. Essentially, the appearance of AUTHORIZATION as an associator indicates that more information about AUTHORIZATION is to be found at the location cited, i.e., AUTHORIZATION within CONTRACT. Thus a citation to AUTHORIZATION must always include CONTRACT. Note that the citation is not of the form

To reiterate, compound keys are not permitted; the reference must begin with the key as an independent associator.

## Targets of a Subject Appear Together

A relationship among two or more data elements forms a subject, which may in turn bear (another) relationship to one or more targets. The distinction between a subject and the reversal of a relationship is important to keep in mind. Specifically, the following configuration is prohibited:

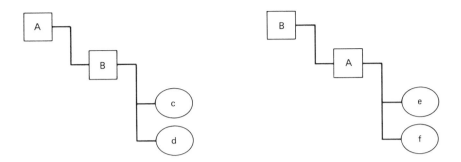

In this case, one of the pair A–B or B–A, must be selected as the subject, and *all* targets of this subject must appear subordinate to it. The reversal B–A or A–B, is not a candidate subject and may have no targets. Either case produces logically equivalent data structures, but the "mixed" case is forbidden. This rule is consistent with the guideline for no redundancy (a subject can only appear once); moreover, once we have identified a subject, everything about it (i.e., all relationships it bears) is recorded in a single location.

### Associator Reversal

The associator reversal convention, which is an important part of the current approach, is a method for insuring that important relationships are defined completely. When associators are used in complicated ways (in deeply nested cascades, for instance) associator reversal becomes a nontrivial exercise. Often, the effort to unravel the associator reversal problem will convince the designer that the original design—the multilevel use of associators—was too complicated. But when the original formulation stands and associators appear in multilevel cascades, the general form of the reversal rule needs to be followed.

The basic rule for associator reversal in cascades can be stated in a way which exploits the decomposition of cascades into constituent relationships.

Let A be a cascade of elements $A_1, A_2, \ldots, A_n$ which forms the subject of a relationship, and let $B$ be an associator which is a target of this relationship. Then to reverse the associator, $B$ must be a key which bears the inverse relationship to the entire subject $A_1, A_2, \ldots, A_n$. Moreover, the same requirement applies to each intervening associator $A_{n-1}, A_{n-2}$, etc. and *its* cascade subject, for we have stressed that *each* element in a cascade is the target of a relationship (and this relationship needs to be reversed.) Thus given the cascade of $n+1$ boxes, $n$ additional assertion templates need to be constructed to express the reversals: There is a distinct reverse relationship under each key cited in the cascade. This is not difficult to do when $n=2$; it is very arduous when $n$ is 3 or more.

In the case of primitive assertions, the reversal is very easy to accomplish. Having recorded one of the following four assertions:

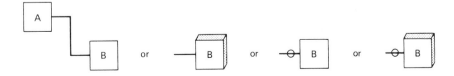

It is very little work to record the reversal; by selecting one of these four (reversed) relationships

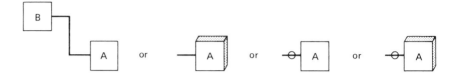

Because it is necessary to choose which pattern of optional/multiple data elements is appropriate, both in the first relationship and in its reversal, there are actually sixteen possible combinations.

Consider, for example, the following assertions in the "forward" direction:

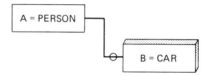

It indicates that the person may own zero or many cars B. Independent decisions need to be made about the reverse relationship:

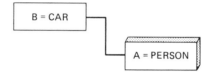

Two questions need to be answered: "Is it possible that a car is owned by no person?" Conceivably, cars in a dealership or cars owned by the Army or cars in the junkyard would not qualify as "owned." Notice how the question forces attention upon the meaning of the concepts (What is a car? What is a person? What does ownership entail?) The result of the first question establishes whether the associator is optional or mandatory in the reversed relationship. The second question is concerned with multiplicity. "Can a car be owned by many persons?" Ordinarily, joint ownership is routinely acceptable, and so the answer is readily apparent in this case.

Though it is easy to record the reversed associator pairs (especially in the primitive cases), the simplicity obscures the importance of what is being done. Associator reversal is not a mechanical process. It is a process for making sure that a relationship has been *completely defined*. Observe, for example, that in choosing one of the four patterns for assertions in the forward direction, the relationship was not well-defined. Although the fact was established that a person can own zero or many cars, the incomplete data structure did not stipulate whether partial ownership counts as ownership, and it did not stipulate whether all the cars in the data base are owned by some person. The associator reversal exercise is required to insure that important relationships in the data base are completely specified.

The rule for associator reversals in the case of more complicated cascades is an intentional compromise between ignoring and becoming enbroiled in complexity. Long cascades of associators are not, normally, reversed completely. Instead, it is *standard* practice to consider a specific subset of the possible reversals by constructing, from the cascade ABCDEF . . . , the "partials" BA, CAB, DABC, EABCD, FABCDE, etc. as illustrated in Figure 5-21. This standard practice forces the designer to consider a reversal problem for each of the cited keys, and it provides a cross-reference to the cascade from each cited key. This standard practice is not even remotely a "complete" reversal of the original cascade. (Remember that a "partial" with DABC is not a relationship from D to ABC. It related DAB to C.) Instead, *standard* reversal serves several useful practical pruposes. In particular, consideration of the standard reversals usually turns up the situations where the original cascade can be expressed in shorter form, where functional dependencies are hidden inside the cascade, or where other significant simplifications can be made. For these reasons, *standard* reversals should always be used for long cascades except in theoretical work.

In this example, note the following:

- The reversal of STATE to DRIVER (ii) is straightforward, and specifies that a STATE may have none, one, or many DRIVERS licensed in it. Other data about the STATE, independent of DRIVER, (such as population) may be recorded, but no additional data may be shown subordinate to DRIVER. Data which is dependent on STATE and DRIVER (such as RESIDENT OF STATE FLAG) must be included with other targets of that subject in the original cascade, according to the rule, Targets of a Subject Appear Together, specified earlier.
- The reversal of VEHICLE (iii) is to the DRIVER-STATE subject. Again there is the opportunity to record independent data about the *new* subjects formed: VEHICLE and VEHICLE DRIVER, but not VEHICLE-DRIVER-STATE as this subject appears in the original cascade. Notice also that in assertions (i) and (ii), the relationship between DRIVER and STATE is multiple and optional (A DRIVER can be licensed in zero, one, or many STATES and a STATE can have zero, one, or many DRIVERS licensed by it). But in (iii), STATE is single and mandatory: for any particular vehicle, a DRIVER is given permission to operate the VEHICLE in exactly one STATE

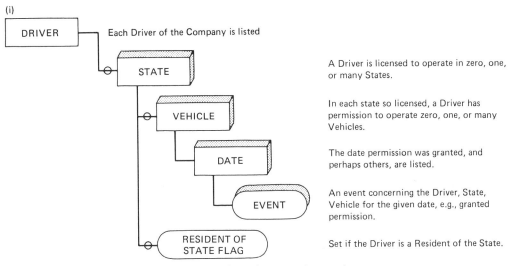

(i)

DRIVER — Each Driver of the Company is listed

STATE — A Driver is licensed to operate in zero, one, or many States.

VEHICLE — In each state so licensed, a Driver has permission to operate zero, one, or many Vehicles.

DATE — The date permission was granted, and perhaps others, are listed.

EVENT — An event concerning the Driver, State, Vehicle for the given date, e.g., granted permission.

RESIDENT OF STATE FLAG — Set if the Driver is a Resident of the State.

Figure 5-21. Cascade reversal example.

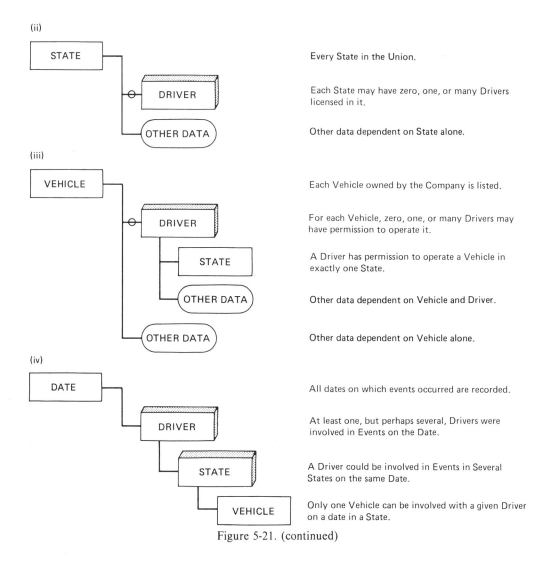

(ii)

STATE

DRIVER

OTHER DATA

Every State in the Union.

Each State may have zero, one, or many Drivers licensed in it.

Other data dependent on State alone.

(iii)

VEHICLE

DRIVER

STATE

OTHER DATA

OTHER DATA

Each Vehicle owned by the Company is listed.

For each Vehicle, zero, one, or many Drivers may have permission to operate it.

A Driver has permission to operate a Vehicle in exactly one State.

Other data dependent on Vehicle and Driver.

Other data dependent on Vehicle alone.

(iv)

DATE

DRIVER

STATE

VEHICLE

All dates on which events occurred are recorded.

At least one, but perhaps several, Drivers were involved in Events on the Date.

A Driver could be involved in Events in Several States on the same Date.

Only one Vehicle can be involved with a given Driver on a date in a State.

Figure 5-21. (continued)

(i.e., a DRIVER cannot operate the same VEHICLE in two STATES, but can operate different VEHICLES in two STATES.) It is the reversal which permits us to specify this additional characteristic of the (compound) relationship.

- The DATE associator is reversed in (iv). The semantics of this assertion are such that no DATE is included in the data base unless an event of interest occurred on it; such an event is then characterized by a DRIVER, a STATE, and a particular VEHICLE (all mandatory). While other data could be included about the subjects DATE-DRIVER and DATE-DRIVER-STATE, none appears in this example.

### Keys Have No Internal Structure

A key is said to have *internal structure* if it carries data about the thing denoted by the key value. In data processing applications, it has been a useful technique to define a thing by combining or concatenating values of what we would call different data elements. For example, to provide a breakdown of account data by year, it is conventional practice to form a compound key ACCOUNT NO.-YEAR and to use this construct as the identifier for a year's worth of account data. In the present notation, this practice is severely constrained, and beginners would be well-advised to avoid compound keys (or data-bearing keys, or structured keys) entirely. The primary reason for avoiding this practice is to avoid the baffling problems that arise when we change one (or more) of the constituent data elements that "make up" the key. The few cases where it is permitted are cases where there is no possibility that the constituent elements will change, but it is extremely rare that a logical design can survive a critic's attack if it carries data in the keys.

*Compound keys are illegal.*
Consider, for example, a shipping company whose vessels travel from port to port on a regularly scheduled basis. We stipulate that there is no foreseeable problem in identifying either a vessel in the fleet or the candidate ports to be visited. But the problem arises when we want to define "Vessel i being engaged in the trip (route segment) between Port j and Port k." The compound identifier "Vessel i, Port j, Port k" comes to mind as the identifier of this route segment. What is wrong with attaching cargo details to such a compound?

The procedure for appraising the merits of this suggestion is quite simple. Examine the effect of changing each component of the combined key:

- Vessel i sinks en route.
- Vessel i never arrives at (and/or never leaves) Port j.
- Vessel i is diverted at sea to Port m, not the original destination, Port k.

This sort of "worst case" thinking is a critical discipline. Admittedly, the worst case is often so unlikely that practical souls will cry out (with justice) that it should be ignored. The logical designer—being equally practical—avoids public emphasis of the worst case when it is an unlikely event. But privately, it is thought through* anyway, for every designer has learned from experience what "it will never happen" really means.

In studying the "Vessel i, Port j, Port k" compound, two cases need to be contrasted. In one case, the triple formed from "vessel, (leave) port, (arrive) port" is the key. In the second case, a new key—call it LEG, for leg of the journey—is used. Side-by-side, these cases appear as shown in Figure 5-22.

The compound key, which uses an illegal triple of values as a key, is extremely imprecise in conveying how the assertion may be accessed. There is no doubt we can access the first assertion template by forming a triple "Vessel i, L-Port j, A-Port k." But imprecision arises when accesses are considered that leave some constituents unspecified. Is it permitted to access the compound key by the following subkeys?

Vessel i only
L-Port j only
A-Port k only

*Logical design demands this kind of discipline. If it is impossible for a key element to change, that impossibility is a valuable fact. On the other hand, if it is possible for ships to sink en route, the logical design must account for that possibility as an equally valuable fact.

Vessel i and L-Port j
Vessel i and A-Port k
L-Port j and A-Port k

In conventional data processing systems that use such compound keys, it is always possible to select the subsets defined by these combinations—as a by-product of searching the whole file. But as noted in No Searching of Files, file searching in not allowed at the key level in a logical design unless the assertions are linked by "Next Pointers." If the designer wishes to provide access by all the above listed combinations of subkeys,

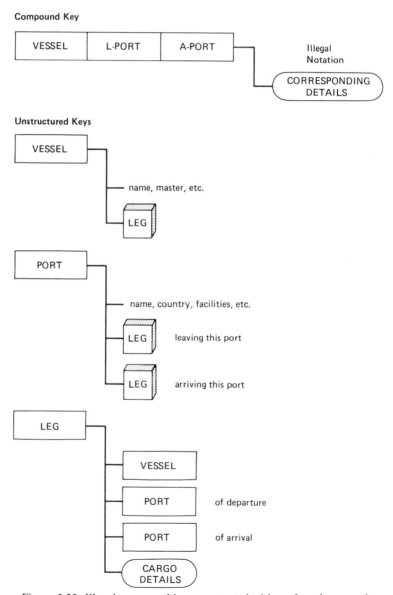

Figure 5-22. Illegal compound keys contrasted with preferred approach.

the correct procedure is to use the second example above in which each LEG is indexed for access by the three subkeys—individually or in combination. The present notation requires the invention of a unique identifier (LEG in this case) for any assertion that is meant to be accessed by multiple paths.

*Constructed keys are poor practice.*
Sometimes the constituent elements used to define an entity are *not* keys in their own right. All we wish to do is to concatenate several data values to provide access to a block of data. It is probably difficult to imagine Vessels and Ports as nonkey items, but if one were a transport broker, it is possible to imagine having no interest in vessels or ports alone, yet ample interest in tracing particular cargoes from place to place. In such a case where Vessel and Port are not keys, it is tempting to use constructed keys using the following notation:

| VESSEL/L-PORT/A-PORT | Poor Practice |

Notice that the key is a single unpartitioned rectangle again and that the value of such a key is formed by combining the three elements given. Access to this key is provided, as usual, by an identity match on the three compounds. Thus this constructed key is consistent with all other rules except for the prohibition against structured keys (or data in the key) which is under discussion.

The foregoing remarks serve to point out the correct practice—how to form constructed keys within the rules if you have to. We now wish to advise the reader *never* to use formulations of this kind as keys. It is much better to rename the construct—call it "voyage segment" or "leg" or some such name. The reason for this warning has nothing to do with correctness. It has to do with keeping things clear and simple.

Consider some other data aggregate in the data base—one representing an event, say—that needs to be linked to the triple under consideration. Using the terminology sketched above, it would show:

A reader looking at this might be misled by the associator name into thinking that the vessel ID of the event and the two ports of the event are recorded under the event. This is not true. The rules say we are not allowed to "look inside" an associator to find data. Rather, we are supposed to make a logical access to the key location and find the data there. In this case, it seems, we get the same answer either way. But there is a difference. In the first (incorrect) interpretation, the data considered to be "right here" appear to be repeated again and again in all the EVENT aggregates, and fewer logical accesses need to be used. In the second (correct) interpretation, data are not repeated and more logical accesses are assumed. Embedding data in the key opens the door to this kind of misinterpretation and imprecision.

The designer who wants to show the data repeated in each EVENT aggregate would, of course, draw:

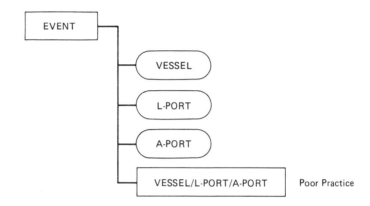

The associator would be used to access data about the voyage segment identified by the triple (e.g., What was the cargo?). The other elements amplify knowledge of the EVENT. This would be perfectly correct, though it shows a flagrant disregard for the principle of holding data in one place. The three elements in ovals clearly belong with the key that is referenced by the associator.

*"Implied pointers" are prohibited.*
The troubles raised by compounding keys do not stop there. For example, in the drawing just discussed, one might be tempted to have an "implied pointer" derived from the presence of VESSEL, L-PORT, and A-PORT in the EVENT aggregate. The method for formation of VESSEL/L-PORT/A-PORT states that a key can be constructed by concatenation, and there can be no quarrel that the above associator could be constructed that way in all cases. The temptation is to omit the associator entirely from the logical design. But of what possible relevance is this to the logical design? The fact that the physical data base design may omit a pointer (and derive it instead from other values) may be of interest when it happens, if it happens. In a logical design, we want to record the fact that the connection *needs* to be made. *How* the connection *is* made is a different problem, and one of the consequences of using these compounds as keys is the distraction that ensues. Attention turns to the rules and artifices of constructing these compounds, to the properties of the component symbols, and to the physical properties of the data base and the accessing mechanism. Since that discussion begins with the observation that a connection is needed, it is evident that most of the effort so expended makes little or no contribution to the logical design effort. While we hesitate to call it a waste of time, it is certainly a distraction. A logical data base design makes no use of "implied pointers."

## GUIDELINES FOR LOGICAL DESIGN

The previous section contained a number of fundamental rules for logical design which are intended to maintain the consistency and clarity of the design, or to force the designer to consider certain key design questions. In this section, guidelines are presented which cover several interesting or challenging design situations. These guidelines or techniques are by no means rules to be religiously applied; rather, they are intended to provide the designer with insight into how to treat various common design problems.

Specifically, we are concerned with promoting guidelines which make the design more precise and at the same time less complex. These are the two highest level goals of a logical design. Precision means reflecting *exactly* what the designer means the design to portray: no more, no less. At the same time, the cost of this precision must not involve undue complexity.

In the beginning of this chapter, we laid bare the essentials of the logical data base design methodology. The methodology is *not* such that an inexperienced person, once introduced to it, can begin to design data bases immediately. Rather, the methodology provides a framework from which the experienced data analyst can approach the logical design of data bases in a consistent and thoughtful manner. The ability to structure data bases comes, to a large degree, with experience. As new situations are encountered and as old approaches prove out or are wanting, the analyst develops a highly tuned design "sense." Having a reasonable methodology to start with is a large plus. So is the experience of others, insofar as it widens the learner's exposure without him having to encounter the situations directly. The final design decisions for which the learner opts may not agree with those chosen by others; however, the exposure to a problem and the reasoning which others have made about it remain valuable. It is this spirit which we present the comments in this section.

## Designing for History

Some of the most interesting and challenging data base design problems arise when there is a need to keep a historical record in the data base. The problem includes (but is far more general than) a requirement to find the values of a few data elements as of some date long past. The problem is also more general than a requirement to search an audit trail to uncover previously recorded data. In a data base designed for history, the whole data base (or, more practically, a major subdata base) can be set back to its state at a previous point in time. A consequence of this ability to set time back is the ability to set time forward as well.

We can think of a data base for which there is a requirement to maintain history as one in which nothing is ever deleted. It grows unchecked, and the designer must take note of the point in time when there is no more "room" for the data base on the devices which held it originally. Historical data bases often span a variety of device types in a hierarchical storage management scheme. The recent data is on disk, data of middle age is on a mass memory of some kind, and really old data is on tapes or something else. The logical designer will make no progress if he spends his time developing or inventing a scheme for managing the (physical) problems posed by the multimedia situation. Instead, the designer should immediately commit himself to using *tags* lavishly, to making these tags as large as necessary so they will *never* be reused, and to allowing these tags to migrate across device boundaries. These premises permit entities to be given permanent identifiers—identifers that continue to apply, regardless of time or the movement of related data from device to device.

The next element of the design of historical data bases is to make repeated use of a particular data structure that has endless uses. This structure—which applies to most entities—regards the entity as having a fixed part and a variable part. The structure is not new; fixed data has always been stored in "header" records, while the variable part has always been stored in "trailer" records. In designing for history, the same essential features of the structure are used again and again. Assign a tag to the entity and let it be the key to the header record. As shown in Figure 5-23, all the data that is used to define the entity or is permanently associated with it goes in the "header." When any of this data changes, we have a new entity. The new entity receives a new header with a new tag, and the new header is linked back (associator chain) to the header that used to represent it. The chain of headers—each is marked with the date and time of the change, of course—tracks the given entity across the various alterations that are considered basic enough to cause the formation of new objects.

This process, the transmutation of entities, is not as fearsome a subject as it may appear. Every entity has certain basic defining conditions that establish it as an object distinct from similar objects. In the case of a life insurance policy, the policy is *defined* by (a) a single person whose life is insured, (b) an owner of the policy and (c) a legal entity who is the beneficiary. A change in (b) or (c) causes the creation of a revised policy related to the old one; a change in (a), the insured, would probably cause the termination of the old policy and the creation of a completely new one. And while an object called a policy is present in the data base, all kinds of variations to it are permitted. The amount of insurance can be raised or lowered, various payment and payout elections can be chosen or revised. These variable elements are carried in the "trailer" records shown in Figure 5-23.

Notice that the trailer records all have unique tags. Each one is uniquely identified by its own distinct identifier—the "Policy Rider" in this example. Each rider points back in time to its predecessor, and there are as many of these snapshots as there are changes to the information contained in the rider.

At the third level, attached to riders, are the events (transactions) that need to be associated with the entity (policy) at any point in time. These provide an audit trail of

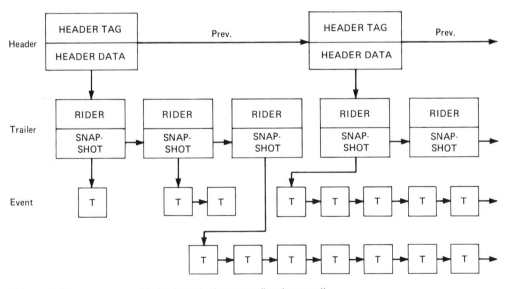

Notes: • All arrows are meant to be shown in the reverse direction as well.
      • "Rider" is another kind of tag.
      • T stands for a transaction. Each transaction also has a unique tag.

Figure 5-23. Three-level chains used for tracking entities historically.

the changes made to the policy. Note very carefully that the events (e.g., change of address notices, payments, etc.) are not attached directly to the header. They are attached to the rider and thus indirectly to the header. This may not be the intuitive way to make the connection, but it is not at all difficult to do. Visualize a payment transaction on policy P. Access the header using P and then find its current rider. Upon processing the new transaction, store it at the head of the chain that emanates from the rider, showing in this manner that the transaction "belongs to" a particular snapshot of the evolving policy.

Observe next that all three chains—the header chain that tracks the entity, the trailer chain that snapshots changes, and the transaction chain—all are altered by placing new additions first. The consequence of these rules is a system of chains (three of them in this example) that extend backward in time. That is, when following any of these chains, the next one in sequence is "older." At this point, the logical designer can comment on the problem of physical file management by expressing considerable indifference (from a logical point of view) as to where the data resides. To make this real, let us assume that the data management system cuts the chains at random points and places everything older than the cut point on a slower device like a mass memory. In other words, the chain continues on a new device once it is old enough. Clearly, a program that is reading the chain, proceeding from the present back into time, will eventually find an associator value that refers to a record not present on the "active" device. Knowing that the record with the cited tag exists somewhere, a query is posed to the physical data management system: where is it? Naturally, the data management system knows where it placed the rest of the chain, and after this slight interruption, the scan proceeds within the alternate storage medium. It will probably be a slower process in the alternate medium, and discussion will surely arise as to whether it is "too" slow. That question is a physical question—one which can only be answered by consulting the cost parameters and the engineering specifications of the candidate devices. What is "too" slow today may well be replaceable tomorrow by a mass storage unit of acceptable cost and speed. The logical designer should contribute to the discussion the following points:

- Read-Only—the "old" segments of chains that have been taken from the "active" data base are all complete. They will never be revised or rewritten. For this reason, the physical designer has the option to use read-only technology in the alternate (and presumably slower) storage devices.
- Variable Purge—the logical design makes no assumptions about the place in the chain where the cut is made. One could cut automatically after three units in each chain. Or one could retire everything that is more than three months old. Or one could have one rule for policies of one type and other rules for policies of other types. The *logical* design avoids prejudging the retirement policy.

The basic building block for a data base designed for history is thus seen to be a structure which has two or three levels of time-sequenced chains. The first two levels represent points in time when the entity undergoes significant changes; the bottom level is a record of transactions against a snapshot of the entity. All three assertion types are time-stamped. Nearly all linkages (associators) into the rest of the data are carried at the middle level—by the assertions identified by the riders in Figure 5-23.

When a historical data base is built from numerous replicas of this molecular data structure, it is relatively easy to recover the status of each assertion at some given time in the past. First, one proceeds down the header chain to the header just earlier than the chosen time. One next proceeds down its rider chain to the trailer just earlier than the chosen time. (To accommodate this easy procedure, one always creates a snapshot of the trailer when a header is changed.) Then, when the right trailer is found, one executes the same procedure on the transaction chain. On completion, one is poised to treat this assertion afresh as if the changes since that time had never happened. Of course, the changes have happened, and we are not allowed to rewrite history as a rule. Consequently, the ability to reset the data base to a time in the past is generally used on a read-only basis.

Yet it was noted earlier that the data base, so constructed, can also be set to a future time if desired. This sort of procedure is used with highly detailed models—models which create tentative changes in the data base. Clearly, if there is a model of this type (they are not commonplace), then the model can add headers, trailers, and transactions with future time stamps to the historical data base in the usual way. When the exercise has been completed, and all has been learned that is needed, the data base can be reset to the present by tracing back the chain as previously described.*

## Exclusive OR Conditions

The exclusive OR is one of several interpretations of the word "or." When OR is used in the exclusive sense, exactly one of the alternatives A or B or C must be fulfilled. When "or" is used in the nonexclusive sense, more than one of the listed alternatives could be fulfilled. Because there are multiple interpretations of what "or" means, logical designers quickly develop the same attitude toward the word that lawyers learned long ago. It is rare to find the word "or" in legal text, and it should be made equally rare in data base work. The reason is that "or" is highly uninformative, subtly misleading, and does not express the facts of a situation very well.

When one writes, "The structure provides for A or B to be present," the words have the ring of authority and they seem to be telling us something. But on closer inspection, the "or" turns out to be uninformative. It is possible

For A to be present alone, of course
For B to be present alone, of course
For *both* A and B to be present
For *neither* A or B to be present

All possible combinations of A and B remain possible, just as all four combinations were possible before we said, "The structure provides for A or B to be present." The sentence, like many that use the word "or," gives very little information. To avoid faulty use of "or," it is valuable to remember to attach other words to it:

A or B (or both)
A or B (but not both)

---

*However, the normal method for accomplishing these (backward and forward) alterations of time is to copy the subdata base that reflects time zero into a new "what if" data space, to run the model and (usually) to erase the "what if" data base once the results have been obtained and verified. Resetting is not normally required when this approach is taken.

A (exclusive) or B = one but not both
A (inclusive) or B = both are possible

Ideally, "or" is avoided entirely.

In a logical design, most instances of an exclusive OR arise when the designer is thinking physically, considering the use a particular storage location to hold two data elements. This is such bad practice we hesitate to show an example. But think of a writing instrument; assume it is either a pencil or a pen. The pen is meant to be filled with ink, but the pencil is automatic and has one of several mechanisms for advancing the lead. Bad practice is to draw something like

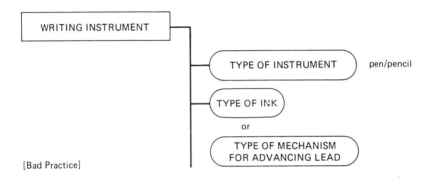

[Bad Practice]

In a departure from standard notation, "or" links two ovals, one of which is not attached to the vertical line. A slightly better practice is to show the type of ink and type of advancing mechanism dependent on type of instrument:

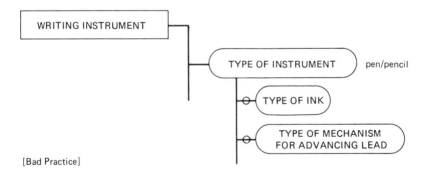

[Bad Practice]

This arrangement makes it explicit that the "ink" and "lead" elements depend on the type of instrument. The exclusive OR becomes rather obvious since TYPE OF INK would not be relevant for a pencil and vice versa. What is not adequately stated in this arrangement is that one of the ink/lead types *must* be supplied. As shown above, it is possible for both elements to be absent, and this may not be the interpretation that is desired. The remedy is not a notational problem but a conceptual one.

In a significant number of cases, the perceived need to use alternation—especially the exclusive OR—is a signal for the need to generalize. This process is considered more carefully below. In the present example, we need to find a shared concept that is one level more general than either TYPE OF INK or TYPE OF MECHANISM FOR ADVANCING LEAD.

The reader may find other good candidates; one choice which serves to illustrate the method is FEED MECHANISM plus MATERIAL TYPE used as follows:

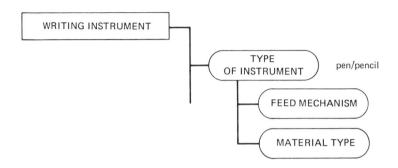

Notice thet *both* FEED MECHANISM and MATERIAL TYPE are mandatory. Not only has the exclusive OR been removed, but also all optionality has vanished. For pens, the FEED MECHANISM is capillary action, hydraulic pressure, gravity, or some such force—for pencils, the mechanism for advancing the lead is to be supplied. On the other hand, MATERIAL TYPE (for pens) recites the TYPE OF INK best suited to the instrument and (for pencils) holds a code for "lead." The lesson, and the reason for this guideline, is to be suspicious of exclusive OR conditions that remain in a logical data base design, for they may indicate either that physical constraints are interfering in the design or that a generalization may need to be made.

### Generalization (Data Element Level)

Perhaps the most significant issue facing the logical data base designer has to do with the selection of the fundamental entities to be treated in the data base. The decisions which the designer must make regarding the selection of entities are the most critical, because they define the very fabric of the design. Slight alterations in the set of primitive entities can transform a rough, unwieldy design into a precise, elegant one.

Traditionally, the selection of entities to be dealt with in a data processing system received little attention. The scope of applications was well defined, the data files needed only to support those applications, and little thought was given to flexibility. The selection of entities was straightforward, most often the objects as they were thought about by the user were accepted uncritically. System analysts and programmers concentrated on the mainstream objects—those which obeyed all the rules. Exceptions or unusual conditions (e.g., parts which could be both purchased *and* manufactured, people who are both agents and policyholders, employees who left the company and returned, and so on), were left to be dealt with later on, or completely ignored. The data base tenets of consistent and well-defined data, and the objectives of a conceptual data model of the enterprise, require us to pay considerably more attention to the choice of fundamental entities.

It needs to be pointed out that both the theoretical and operational apparatus now at hand need to be extended to deal with the problems of entity selection. Both the data models (CODASYL networks, relations, hierarchies) and the data base management software available to the practitioner still reflect the thinking, as far as entity selection goes, of the narrow, single-application orientation briefly reviewed above. For example, consider the simple case of employee and applicant. Are these to be treated as:

— Independent but related entity types?
— Entities which are instances of the more general type person?
— Characteristics of the entity type person?

Certainly, great advances will be forthcoming soon on the theoretical and operational area dealing with these problems. Meanwhile, we have to make do with the tools at hand.

Restricting our attention for the moment to data elements which are not keys or associators, let us examine a portion of the assertion in the NPD example dealing with Contract Items and repeated here as in Figure 5-24. Consider the elements PLANNED RESOURCE USAGE AMOUNT and TYPE OF PLANNED RESOURCE USAGE AMOUNT. Where did these elements come from? In all likelihood, they would *not* be found as part of the real world problem which this data base addresses; at least they wouldn't have prior to the data base design effort. In particular, the data element TYPE OF PLANNED RESOURCE USAGE AMOUNT was invented, so to speak, by the designer to achieve some purpose. That purpose is simplification and flexibility. To grasp the situation more fully, consider what the design in Figure 5-24 might have looked like prior to the generalization. This is depicted in Figure 5-25.

The process of generalization described here is quite straightforward. Several differ-

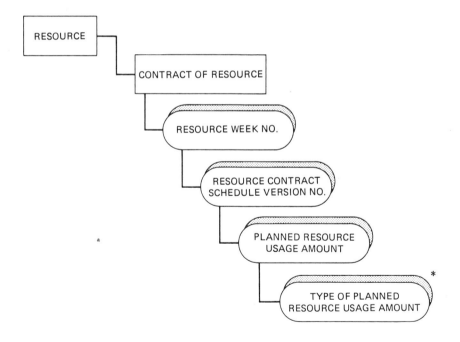

*Recall that if the same PLANNED RESOURCE USAGE AMOUNT can occur for two or more types, then this element must be multiply occurring.

Figure 5-24. Contract Items—a portion of the assertion template from the NPD example.

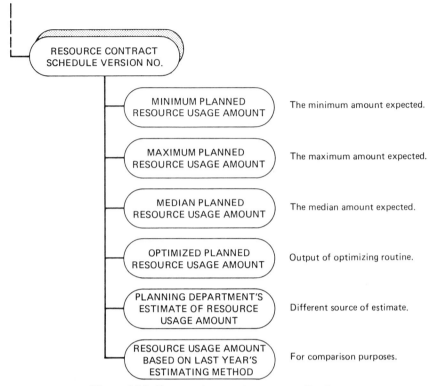

Figure 5-25. Contract items prior to generalization.

ent data elements all defined over the same domain are combined into one multyply-occurring data element, and a type indicator to distinguish among them. What benefits does this kind of generalization bring to the design, other than the obvious one of reducing the overall number of different elements (in the case from six to two)? Perhaps the most significant advantage is flexibility. For instance, if sometime in the future we wish to record the accounting department's estimate, then in the initial method we would have to define a new data element:

ACCOUNTING DEPARTMENT'S ESTIMATE OF RESOURCE USAGE AMOUNT

With the generalized design, no new element needs to be created; instead a new allowable *value* is introduced for the data element:

TYPE OF PLANNED RESOURCE USAGE AMOUNT

Similarly, if we decide that the optimized estimate no longer needs to be provided for in the data base, then very little needs to be done to implement this. Specifically, either of these changes can be accommodated without a change in the data base design.

Another benefit of generalization is a possible reduction in programming effort. This may not appear to be the case at first glance, especially if there were only three or four distinct elements be begin with. Having each as a separate element allows the programmer to pick out the value directly by using the proper element name. But suppose there are 20 or 30 such elements. And suppose that the same processing routine could apply to any of these—clearly we don't want to write the same routine 20 times with just the element name changed. More likely, we are apt to write the routine once, moving the particular element desired to a common element used by the one routine, and perhaps moving the resulting calculation value back to the proper element name for output. In these cases, it is more straightforward to use the multiply-occurring element, testing on the type indicator for the one desired.

Many opportunities for simplifying in this manner are readily apparent. For instance, we are quite likely to store each of the last 12 months' value of some element as an array of 12 occurrences of the same element. In this case, the TYPE is understood as the subscript, and reflects to which month the associated value corresponds. Other opportunities are not so apparent, and the designer has to look for them.

Care should be taken not to confuse the technique of data element simplification with the notational convention use of "label" to represent a family relationship as introduced previously in this chapter. The use of label is understood to be merely a temporary shorthand—later on as the design progresses, each and every member of the family will be identified and fully defined as a stand-alone data element. When we do not know all of the members of the family at present, and their delineation right now is not crucial, we can use the label shorthand to indicate that several similar elements will eventually need to be defined. For example

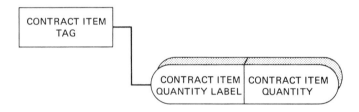

might eventually be expanded to

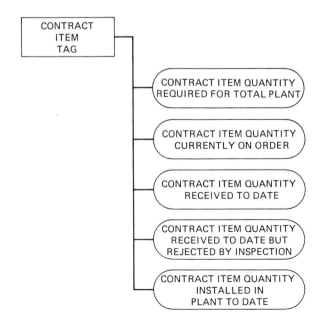

If we compare the two examples, namely,

TYPE OF PLANNED RESOURCE USAGE AMOUNT
and
CONTRACT ITEM QUANTITY LABEL

we can gain an appreciation of when to use the generalization technique, and when not to use it. First, in both cases, all of the potential data elements in question must be defined over the same domain (e.g., all ⟨resource usage amounts⟩ or ⟨item quantities⟩). As previously mentioned, some effort to unify domains may be required prior to applying the generalization technique, or determining if it is indeed applicable. Another requirement for generalization is that each of the elements be processible in the same way. For example, we can easily imagine several applications which use a PLANNED RESOURCE USAGE AMOUNT: the applications are not particularly sensitive to precisely which amount is used (maximum, minimum, the planning department's guess, etc.). Today, an application could be based on one TYPE of these amounts, tomorrow on another TYPE, depending on which kind of plan we are interested in. Not so in the case of the various contract item quantities—we would be hard pressed to find a usage in which the quantity required for the total plant was interchangeable in the manner described with the quantity received to date.

The benefits of the generalization technique are related to flexibility—so the presence of variability in the list of elements is a strong (but not absolutely mandatory) requirement. Again, for any CONTRACT ITEM we are likely to want all of the quantity related data elements; but for any RESOURCE CONTRACT SCHEDULE we may only want to record one or at most a few of the possible types of planned resource usage amounts. On top of this, it is likely that we will want to introduce new types of planned amounts in the future.

Notice that the technique of data element generalization involves only a slight change in the selection of entities. In our example, we are still dealing with the fundamental entity of (resource usage) amounts (actually the entity referenced here is a dimensionless cardinality—see Chapter 4).

## Generalization (Key-Level)

Here we consider a kind of generalization similar to that discussed above with regard to nonkey data elements, but now focusing on the data base keys instead.

Consider the following substructure which might appear in a key-level overview of the data base:

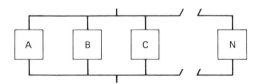

What we intend to portray here is a series of keys which appear to be treated very similarly in the data base. Our initial design shows that for the most part, each of the keys enters into the same or almost the same relationships with other keys. This is evident by our ability to form a common set of lines to and from this group of keys and other keys in the overall structure diagram. The individual assertions for each key likewise are very similar, if not exactly the same. Furthermore, when we think about the processing which will be done to the assertions, each will receive similar processing. A transformation should then be considered which accomplishes the following generalization:

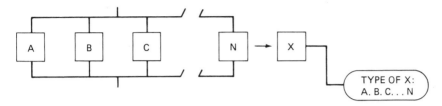

This transformation is in principle quite similar to the one discussed above with respect to nonkey elements. However, since key elements are more intricately woven into the fabric of the data base, there are important differences.

Recall the discussion in Chapter 4 dealing with the issue of classifying entities into domains. We concluded that discussion with the observations that choices were indeed available, and that different choices were dependent on differing points of view (e.g., "people" and "corporations" vs. "legal entities"). The process of key-level generalization is analogous to combining previously separate domains into a single domain—i.e., of viewing different kinds of entities as variations of the same basic type (essentially a process of generalization). Sometimes this generalizing can be done with confidence early in the design process—when the initial choices of domains are being made. However, the decision remains subjective and vulnerable to differing points of view. Often the rationale for combining or "generalizing" does not appear until the overall structure of the data base begins to take shape and certain points of view are in fact emphasized over others.

Thus many of the entity types corresponding to the initial classification into domains will be the subject of assertion templates in the data base; the designer can then recognize that several assertion templates are quite similar (particularly including the associators in the templates, indicating that the keys enter into similar relationships with other keys).

Still, the opportunities for generalization either during the domain definition process or once an initial structure emerges, are often overlooked. If the terminology already in use suggests it, then the opportunity becomes apparent. For example, a data base which must deal with COD ORDERS, PREPAID ORDERS, and CHARGE ORDERS is likely to be initially organized to consider these as variants of the entity type CUSTOMER ORDER. But it will not be until the structure of the data base has been further fleshed out when the designer decides to generalize CUSTOMER ORDER and INTERPLANT TRANSFER into a single entity type, REQUEST FOR SHIPMENT.

Note that in order to achieve key-level generalization, some unification of the previously independent domains involved might be required. If a CUSTOMER ORDER and an INTERPLANT TRANSFER could have the same identifier, then an undesirable one-to-many correspondence (to be discussed next) is established. The use of an internal identifier (i.e., TAG) may be called for.

Again, the advantages of generalization are numerous. First, the design itself is simplified, requiring fewer assertions and data elements. Programming will be simplified because one routine will work on the single structure to the degree that processing is similar. Thus we do not need separate routines to compute the freight routing of CUS-

TOMER ORDERS and INTERPLANT TRANSFERS, but just one routine for REQUESTS FOR SHIPMENT.

Note, however, that where differences do exist they must be tested for and taken care of in the program. Thus if only charge order type of REQUESTS FOR SHIPMENT have credit ratings, the program must determine if this is a charge type, and process it accordingly. Of course, when the differences become great, it is better to stay with the separate entities and treat each one distinctly.

While the guidelines on how to set up an initial classification of entities into domains, or whether to generalize several keys into one are meager, nevertheless there are a few general guidelines which appear to make sense. We can identify the following ones (in order of importance):

1. Do not partition a set of entity types into finer domains (i.e., do generalize the keys), if the distinctions are not likely to be useful in the data base. Thus making a distinction between right-handed and left-handed people is probably not of major significance; a single entity type PERSON is adequate.
2. Do not partition (again, do generalize) classes which are inherently fuzzy. Thus the distinction between fruits and vegetables is probably fuzzy. The distinction is better made within an assertion.
3. Do not partition classes where an entity could change classes. Thus if a part could be a manufactured part one day and a purchased part the next, a single entity type is probably best.
4. Do separate into distinct entity types (i.e., do *not* generalize keys) when the assertions for each subclass (key) are quite different. Thus, while CONTRACT and PUR-CHASE ORDER in the NPD example share some characteristics (both are documents, both have dates of issuance, signatures, etc.) for the most part they would have different assertion types in the data base. If we did try to simplfy them, say into LEGAL DOCUMENT, the resulting assertion type would have an overwhelming number of optional targets (depending on whether it was a purchase order or a contract). In other examples, there could be more similarity than differences and the generalization should be consummated (e.g., in some kind of document retrieval system).

In the end, however, the designer's judgment prevails.

The kind of key-level generalization described so far is the most common, but there are other types. Consider the following transform:

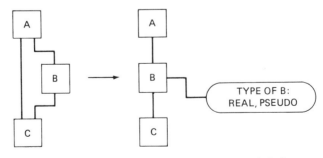

This is the case where the key C is usually related to A through B; however, occasionally C relates directly to A.

An example might be:

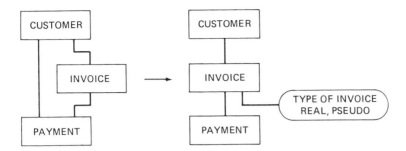

Usually a payment is credited to an invoice. But occasionally we can't tell which invoice is to be credited or there is no invoice (i.e., the customer shows a credit), in which case the payment is related directly to the customer. Alternatively, the designer should consider generalizing the concept of invoice to include a pseudoinvoice, thereby considerably simplifying the design. Adequate definition of a pseudoinvoice is required.

### Noncontrolled Identifiers

Up to now, we have been insisting that identifiers be assigned to entities in one-to-one (or at most many-to-one) correspondence. Unfortunately, most real world data bases contain ambiguous identifiers. The use of employee numbers, Social Security numbers, and most other external (i.e., noncontrolled) identifiers usually results in one-to-many mappings. Symbol strings tend to be reused. In this section, we review the unpleasantness which results from the use of noncontrolled identifiers and suggest some design techniques to minimize the problems.

Examination of the hypothetical inventory of entity-identifier pairs introduced in Chapter 4 will show four cases. In the first case, Figure 5-26a, each identifier is assigned to exactly one object (right-hand member). This is a perfect one-to-one correspondence between the symbols and the objects, and all the objects are uniquely identified in one and only one way. The second case, Figure 5-26b, however, is far more common. Some objects have several synonymous identifiers assigned. This is a many-to-one correspondence between the symbols and the objects. The other two cases, finally, involve ambig-

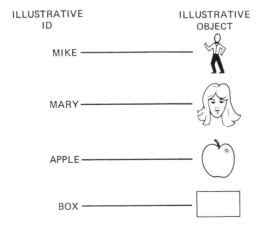

a) One-to-one Correspondence (Unique Identification)

Figure 5-26. Hypothetical inventory of entity-identifier pairs.

ILLUSTRATIVE
ID

ILLUSTRATIVE
OBJECT

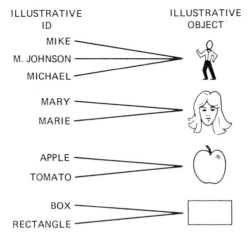

b)  Many-to-one Correspondence (Synonymous Identification)

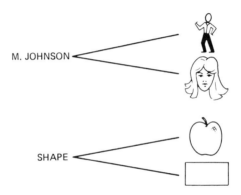

c)  One-to-many Correspondence (Ambiguous Identification)

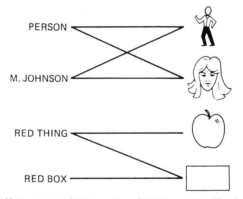

d)  Many-to-many Correspondence (Ambiguous Identification)

Figure 5-26. (continued)

uous identifiers: the same symbol is used to identify more than *one* object, which results in a one-to-many or many-to-many correspondence.

One-to-many mappings occur when identifiers are reused. A familiar case is the Personnel Data Base in which Employee Numbers are reissued after an employee retires or leaves the company.

Over the years, the Employee Number 1234 may have been assigned to a dozen people, including the one to whom it is currently assigned. Perhaps the fact that '1234' identifies many people only becomes significant when we develop the Employee Benefits portion of the data base, for now the data base becomes seriously concerned with employees who have left or died. We cannot utilize Employee Number to look up the addresses of retired or ex-employees because the mapping has become one-to-many. Given the value of an Employee Number, the data base doesn't know what (or who) it is talking about.

We can try to disambiguate the external identifier by using the date the employee joined the company in one of two ways. First, we may interpret the symbol string resulting from the combination of Employee Number/Date as the entity identifier. In this case, we cannot correct an error in the date without destroying the identifier. But at least it reduces the possibility of a one-to-many mapping.*

We could always ask for the date whenever the possibility of ambiguity arises—e.g., are you interested in the Employee Number 1234 who joined the company 10/1/63 or the Employee Number 1234 who joined the company 3/15/65? In either case, what do we do about the employee who leaves the company and returns? If the Personnel Department assigns the same Employee Number, we would need two records, both showing 1234 but with different start dates (hopefully cross-referenced). If they assign a different Employee Number, we get a many-to-one mapping.

Moreover, we also have the problem of two employees having the same number at the same time—if for instance, a new company is acquired and has a duplicate numbering scheme. What about the employee who is then forced to change his employee number? Does he lose his seniority if the date used is today's date? If we use his original date with a new number, we might create another duplicate. We will also get a wrong answer to a question about how many employees the company has as of a certain date!

Many-to-one mappings result from having multiple identifiers for the same object. When several identifiers within the inventory refer to the same object, counts will be in error, unless special steps are taken to equate the equivalent identifiers. (The data base must regard the entity identifiers as distinct unless told otherwise.) If an equivalence among alternate identifiers is declared, then the identifiers are said to be aliases of one another. Cases of many-to-one mappings frequently occur where the objects to which the identifiers refer are recognized to be the same some time after the identifiers have been assigned. For example, consider the various account numbers which a person has with the same bank, or various customer numbers which a firm has with different divisions of the same vendor. In either case, the bank or the vendor want to recognize the same CUSTOMER, both for marketing reasons and so that when the customer submits an address change, it can be reflected in all the proper places. Generally, complex cross-referencing schemes are used to deal with many-to-one mappings.

When entity identifier mappings are one-to-one (and not varying over time),** they usually involve the assignment of internal system-controlled entity identifiers along the lines of the TAG concept previously introduced. Cross-references between the internal TAG and various (ambiguous) external identifiers are then used to relate to the outside world. The external identifiers no longer serve as entity identifiers of the objects, but as identifiers of themselves. Thus Employee Number becomes an entity type in and of

*It also introduces the problems of nonatomic identifiers discussed previously.

**Actually, we should say the one-to-one mappings hold over long periods of time. Since entity identifiers will always be of a maximum length, they can only uniquely identify a given number of entities. It is impossible to guarantee a one-to-one mapping over all time without assuming an infinite machine.

itself. It can be assigned to different employees at the same or different times, and serve to *describe* an employee at a given time (through an assertion) but not to *identify* him.

Noncontrolled identifiers also occur whenever meaning is introduced into the symbol string assignment process, often as part of a nonatomic identifier (i.e., the identifier is composed of more than one atomic unit, such as the Employee Number/Date example considered above).

We have become so accustomed, in our society, to seeing structured meaningful strings as identifiers that our strong preference for meaningless (pure) identifiers needs amplification. How many times have we seen an account number or part number and wondered what the digits mean? There is no question that meaningful strings are used as identifiers in ordinary experience and used as identifiers in data bases. But each use has perils. An obvious one is this: If 'A1234' is a part made out of aluminum (as signified by the prefix 'A') and we later decide to make the part out of titanium (whose code is 'T') then the new part number should begin with 'T'. Let's use 'T4567,' since nothing says that the last digits need to match. (indeed, there may already be a 'T1234' in the data base.) So now we have two part numbers, 'A1234' and 'T4567.' They either identify *two* parts in the entity inventory, or the *same* part. If we think they are two different parts, there is no problem. But if we want to treat them as the same part, problems arise. For instance, if we count the number 'A' identifiers and 'T' identifiers in the entity inventory, we might now find six A's and four T's. This does not necessarily mean there are six parts made out of aluminum (indeed, 'A1234' is going to be made out of titanium but was counted as 'A'). Since this part has two identifiers, it was counted twice: there are not ten but at most nine *parts* in the set we tried to count. So we get into a box if an object changes its code property without becoming a new object. Either the property code ('A' or 'T') loses reliability, or we commit to removing all references to the old ('A1234') code when there is a change, or we forbid the organization from thinking the part has remained the same. None of these alternatives is particularly attractive.

It is incumbent upon the designer to analyze carefully the entity identification schemes to be used in the data base design, and their implications for the long term. The designer should consider an external identifier as an entity in itself, substituting an internal identifier and appropriate cross-references, whenever the kinds of problems discussed above appear likely.

## Specialization

In a previous section, we considered the technique of key-level generalization, in which previously independent keys were combined into a single key. In this section, we take up the idea of splitting apart a previously single key into two (or more) keys; we name this process "specialization." There are certainly cases in which the designer might have attempted to combine several distinct concepts into one entity type, but later decided against this option and declared several independent entities. Such cases trivially fall into the category of specialization. Of greater importance, however, are those cases in which the designer truly fails to recognize important differences in various aspects of an entity type. Here the designer needs to be on the lookout for indications that discrimination among the aspects of an entity type is warranted.

Two sorts of conditions warrant specialization. The first constitutes a failure to analyze a functional dependency properly. For example, the designer may initially depict a steamship data base design as follows.

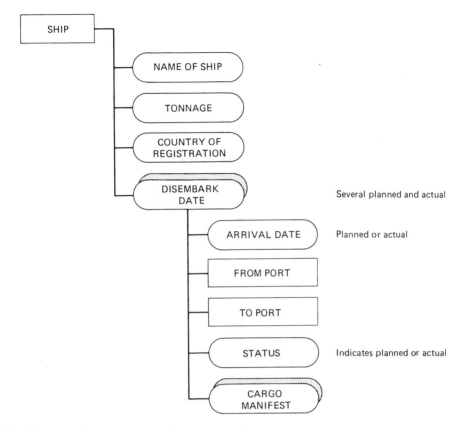

The idea here is that a series of both scheduled future and actual past trips are shown dependent on SHIP. When the ship sails, the status is changed from planned to actual. Problems arise when one ship is substituted for another at the last minute: a wealth of data has to be transferred to the new SHIP. The error seems to be that while an actual trip is functionally dependent on SHIP, a planned one is not. The specialization process is involved to discriminate between a SHIP and a VOYAGE. A VOYAGE can be planned independently of SHIP. So we might have:

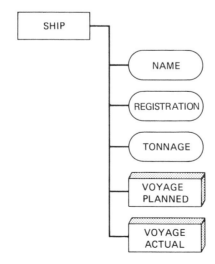

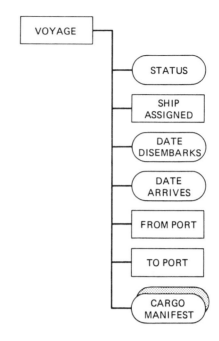

A second and more difficult situation to uncover arises when the users or other "informants" who are describing the real world of interest fail to discriminate two or more entities. To some degree, it may be a linguistic problem—the same word is being used to refer to slightly different aspects of the same thing, and most likely existing systems, manual or automated, fail to make the distinction as well. This situation is extremely difficult to uncover, particularly early in the design. Only when many of the details are being filled in does the designer sense something is wrong. One example from an actual case history will suffice. A company is engaged in the mail-order business and publishes "catalogs" offering its products. Users talk of budgeting, planning, mailing, and measuring the sales of each "catalog." So the designer begins with an entity called Catalog and builds up an assertion template required to meet the information needs as the users talk about catalogs. Only until much later does the designer realize that "catalog" should really be three entities:

Season Catalog: Really a selling campaign or program under a particular name for a season.

Catalog Type: A pamphlet offering specific merchandise for sale. There may be several per season catalog with minor differences. All have the same name printed on them.

Mailed Catalog: A copy of a Catalog Type is mailed to several sets of selected customers at a given point in time. In some senses, the June mailing to the "A" customers in the East is a different "Catalog" from the same mailing to the West.

The key to the designer recognizing that there are actually three entities is that different things happen to each:

Season Catalogs: Planned and budgeted at an overall level; P & L are measured here.

Catalog Types:    Budgeted at the merchandise item level and have pages.

Mailed Catalogs: Actually mailed, and sales are measured for them.

Users, however, use the word "Catalog" to refer to all three entities.

### Self-Defining Data Elements

The technique for constructing self-defining data elements is by no means a new one. Yet it is seldom used when it readily could be. It involves attaching data element *names* to values stored in the data base.

Consider a data base in which a fairly large number of targets apply to the subject (key) of an assertion. The most straightforward design for the situation is, of course, to declare each such target to be a regular data element according to the definitions and rules previously covered in this book. For example, let's examine some targets that might apply to the key PART, as given in Figure 5-27. In studying this assertion, note that a few of the elements are mandatory—e.g., all parts must have a weight and name recorded. However, many of the elements describing a part are optional—not all parts have holes or flanges, or are appropriately described by color or density. Assume that the list of potential part characteristics is quite long—say on the order of 30 or perhaps even 100 elements. Moreover, some of the characteristics can occur multiple times (e.g., a part can have several colors). Now any particular part will in fact only have a small

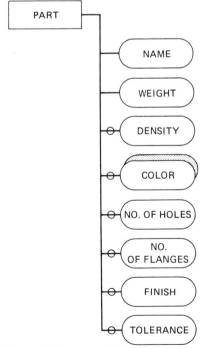

Figure 5-27. Potential for self-defining data elements.

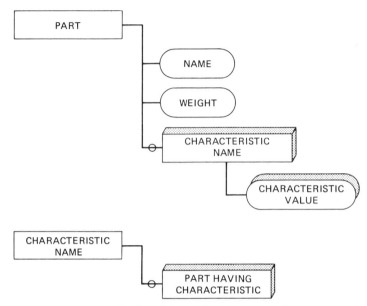

Figure 5-28. Self-defining data element design.

subset of these elements actually applied to it—thus any given assertion occurrence will contain only a few occurrences of the targets.

On top of this description of the situation, we add the requirement that the list of characteristics of parts changes frequently. Thus, for argument sake, let's say that two or three new part characteristics are developed monthly (e.g., part toxicity, part strength, etc.). And a certain time period after a characteristic no longer applies to any part, it is to be deleted as a legitimate characteristic. Under the design shown in Figure 5-27, such additions and deletions would have a direct impact on the logical data structure. And even with data element level data independence, changes like this would be cumbersome to implement continually in any data base management software package, to say nothing of the difficulty because of so many optional elements.

The self-defining data element technique addresses these problems in the following way. Each characteristic no longer appears as a fixed data element. Rather, a design along the lines of Figure 5-28 is utilized. Here the fixed characteristic elements have been replaced with a pair of data elements, CHARACTERISTIC NAME and CHARACTERISTIC VALUE, which can occur a variable number of times. The element CHARACTERISTIC NAME is intended to contain the name of the data element whose value appears as CHARACTERISTIC VALUE. In other words, we have unified previously unrelated entities (colors, density, shelf-life, etc.) into a single kind of entity: part characteristic. It is important to note that this technique has important differences from the data element or key-level generalization technique. Here the unification is being made across different entities and no standardization of domains is implied. Thus the peculiar data element CHARACTERISTIC VALUE cannot be interpreted without its counterpart. The domain of the value cannot be specified until the characteristic name is given. The data element CHARACTERISTIC NAME has as its domain Data Element Name, and can be regarded as a sort of *meta* data element.

With this scheme of things, new kinds of characteristics can be applied to parts with no change to the data base structure. Notice that in Figure 5-28 we left as individual elements PART WEIGHT and PART NAME because they applied to *all* parts. Moreover, we chose to make CHARACTERISTIC NAME an associator, so the reversal provides an index to parts which actually have the characteristic. The use of a code instead of name for the characteristic would also be appropriate. In this way, the name could be stored only once as a target of the code.

## REFERENCES

1. Navathe, S. "Schema Analysis for Data Base Restructuring," *ACM Transactions on Database Systems,* **5**:2, June 1980.

   As a prerequisite to restructuring hierarchical and network data bases, an analysis must be made to uncover the true underlying nature of relationships. For example, consider the CODASYL set:

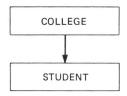

   It may well be that records referring to the same student appear under different colleges, thus reflecting a many-to-many relationship rather than the one-to-many relationship the schema suggests. This paper discusses this and similar problems, some having to do with compound identifiers, from the restructuring point of view. It points out that clarity of design and design notation is required to preserve the data base meaning when restructuring.

2. 1978 New Orleans Data Base Design Workshop Report, published by IBM as Computer Science Research Report RJ2554 (33154), July 13, 1979.

   This report contains the results of a workshop on data base design and summarizes a number of design methodologies.

3. Jefferson, David. *Data Base Design,* David W. Taylor Naval Ship Research and Development Center, June 1976 (AD/A-035945).

   A comprehensive data base design discussion covering both logical and physical aspects of design.

4. Hammer, M., and McLeod, D. "The Semantic Data Model: A Modelling Mechanism for Data Base Applications," *Proceedings of the 1978 International Conference on the Management of Data,* ACM, 1978.

   The methodology described in this paper covers a formal model for capturing a high level of the semantics of a data problem.

5. Palmer, I. "Record Subtype Facilities in Database Systems," *Proceedings of the 4th International Conference on Very Large Data Bases,* 1978.

   This paper contains a proposal to deal with multiple levels of generalization in a CODASYL environment. Compare with the reference below, and with the Smith and Smith reference in Chapter 4.

6. Bachman, C., and Daya, M. "The Role Concept in Data Models," *Proceedings of the 3rd International Conference on Very Large Data Bases,* 1977.

   Here again is a proposal to deal with multiple levels of generalization, by stipulating that an entity can have several "roles." For example, employee and consultant are two roles for persons. This proposal seems to be limited to two levels in a generalization hierarchy.

7. Housel, B., Waddle, V., and Yao, S. "The Functional Dependency Model for Logical Data Base Design," *Proceedings of the 5th International Conference on Very Large Data Bases,* 1979.

   Yet another modeling scheme for representing a logical data base design with a high level of semantic information. Also included is a notation for specifying transactions.

# 6

# Miscellaneous Topics

This final chapter treats three topics in logical data base design. First, the notion of correspondences is introduced. A *correspondence* is concerned with the relationship between two sets A and B, in both directions. It is considerably more powerful than the more restricted "mapping" of just A to B, and an analysis of the correspondences exhibited in a particular design can reveal important insights into how the data base will function.

Next we turn to the topic of *documenting* a logical design. Communicating a design to others, both users and technicians, is a prerequisite to a successful design effort. Guidelines for preparation of good documentation material are presented.

Finally, the third section consists of a comparison of the methods introduced in this book with both the CODASYL and relational approaches.

## CORRESPONDENCES

### Establishment of Correspondences

When the data base design provides keys which are defined over two sets of entities (domains) A and B, *and* a reversed associator pair is used to relate these two sets, the sets are placed (by that relationship) into one of sixteen possible correspondences. The correspondences, which provide a classification of the relationship between the sets, are based on two features of the relationship. The first feature is concerned with *fanout,* i.e., with how many things are being related. Four different fanout conditions (one-to-one, one-to-many, many-to-one, and many-to-many) are possible. The second feature is *coverage:* does the relationship apply to all A and all B, or does the relationship exclude some A's, or some B's. Thus correspondences describe a relationship by pointing out it is a "many-to-one correspondence between some A's and all B's." One of the principles of a logical data base design is that correspondences are *invariant*. That is, if the logical designer goes to the trouble of defining a relationship so completely that a correspondence is defined, then that correspondence between the sets is not meant to be compromised. Correspondences are meant to be preserved.

Correspondences are not difficult to define when there is complete information about the relationship from A to B and also about the relationship from B to A. For example, consider the relationship between the set of passengers aboard an airplane and the set of seats on that airplane. Ordinarily, every passenger is allocated exactly one seat, there are never more passengers than there are seats, and some seats may be unoccupied. The foregoing remarks describe a "one-to-one correspondence between all passengers and some seats." If we now alter one of the remarks to make allowance for very large per-

| Code Name | Long Name | Converse Code |
|---|---|---|
| mmss | A many-to-many correspondence between some A and some B. | mmss |
| mmsa | A many-to-many correspondence between some A and all B. | mmas |
| mmas | A many-to-many correspondence between all A and some B. | mmsa |
| mmaa | A many-to-many correspondence between all A and all B. | mmaa |
| moss | A many-to-one correspondence between some A and some B. | omss |
| mosa | A many-to-one correspondence between some A and all B. | omas |
| moas | A many-to-one correspondence between all A and some B. | omsa |
| moaa | A many-to-one correspondence between all A and all B. | omaa |
| omss | A one-to-many correspondence between some A and some B. | moss |
| omsa | A one-to-many correspondence between some A and all B. | moas |
| omas | A one-to-many correspondence between all A and some B. | mosa |
| omaa | A one-to-many correspondence between all A and all B. | moaa |
| ooss | A one-to-one correspondence between some A and some B. | ooss |
| oosa | A one-to-one correspondence between some A and all B. | ooas |
| ooas | A one-to-one correspondence between all A and some B. | oosa |
| ooaa | A one-to-one correspondence between all A and all B. | ooaa |

Figure 6-1. The sixteen correspondences between two sets.

sons or invalids who need to lie down, then there are passengers who may be allocated more than one seat. Under this revised set of provisions, we have a different correspondence, "a one-to-many correspondence between all passengers and some seats." Whenever two keys are related by a pair of reversed associators, a correspondence is (automatically) created between the sets. The sixteen correspondences are listed in Figure 6-1.

Notice that all the correspondences are given both short names and long names in accordance with a standard syntax. The names are constructed by making the indicated choices of "many, one" and "some, all" in:

$$A \begin{Bmatrix} \text{many} \\ \text{one} \end{Bmatrix} \text{to} \begin{Bmatrix} \text{many} \\ \text{one} \end{Bmatrix} \text{correspondence between} \begin{Bmatrix} \text{some} \\ \text{all} \end{Bmatrix} A \text{ and } \begin{Bmatrix} \text{some} \\ \text{all} \end{Bmatrix} B$$

It is also useful to abbreviate using just the initial letters:

$$\begin{Bmatrix} \textbf{m} \\ \textbf{o} \end{Bmatrix} \begin{Bmatrix} \textbf{m} \\ \textbf{o} \end{Bmatrix} \begin{Bmatrix} \textbf{s} \\ \textbf{a} \end{Bmatrix} \begin{Bmatrix} \textbf{s} \\ \textbf{a} \end{Bmatrix}$$

This produces names like **mosa** and **mmaa** as shorthand for the full name.

The correspondences between A and B are always directional, from A to B. The converse correspondence, in the reverse direction, can easily be calculated by altering the order of the letters:

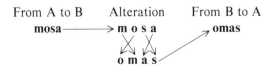

Thus, the converse correspondence can always be written down by inspection. For reference, the converse correspondences are also shown in Figure 6-1.

Each pair of reversed* associators yields one of the sixteen correspondences. Each correspondence is a macroscopic statement about both sets taken together as a whole.

The correspondences are an inescapable by-product of declaring a reversed associator pair. The first feature, fanout, is a consequence of whether the two associators are shown in planar or solid boxes, in various combinations. For the relationship from A to B:

| Is B multiple under Key A? | Is A multiple under Key B? | Fanout |
|---|---|---|
| Yes | Yes | many A to many B |
| Yes | No | one A to many B |
| No | Yes | many A to one B |
| No | No | one A to one B |

The second feature, coverage, is a consequence of whether the two associators are marked mandatory or optional, in various combinations. For the relationship from A to B:

| Is B optional under Key A? | Is A optional under Key B? | Coverage |
|---|---|---|
| Yes | Yes | some A to some B |
| Yes | No | some A to all B |
| No | Yes | all A to some B |
| No | No | all A to all B |

Figure 6-2** provides a synopsis of the way these features define the sixteen correspondences.

In Figures 6-11 through 6-26 (which are located at the end of this section for reference), each of the sixteen correspondences is discussed further. The diagram of each one is based on an example that is meant to illustrate the properties of the correspondence more intuitively. Note the remarks that outline the rules for adding new keys, deleting relationships, etc. These rules are needed to maintain the integrity of each correspondence. Once the designer has drawn the forward and reversed associators, all of the apparatus which goes with one of these correspondences is invoked, and material drawn from Figures 6-11 through 6-26 can be incorporated in the documentation of each of the associators.

### Relationships Among Correspondences

There are a few relationships among the correspondences themselves that deserve to be treated briefly. First, some are more "permissive" than others in the sense that the permissive ones include the more restrictive ones. Second, the correspondences can be compounded in two ways: "serially" by chaining them, and "vertically" (when one enters into many correspondences). These properties are investigated in this section.

---

*When the associators are not reversed in pairs, a correspondence is not established. Instead, the relationship must be regarded as a *mapping* from A to B; mappings are much weaker than correspondences since they lack any constraint on the B to A relationship.

**It may be of some comfort to the reader to learn that nearly everyone finds it difficult to determine, from the pattern on the charts, that the correspondence shown is, say, "A **mosa** B." The patterns are so regular that they resist being committed to memory. Designers who care to study correspondences are urged to make heavy use of Figure 6-2 since establishing correspondences mentally is likely to introduce errors in transcribing the facts.

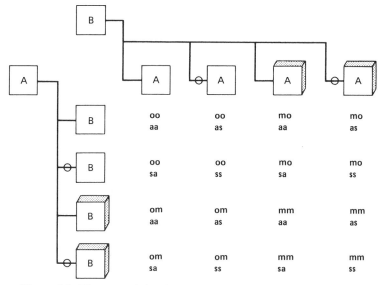

Figure 6-2. Elements of the sixteen correspondences between A and B.

**The Inclusion Relationship.** There is an important inclusion relation that holds between correspondences. For example, **mosa\*** includes **oosa.** This is easily seen:

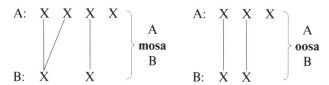

The correspondence at the right (**oosa**) describes a subset of the **mosa** correspondence. It illustrates the self-evident rule that "many-to-one" includes "one-to-one." Similarly, **moss** includes **mosa:**

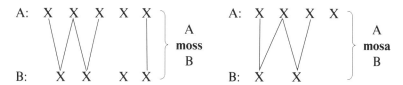

This is a case of the rule "some" includes "all." When we say "Some persons have employee numbers," we include the possibility that *all* do.

The full-scale inclusion relation that holds between pairs of correspondences can be drawn as shown in Figure 6-3. The correspondences at the top of the page include those connected below. The lowest correspondence **ooaa** is included directly or indirectly in all the others. In general, the correspondences with *m* and *s* in their names tend to be permissive, those with *o* and *a* tend to be restrictive. Any given correspondence (like **oosa**) can be implemented by embedding it in a more permissive correspondence (like **mosa**).

*"A *many-to-one* correspondence between *some* A and *all* B."

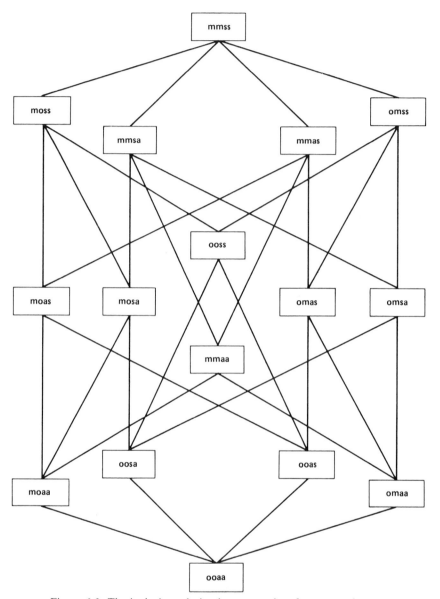

Figure 6-3. The inclusion relation between pairs of correspondences.

**Compound Correspondences.** Correspondences can be compounded in two ways, serially and vertically. The serial arrangement concerns chaining from set A to B to C, etc., and is a relatively simple concept. The vertical arrangement, which arises when a particular key A has two or more associators B and C listed under it, is somewhat more complex, for it concerns itself with cases when the relationships may "interfere" with one another. These two types of compounded correspondences will be treated in turn.

*Serial compounding.* The compounding of correspondences serially is concerned with taking a series of steps through the network of associations provided by the indicated relations. See Figure 6-4.

The first reversed associator pair (AB, BA) in the data base establishes a correspondence. Now we also have another pair (BC, CB) that establishes a second correspondence in the data base at the same time. The question asked is: What is the nature of the correspondence between A and C, given AB and BC?

The type of correspondence that is implied between two sets which are related through compound correspondences is determined by the following rules:

- If any correspondence has a "many", then the compound has a "many."
- If any correspondence has a "some", then the compound has a "some."

Thus: if A to B is        **oosa**
     and B to C is       **ooaa**
     then A to C is      **oosa**

Further:
     if C to D is        **mosa**
     then A to D is      **mosa**

In other words, A **oosa** B **ooaa** C = A **oosa** C
                A **oosa** B **ooaa** C **mosa** D = A **mosa** D

All compound correspondences tend to degenerate in the direction of **mmss.** That is, each step in the compounding represents an additional opportunity for a "many" or a "some" to be encountered and to be introduced into the compound correspondence. The

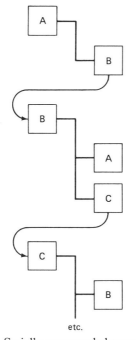

etc.

Figure 6-4. Serially compounded correspondences.

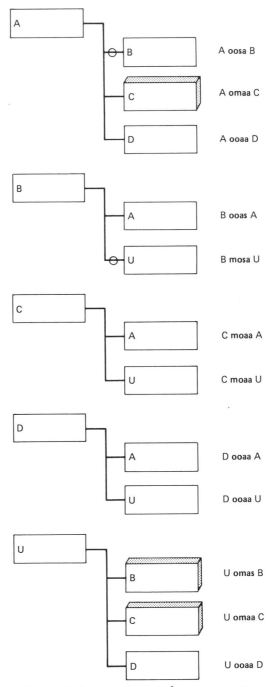

Figure 6-5. An example of vertical compounding.

process of compounding always tends upward in the diagram of Figure 6-3, the direction of decreasing constraint.

*Vertical compounding.* When a key participates in many correspondences, it appears on the charts as follows:

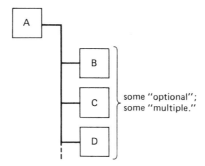

The interesting questions that arise in design are illustrated in Figure 6-5 and summarized in the schematic in Figure 6-6.

In these figures A and U exhibit vertical compounding. That is, A and U are related by three serial correspondences:

| | |
|---|---|
| ABU | A **mosa** U = (A **oosa** B **mosa** U) |
| ACU | A **mmaa** U = (A **omaa** C **moaa** U) |
| ADU | A **ooaa** U = (A **ooaa** D **ooaa** U) |

But is it "meaningful" for A and U to be related by three different correspondences? How can the relationship A-U be one-to-one, many-to-one, and many-to-many at the same time?

In developing the answer, it is important to distinguish between the declared correspondences (AB, for example), the calculated serial correspondences (ABU, for example) and the actual correspondence A-U one would find in the data base. While one can calculate many serial correspondences between two endpoints, inspection of the working data base leads always to exactly one observed correspondence between those points.

In Figures 6-7 and 6-11 through 6-26, each of the correspondences is marked to indicate whether the given correspondence forces a relationship between the size N(A) of set A and the size of the second set N(B). Sometimes there is no relation established, a situation that applies to the "some-to-some" relationships, among others. In some many-to-one correspondences, the first set cannot possibly be smaller than the second. Sometimes, as in some one-to-one correspondences, the sets must be equal in size.

From Figures 6-7, 6-8 or 6-11 through 6-26, we can determine the following:

| | | |
|---|---|---|
| ABU | **mosa** | $N(A) \geq N(U)$ |
| ACU | **mmaa** | not related |
| ADU | **ooaa** | $N(A) = N(U)$ |

The correspondence A-U observed in the data base is a consequence of the rules which

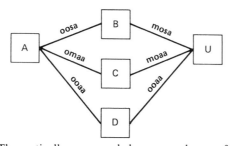

Figure 6-6. The vertically compounded correspondences of Figure 6-5.

|  | **aa** (all A to all B) | **as** (all A to some B) | **sa** (some A to all B) | **ss** (some A to some B) |
|---|---|---|---|---|
| **o o** (one A to one B) | $N(A) = N(B)$ | $N(A) \leq N(B)$ | $N(A) \geq N(B)$ | no relation |
| **o m** (one A to many B) | $N(A) \leq N(B)$ | $N(A) \leq N(B)$ | no relation | no relation |
| **m o** (many A to one B) | $N(A) \geq N(B)$ | no relation | $N(A) \geq N(B)$ | no relation |
| **m m** (many A to many B) | no relation | no relation | no relation | no relation |

Figure 6-7. Relationship of set sizes under the sixteen correspondences.

keep each of the sets consistent with the correspondences that apply to it. The only way to meet all the above requirements is to keep $N(A) = N(U)$. Even though the correspondence ABU is **mosa,** the other path via D keeps A and U in one-to-one correspondence.

What may not be obvious on the surface is that this has an impact on the A-B-U path in the data base. $N(A) = N(U)$ forces both A-B and B-U to be **ooaa** correspondences. Observe first that

| AB | **oosa** | $N(A) \geq N(B)$ |
|---|---|---|
| BU | **mosa** | $N(B) \geq N(U)$ |

forces $N(A) = N(B) = N(U)$. The only way A-B can be a one-to-one correspondence between two sets of equal size *and* hit all members of B is for it to map *all* (not just some) members of A onto all members of B. Thus, A-B is going to be forced to a **ooaa** in the data base even though the more permissive **oosa** was declared. A similar argument applies to B-U; again, a more restrictive relationship would be found implemented in practice than the designer declared. The fact that B is constrained to the same size as D, even though B does not "point to" D may be a surprise.

Such a surprise generally serves as a warning that something is amiss. It may be something very simple. For example, the above A-B **oosa** correspondence rested, in part, on an "optional" associator from A to B. Perhaps that choice seemed correct early in the design, but if it were reviewed now it might turn out to need a mandatory associator. This repair would make A-B **ooaa** to solve part of the problem.

More seriously, the interference among the compound correspondences may indicate a flaw in the designer's understanding of the data problem. One of the most valuable aspects of using correspondences to critique a design is that they sometimes signal such misconceptions. By construction, the correspondences check the declared interconnections in the data (e.g., the associators) and the way these play against the data base

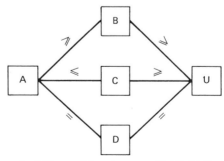

Figure 6-8. The network of Figure 6-6 redrawn to highlight the set size relationships.

rules that govern the structure. Because they check a great deal, the designer should take pains to understand any cases of interference that are uncovered.

Remark: It is a natural thought, when viewing complex networks which can be constructed in data base designs, to wonder if there are not conditions which are "impossible." For example, it can be imagined that constraints exist among three sets A, B, C so that A is larger than B, B is larger than C, and C is larger than A. In schematic form:

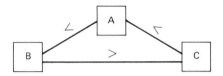

The absurd conclusion that A is larger than itself would signal the existence of some flaw in setting up the constituents parts of the loop.

The present notation offers no such cases. The reason can be seen by inspection of Figure 6-7 where all the set size relations (including "no relation") permit the two sets to be equal in size. The worst that can happen, in other words, is that the data base will become, in a sense, "tightly bound"—preserving very tight one-to-one correspondences which may not have been intended. Even an error on the part of the designer will not set up a condition that is impossible, contradictory, or absurd. At some future date, when there is better insight into what it means to "make a mistake" in a logical design, it may be obvious that certain loops or too tightly bound sets are best forbidden. This notation falls a few steps short of that kind of objective, adhering instead to the principle "If the designer says it is so, then there has to be a data base which reflects those instructions." It remains to be seen whether the art of logical design should evolve along these "everything is possible" lines or whether constraints should be added that prevent the construction of data base "mistakes."

## Precedence Implications of the Correspondences

If two sets A and B are tightly bound by an **ooaa** correspondence, i.e., a relationship that is one-to-one and exhausts both sets, the process of adding (creating) a new A value must be strictly controlled. The new A must be placed in correspondence with one B. All B's already on file are already attached to one A and may not be attached to another A if the one-to-one requirement is to be preserved. Therefore a new B must be created. But the new B, by the same reasoning, requires a new A, which is what we were attempting to accomplish when this process began a few sentences ago. There is only one way to create a new A (or a new B for that matter) in a **ooaa** correspondence. That is to create a new A, a new B and a new AB link between them simultaneously.

In Figure 6-9, this observation is recorded under **ooaa** by the entry "A requires B and B requires A". Other entries in the figure record the result of analyzing all the other correspondences from the point of view of precedence. While the **ooaa** correspondence requires both A and B (and AB) to be created concurrently, most of the other correspondences suggest that there is a "natural" order in which new values of A and B should be created. In the second column, which shows the "all-to-some" correspondences, it is noted that A requires B. In other words, before we can create a new entry for a new value of A, it is necessary that we make preparations by finding (or placing) at least one value of B on the file. Work on B should be done first *before* A is added. The "natural" precedence for these correspondences is to add B first, then A.

On the other hand, the last two columns, which show the **sa** and **ss** correspondences, permit an A to be created without reference to B. The new A may thus be entered before a new B is created if desired: A first, then B. For completeness, correspondences in the last column **ss** also show that B is independent of A so that the values may be entered in either order.

These precedences induce interesting patterns ("natural" sequences) on a logical data structure. The patterns are most visible when the key-level overview (e.g., the network diagram in Figure 6-6) is studied. To show the pattern, the correspondences used in Figure 6-6 are redrawn in Figure 6-10 and heavy arrows are used to show the natural transaction flow. Thus, if A should be entered before B, the arrow points from A to B so that one may follow the arrows to visualize the "natural" sequence of creating new entries. The figure also shows keys connected by double arrows that look like butterflies. These link keys in which both A and B (and AB) must be added simultaneously. Finally, when it makes no difference which value is entered first, there is no arrow on the connecting line.

We have already examined these same correspondences from the point of view of set size, and that earlier discussion established that there were indirect constraints that forced A, B, C, D, and U to be very tightly bound. Figure 6-10 exhibits the same kind of binding. At a glance, A, C, D, and U are seen to be so linked by butterflies that no "natural" sequence for entering them exists. All four have to be entered as a four-way

| | | (all A to all B) **aa** | (all A to some B) **as** | (some A to all B) **sa** | (some A to some B) **ss** |
|---|---|---|---|---|---|
| (one A to one B) | oo | A requires B and B requires A | A requires B | A is independent of B | A is independent of B and B is independent of A |
| (one A to many B) | om | A requires B and B requires A | A requires B | A is independent of B | A is independent of B and B is independent of A |
| (many A to one B) | mo | A requires B and B may require A | A requires B | A is independent of B | A is independent of B and B is independent of A |
| (many A to many B) | mm | A requires B and B may require A | A requires B | A is independent of B | A is independent of B and B is independent of A |
| Precedence | | A, B simultaneous | B first then A | A first is OK | Either A or B may be first |
| Symbol | | A ▶◀ B | A ◀ B | A ▶ B | A —— B |

Figure 6-9. Precedence relations governing creation of a new "A" for the sixteen correspondences between "A" and "B."

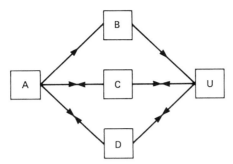

Figure 6-10. The precedence pattern for the network of Figure 6-6.

simultaneous group. Only B remains with a little freedom. Even though the endpoints A and U have been entered together, it is possible to proceed from A to a new B and then from that B to an existing U as the arrows suggest.

There is nothing "illegal"* about any pattern of arrows that may emerge from such an analysis. The arrows distill what the designer declared on the charts and show the pattern that is there. Hopefully, that pattern is consistent with the designer's expectation. If not, as before, any surprises should be investigated at the detailed level provided by the original associator links. Some designers, through personal preference, take pains to avoid conditions that assume simultaneous updates. At the present state-of-the-art of data base management systems, this policy has great merit, for few DBM's are able to provide this capability. But the application of a rule that implies no simultaneous updates (or deletes) is *not* part of this notation or of this approach. Designers who relax the requirements which the data problem presents (e.g., a complex binding like the one shown in Figure 6-10) take the risk of recording a design which solves a different problem than the one they were given. While cases of strong binding, with many simultaneous updates, must be scrutinized carefully as a check on the correctness of the design, the designer's first responsibility is to present an accurate statement of the data problem. Relaxing some of the constraints (to avoid simultaneous updates or for any other practical purpose) embeds the real problem that was given in another structure that is easier to deal with. When this embedding is done gracefully, by making only one or two changes in the logical data structure, hardly anyone would doubt that the designer had made a significant step forward in simplifying the data structure and providing a more practical approach. But it simply is not fair to allow the logical designer to restate the real problem for his own convenience, and relaxation of requirements should therefore be pursued with great self-control.

It is recommended that designers adopt the following policy. When a cluster of keys is discovered—like the four-way cluster A, C, D, and U in Figure 6-10—which are in mutual one-to-one correspondence, first check the charts and the detailed relationships (associators) to verify that the cluster is real. If the cluster remains after this review, see what happens if the cluster is treated as a single entity. That is, investigate whether A, C, D, U can be treated as facets of the same thing. In some cases this is the "message" which the analysis is trying to convey, for the logical data structure is not making any noteworthy distinctions among the four keys. It is keeping them tightly in one-to-

---

*See the Remark at the end of the preceding section. The same comments apply here to precedences as applied before to the set size relationship. In the present notation, there is no way to form a contradiction. At worst, set sizes are forced to be equal and updates are forced to be simultaneous. There are no impossible data structures in this notation.

one correspondence, and it is doing "four times as much work" to administer four of them as it would if there were a single entity. We cannot supply a cookbook for this process of replacing the cluster by a single key, but the designer should be quick to seize the opportunity if the cluster shows the properties which permit the four keys to be unified. Clearly, such a change could reduce the number of keys that are tightly bound, and the result would probably be a preferable design.

But note our caution, our use of the word "probably." Application of guidelines in the design of a data structure must always be controlled by the facts at hand. Any rule that permits a new, simpler structure to be constructed has in it the seeds of the destruction of the whole data base. Repeated application of the guideline can easily produce a runaway situation. Ultimately, under some interpretation, any data base can be represented as a structure in which one data type "thing" is embedded in the following structure:

The curved lines represent a variety of **mmss** correspondences of "things" to other "things." Our cautionary words are a warning that it is possible to trivialize a data structure by excessive or blind adherence to rules of simplification.

## ooaa

A one-to-one correspondence between all A and all B.

Example:    A = STATE            A state of the U.S.

B = GOVERNOR        The chief executive of a state of the U.S.

Assumptions: Every state has exactly one governor. Every governor heads up exactly one state:

Picture:

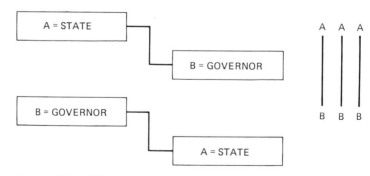

Remarks:    N(A) = N(B)

This correspondence can only be altered by using a special procedure that adds/deletes both A = STATE and B = GOVERNOR and also the A-B link simultaneously. The **ooaa** correspondence is considered the "most restrictive" correspondence because of the presence of all these constraints.

Figure 6-11. Individual correspondence **ooaa**.

## o o a s

A one-to-one correspondence between all A and some B.

Example:     A = EMPLOYEE          A person currently employed

             B = EMPLOYEE NO.      A set of numbers assigned or reserved for assignment
                                   to employees

         Assumption:  There are some employee numbers that do not correspond to current
         employees.  There is exactly one employee number for each current employee.

Picture:

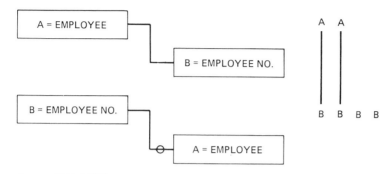

Remarks:     N(A) ⩽ N(B)

To create an A = EMPLOYEE, an unassigned value of B = EMPLOYEE NO. must be linked to A
    first.  An unassigned value or B = EMPLOYEE NO. already on file may be chosen, or a new
    value of B may be added to the file first, then the new A linked to the old B may be created.

Key A = EMPLOYEE may be deleted without altering the correspondence.

Figure 6-12. Individual correspondence **ooas.**

## o o s a

A one-to-one correspondence between some A and all B.

Example:     A = EMPLOYEE NO.      A set of numbers assigned or reserved for assignment
                                   to employees

             B = EMPLOYEE          A person currently employed

         Assumption:  There are some employee numbers that do not correspond to current
         employees.  There is exactly one employee number for each current employee.

Picture:

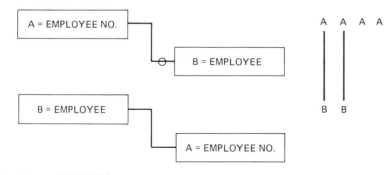

Remarks:     N(A) ⩾ N(B)

A new A = EMPLOYEE NO. may be created without altering the correspondence

If an A = EMPLOYEE NO. is deleted, the B = EMPLOYEE assigned that number must be deleted
    first.

Figure 6-13. Individual correspondence **oosa.**

# o o s s

A one-to-one correspondence between some A and some B.

Example:     A = AUTOMOBILE ID

                 B = LICENSE PLATE NO.

                 Assumption:  There are automobiles that do not have license plates, and there are license plates that do not correspond to automobiles.  An automobile, however, can have but one license plate number.

Picture:

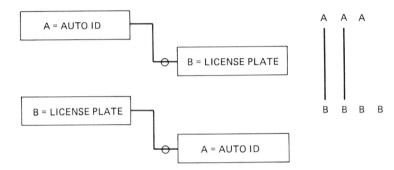

Remarks:     N(A) not related to N(B)

A new A = AUTO ID may be created without altering the correspondence, provided it does not have more than one B = LICENSE PLATE or relate to a B = LICENSE PLATE already assigned.

An A = AUTO ID may be deleted without altering the correspondence.

Figure 6-14. Individual correspondence **ooss.**

# o m a a

A one-to-many correspondence between all A and all B.

Example:     A = MONTH                    A given set of days.

                 B = DAY                      The set of days in a 100-day period.

                 Assumptions:  All the months are listed.  Also, each day belongs to exactly one month.

Picture:

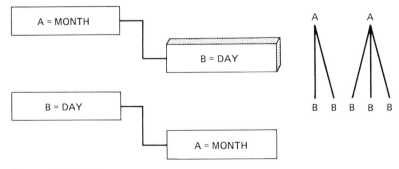

Remarks:     N(A) ≤ N(B)

To create an A = MONTH, the set of B = DAYS therein must be already on file.  This is a problem: before we can add a B = DAY, the A = MONTH must be on file.  Therefore, a special procedure to add one A = MONTH and one of its B = DAYS at the same time must be used to stay within the requirements of the correspondence.

If an A = MONTH is deleted, all of its B = DAYS must be deleted first.

Figure 6-15. Individual correspondence **omaa.**

## omas

A one-to-many correspondence between all A and some B.

Example:     A = SHIP           A set of manned ships

               B = SAILOR       A person who is not necessarily on a ship

Assumptions: Not every sailor is on a ship. Also, a ship must have one or many sailors aboard since only manned ships are considered.

Picture:

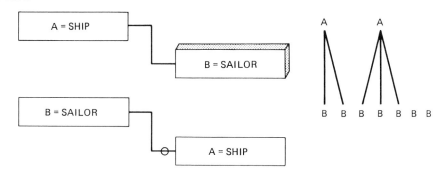

Remarks:     $N(A) \leqslant N(B)$

To create an A = SHIP, at least one B = SAILOR must be linked to A first. This B = SAILOR may either already be on file and unassigned or else this B = SAILOR must be placed on file before A = SHIP may be added.

Key A = SHIP may be deleted, without affecting the correspondence.

Figure 6-16. Individual correspondence **omas.**

## omsa

A one-to-many correspondence between some A and all B.

Example:     A = BIRTHDAY      A set of days

               B = PERSON         A set of persons

Assumptions: There may be days which are nobody's birthday. Also, every person has a known birthday.

Picture:

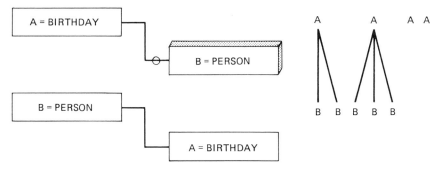

Remarks:     $N(A)$ not related to $N(B)$

(This important correspondence is noteworthy for being the relationship of an **owner**, record to the **member** records of a **set** in the CODASYL approach. View BIRTHDAY as owner in this example.)

An A = BIRTHDAY may be added without affecting the correspondence.

If an A = BIRTHDAY is deleted, all B = PERSONS have that BIRTHDAY must be deleted first.

Figure 6-17. Individual correspondence **omsa.**

## omss

A one-to-many correspondence between some A and some B.

Example:    A = CAR               A set of cars

                   B = PERSON       A set of persons

                   Assumptions: The relationship of interest concerns people who are riding in cars. Some people are not riding in cars (e.g., pedestrians). Some cars are parked with no people in them.

Picture:

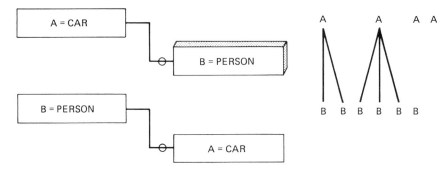

Remarks:     N(A) not related to N(B)

To add an A = CAR has no effect on the correspondence provided its B = PERSON passengers are not already assigned to other A = CARS.

There are no restrictions on deleting A = CAR.

Figure 6-18. Individual correspondence **omss.**

## moaa

A many-to-one correspondence between all A and all B.

Example:    A = DAY               The set of all days in a time period 100 days in length

                   B = MONTH       A set of consecutive days

                   Assumptions: Each day belongs to exactly one month.

Picture:

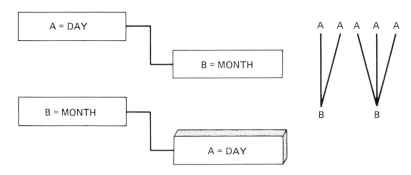

Remarks:     N(A) > N(B)

To create an A = DAY, it is necessary that a unique B = MONTH already on file be linked to it first.

If an A = DAY is deleted which is the sole A = DAY of a B = MONTH, then the B = MONTH must be deleted.

Figure 6-19. Individual correspondence **moaa.**

## moas

A many-to-one correspondence between all A and some B.

Example:     A = PERSON          A set of persons

             B = BIRTHDAY         A set of days

             Assumptions:  There may be days which are nobody's birthday.  Also, every person
             has a known birthday.

Picture:

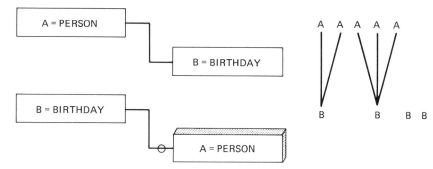

Remarks:      N(A) not related to N(B)

To create an A = PERSON, the B = BIRTHDAY must be linked to A first.  This B = BIRTHDAY
     must either be already on file or it must be added first.

An A = PERSON may be deleted without affecting the correspondence.

Figure 6-20. Individual correspondence **moas.**


## mosa

A many-to-one correspondence between some A and all B.

Example:     A = SAILOR          A person who is not necessarily on a ship or boat.

             B = SHIP            A set of manned ships

             Assumptions:  Not every sailor is on a ship.  Also, an unmanned ship must have one
             or many sailors aboard.

Picture:

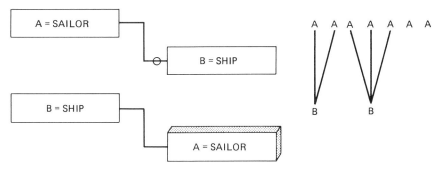

Remarks:      N(A) ⩾ N(B)

An A = SAILOR may be created without affecting the correspondence provided he is assigned to
     at most one B = SHIP.

If an A = SAILOR is deleted who is the sole person on a B = SHIP, then B = SHIP must be deleted.
     It is unmanned.

Figure 6-21. Individual correspondence **mosa.**

## moss

A many-to-one correspondence between some A and some B.

Example:  A = PERSON          A set of persons

B = CAR          A set of cars

Assumptions:  The relationship of interest concerns people who are riding in cars. Some people are not riding in cars; e.g., pedestrians.  Some cars are parked with no people in them.

Picture:

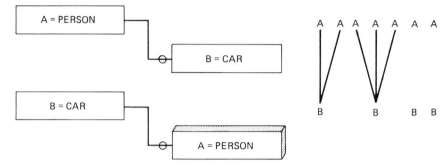

Remarks:     N(A) not related to N(B)

An A = PERSON may be created without affecting the correspondence provided the person is assigned to at most one B = CAR.

An A = PERSON may be deleted without affecting the correspondence.

Figure 6-22. Individual correspondence **moss.**


## mmaa

A many-to-many correspondence between all A and all B.

Example:  A = DOCTOR              A set of doctors

B = HOSPITAL          A set of hospitals

Assumptions:  Each doctor must be affiliated with one or more hospitals.  Also, each hospital must be staffed by one or more doctors.

Picture:

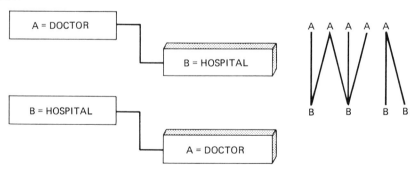

Remarks:     N(A) not related to N(B)

To create a new A = DOCTOR, an old B = HOSPITAL must be linked to A first.  But if a new B = HOSPITAL needs to be created at the same time, the new A = DOCTOR is the new B = HOSPITAL's sole practitioner to date.  In this case, the new A = DOCTOR and the new B = HOSPTIAL must be added simultaneously.

If an A = DOCTOR's last (only) B = HOSPITAL affiliation is deleted, the A = DOCTOR must be deleted.

Figure 6-23. Individual correspondence **mmaa.**

# mmas

A many-to-many correspondence between all A and some B.

Example:    A = SOCIETY            A set of organizations

              B = PERSON             A set of persons

              Assumptions: The relationship of interest is the membership relationship. Every society must have at least one member. (Not all persons are members of societies, however.) Clearly, a society may have many members and a person may belong to many societies.

Picture:

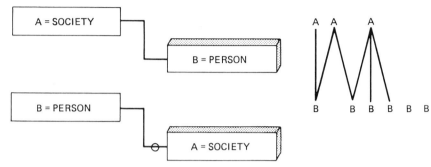

Remarks:      N(A) not related to N(B)

To create a new A = SOCIETY at least one B = PERSON (member) must be linked to A first. This B = PERSON may already be on file, or else it must be placed on file first.

An A = SOCIETY may be deleted without affecting the correspondence.

Figure 6-24. Individual correspondence **mmas.**


# mmsa

A many-to-many correspondence between some A and all B.

Example:    A = PERSON            A set of persons

              B = SOCIETY           A set of organizations

              Assumptions: The relationship of interest is the membership relation. Not every person belongs to a society. Every society has at least one person (member).

Picture:

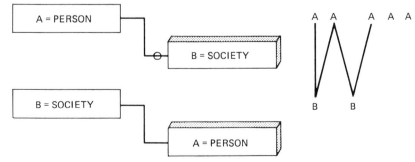

Remarks:     N(A) not related to N(B)

An A = PERSON may be created without affecting the correspondence

If an A = PERSON is deleted who is a B = SOCIETY sole member, then the B = SOCIETY ceases to be defined and must also be deleted.

Figure 6-25. Individual correspondence **mmsa.**

## m m s s

A many-to-many correspondence between some A and some B.

Example:     A = PERSON          A set of persons

B = POLICY          A set of insurance policies

Assumptions: Some persons are not insured. Some persons are covered by more than one policy. Some policies do not cover people (they cover companies). Some policies cover multiple people (group coverage).

Picture:

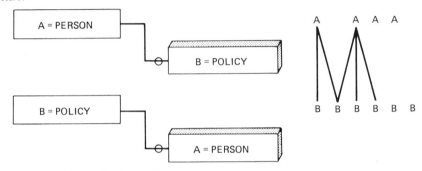

Remarks:     N(A) not related to N(B)

An A = PERSON (or a B = POLICY) may be created or deleted without affecting this correspondence. It is this freedom from constraints which makes **mmss** "the most permissive" correspondence.

Figure 6-26. Individual correspondence **mmss**.

## DOCUMENTATION OF A LOGICAL DESIGN

### Need For Dynamic Documentation

The amount of documentation needed for a logical design varies greatly. In general, small designs require relatively little documentation, but as the size of the data base or the number of participants increases, the need for a careful written record becomes more intense. Every logical designer is required by the nature of the work to develop a habit of recording relationships in complete, precise, unambiguous language. Every logical designer is also required to become skilled in writing definitions (notably of data elements) and to become adept at recording exactly what was decided at a meeting. All these skills are sharpened by the experience of developing data base documentation. Consequently, it is almost unthinkable to develop a data base design without documenting it, either because the job demands it, or because somebody needs the experience, or because it is simply the natural thing to do. Except when one is designing a data base for personal use, a logical design does not exist until it is fully documented.

Organizations or people who are approaching logical design for the first time regularly forget that there is a *process* involved. This process has been described throughout this book, and we have made no secret of its iterative, trial and error, even exploratory nature. During this process, while relationships are being considered, entities are being defined, and the problem is being appreciated, everything is dynamic. Any documentation that exists during the process is subject to change, and it is changed frequently. It is therefore necessary to make use of working documents that are easy to change, easy to keep up-to-date, and so constructed that a concept can be altered without the need to reissue pages and pages of documentation. These requirements, which apply during the formative stages of a design, also apply later on when the data base has been implemented: every data base changes, and it is valuable to have an easy way for the documentation to track these changes. But all concerned should appreciate that there is a difference in scale and a difference in timing before and after the design is frozen. It is relatively easy to track changes in an established data base. Since careful consideration must be given to the impact of the change on programs, users, and other areas of the data base, the process takes weeks and few changes are regularly made. But during the design process, changes take place daily, and the rate at which these changes are made is impressive.

Data dictionaries, automated tools for the management of data base documentation are well-suited to the record-keeping required for physical designs and implemented data bases. When changes occur fairly slowly—as they do when the data base is operational—the data dictionary has much to offer. Some of the data dictionary products on the market are developing a capability to distinguish a logical design from a physical design and to carry the logical design documentation as well. But, so far, no data dictionary has been marketed which operates at the pace of the logical design process. Automated dictionaries currently stress deliberate record-keeping of the final product, and we have often recommended their use for this purpose. When it comes to the day-to-day task of tracking the logical design process, using a standard data dictionary is impractically slow.

There are new tools coming to support the design process. They are generally called "design aids." Their role is to support the design group's creative efforts, imposing hardly any disciplines or obstacles—and imposing even those with a light touch. Using on-line update techniques, they print out changed documentation almost immediately, redraw pictures, and highlight what has been altered.

## An Approach to Documenting a Logical Design

In the meantime, there is value in devoting a small amount of space to some documentation methods which use apparatus that is generally available: office typewriters, copiers, forms, and three-ring notebooks. These tools have their limits, but it is possible to use them to track a logical design through its most turbulent periods. It is the approach, however—not the paper and pencil technology—that deserves to be understood then adapted to each designer's style. The approach is tied, of course, to use of the notation we have described throughout this book.

First, one needs to develop the charts depicting assertion templates. That process has been described at length, but now we want to dwell on documentation. Note that the graphic quality of the template charts is quite important. These should be neatly done, and not crowded onto the page so that the overall chart becomes difficult to read. The data structure of the template should be readily "pictured" by the reader. Because the charts will change frequently during initial development, and somewhat less but still regularly afterward, it is important to date each version of each template.

The notes which are included to the right of each element in the NPD data base are optional, and are not meant to replace a full specification of each element. These notes, however, can be used to reduce the necessity to refer to other documentation, and are more useful in the earliest stages of a design before more formal documentation of data elements is warranted. Preparation for the more formal documentation should begin when the early concepts have solidified and meaningful assertion templates are taking shape. To do this, create a notebook that allows a whole page to each "outline" on the charts. In other words, there will be one page of documentation for each data element.

Clearly, each page needs to be cross-linked to the charts to permit a reader to understand which data element is being described and to see its context at a glance. Some data element "locator" or numbering scheme needs to be invented for easy reference and cross-reference purposes. One scheme we use is to assign each key to a logical page number (which could require several sheets of paper) and merely sequentially number each element within the key. There is no particular requirement to maintain the elements in numbered sequence, so adding and deleting elements is easy.

Next we add a "series" letter or letter pair used to distinguish one data base design from another. The "series" code is useful for people who work on the design of many data bases, but it is also used to distinguish "subsystem" data bases that are designed separately and integrated later. The resulting "locator" is of the form PSK.L, as in 5A3.11, where

P = Page number (e.g., logical page 5 of the charts)
S = Series (e.g., series A for "Accounting")
K = Key number (e.g., reference is made to the third key on logical page 5 of the charts for Series A)
· = Separator between key number and data element number
L = Line (e.g., data element 11 under the third key, a named shape that will be found on the chart)

One further convention is most helpful. Because the key always appears first in the assertion template, it is natural to treat it as falling on line 0. Thus the key in the above example would have locator 5A3.0. All keys have locators with a zero after the "decimal point."

Adherence to this method for numbering data element sheets produces, at once, a notebook in which each sheet is inscribed with the locator (e.g., 5A3.11) of some element on the charts. Each page should also contain, prominently, an exact copy of the data element name as it is written in the shape on page 5 of the charts. This completes the "set up," provided the logical pages of the charts have been numbered 1A, 2A, 3A, etc. The series letter always appears on each page of the charts *after* the page number to conform to the sequence PS in the locator PSK.L. This method of setting up the notebook (or any other physical design with the same logical structure) has proved to be amply adaptable to reshuffling—yet easy and obvious to use.

Given this general format for the design notebook, the serious work of data element documentation can begin. We use a form for data element sheets (Figure 6-27) that contains a grille on the right-hand side. In this grille, we record the locators of other data element sheets which contain information of documentary interest to the given one. Very few people enjoy the administration of cross-references, and nearly everyone we know has begun to document data elements confident that *he* would have no need for this feature. But those attitudes do not take into account the *process* of logical design—the turbulent reformulation of ideas. It is virtually impossible to write a little story about a data element in a single place. The story is spread out over several data element sheets for a very simple reason. It happens that way, and it is far too much trouble to restructure the documentation to undo it once it has happened.

Consider this example to illustrate the point. Begin with a key that represents an insurance policy, where POLICY is element 3K6.0 on the charts. There is a data element sheet for the key, of course, and it is natural to write a little story about the POLICY on

┌─────┬──────┬─────┬──────┐
│     │      │     │      │
└─────┴──────┴─────┴──────┘
 Page  Series  Key   Line

┌────────────────────────┐
│                        │  **KIND:**
└────────────────────────┘
    Data Element Name

**FUNCTIONS:**


**COMMENTARY:**

| NOTE | P | S | K | L |
|------|---|---|---|---|
|      |   |   |   |   |
|      |   |   |   |   |
|      |   |   |   |   |
|      |   |   |   |   |
|      |   |   |   |   |
|      |   |   |   |   |
|      |   |   |   |   |
|      |   |   |   |   |
|      |   |   |   |   |
|      |   |   |   |   |
|      |   |   |   |   |
|      |   |   |   |   |
|      |   |   |   |   |
|      |   |   |   |   |
|      |   |   |   |   |
|      |   |   |   |   |
|      |   |   |   |   |
|      |   |   |   |   |
|      |   |   |   |   |
|      |   |   |   |   |
|      |   |   |   |   |
|      |   |   |   |   |
|      |   |   |   |   |
|      |   |   |   |   |
|      |   |   |   |   |
|      |   |   |   |   |
|      |   |   |   |   |
|      |   |   |   |   |
|      |   |   |   |   |
|      |   |   |   |   |
|      |   |   |   |   |
|      |   |   |   |   |
|      |   |   |   |   |
|      |   |   |   |   |
|      |   |   |   |   |
|      |   |   |   |   |
|      |   |   |   |   |
|      |   |   |   |   |
|      |   |   |   |   |

Figure 6-27. Date element sheet.

the key's worksheet. This text points out what a policy is and proceeds to point out the subtle differences between owner, named insured, beneficiary, etc. The role of medical information, date of birth of the insured, and similar observations are crucial to the understanding of a POLICY, for a policy cannot exist unless these conditions are met. So they are discussed on the key's page. A few pages later, (e.g., 3K6.7) where the data element BENEFICIARY is up for description, it is foolish to repeat what was already discussed. This is the time to place "SEE 3K6.0" in the grille on the BENEFICIARY sheet, to include the key's text by reference. In keeping with our practice throughout this book, we reverse this cross-reference. That is, leafing back to the sheet for POLICY (3K6.0), we note REF 3K6.7 in its grille area. REF is the converse of SEE, and the key's grille now shows that some other data element discussion, namely that on page 3K6.7, is dependent on what is written on that page. The designer/documenter should take care to check that dependency wherever the premises noted on the key's page are altered significantly. The discipline of writing with cross-references is neither difficult to learn nor tedious. All that is necessary is an honest respect for the enormous amount of detail that needs to be written down to document a logical data base design thoroughly.

Let us continue one more step with the example of POLICY. At the time we described BENEFICIARY, it surely came to mind that there is a rule, for this kind of policy, that the beneficiary must be some stipulated blood relative of the owner. This is only an imaginary rule, but it makes our point beautifully. That rule, which relates beneficiary, owner, and family relationships, clearly has bearing on at least three data elements. It is pointless to state the rule three times on three different pages, especially since we are not at all clear, when we first write it, what the precise, formal, even legal statement of the rule should be. Cross-referencing is vital in data element documentation because of the interplay of these factors—needing the same statement in several places, and needing great freedom to change it. It is for these reasons that the principle of storing data in one place and referring to it by pointers is used to guide the documentation process. Needless to say, the discipline also encourages the designer/documenter to be alert to functional dependencies.

Once the grille is used for text cross-reference, it is easy to extend its use to serve other purposes. One step we heartily recommend is to cross-reference keys and associators. Begin with an associator sheet, say 15K2.3. Assume that associator cites POLICY, the same POLICY key illustrated above. Observe that there is no clue on that associator page 15K2.3 that indicates where to find the sheet on POLICY. One could go back to the charts and search through the Keys, but this is not easy when the data base contains several hundred keys. So we advise doing the lookup routinely whenever an associator sheet is first created. Write KEY 3K6.0 in the grille to permit a subsequent reader to understand quickly what (where) this associator is pointing to. Again, in keeping with our conventions, turn back to page 3K6.0 and write ATR 15K2.3. This says that there is an associator which points to this key located at 15K2.3.

To summarize, the two important cross-reference pairs are:

SEE   More information available at:
REF   Another element cites this text

and

KEY   This associator points to the key at:
ATR   This key is referenced by an associator at:

Adherence to these conventions, together with a reasonable effort not to be repetitive, produces a documentation notebook in which one can record details of the properties of the data, even as the concepts are being developed.

Within this framework, or any other, some guidelines are needed to define what should be written down. The first guideline will strike many readers as counterintuitive: do not attempt to write a *complete* data element *definition* on the data element worksheet. The reason this guideline is helpful is that it is a reminder that data element definitions cannot be written during the logical design process. They can be (and are) written at the *end* of the logical design process. But as one is working on the problem, most attempts to *define* a data element will flounder because other data elements, needed in the definition, are themselves poorly defined. Consider POLICY, OWNER, BENEFICIARY above. Reflection will show that a POLICY depends on what the other two turn out to be, and vice versa. Even if one succeeds in writing a satisfying definition at this stage, it is virtually certain that conditions will arise later to change it. For example, the definition will fail to take into account a little-known fact like "If the owner is an agent of a foreign government whose assets in the U.S. have been frozen, then . . ." Is the policy still a policy? Is it void? Does it lapse? The guideline reminds us to avoid the pretense of thinking our notes are data element definitions. They are not. They are notes, comments, facts, and relationships from which definitions can be created later.

Once again, remember that the whole story about a data element appears on many sheets. The final definition must be written when the whole story is assembled and analyzed.

All the notes and comments in a design document should be written with the same precision of language and clarity of thought one customarily uses in writing definitions. But leave the actual composition of a complete definition for last. Otherwise, the documentation process bogs down and becomes a legalistic exercise of playing with words; constant rephrasing of ill-formulated definitions is not a smooth way either to achieve a well thought out design or to construct a design document.

Documentation during the design process should stress the description of domains, data elements, and relationships. Use the data element sheets associated with keys (they have locators ending in .0) to discuss the domain over which the key is defined. The key value generally identifies, uniquely, an individual member of the domain. When this is not true, take extra pains to point it out, for readers of the documentation will be predisposed to assume the key is a unique identifier. When employee numbers are reused, EMPLOYEE NUMBER = 3164 could define both a current employee and a past employee. This possibility should be noted prominently in the documentation provided for the key and its domain.

For all data elements except keys, record a clear statement of the function of the data element. "This particular data element is needed here for the following purposes." Notice that saying why an element is needed forces one to review all its principal uses and some unusual uses. This examination of its uses is very valuable, for it often happens that these uses are forgotten with the passage of time when the designer's attention has been diverted elsewhere. The documentation should be a reminder, when the element is examined again, that there were specific reasons for including it and what those reasons were. Even innocuous data elements—dates, addresses—need this sort of treatment. We routinely find that later work causes the creation of a date or address data element elsewhere in the structure. Sometimes the new date is positioned in a far better place than the old date and serves all its purposes. Sometimes the new date is far inferior to the one that was previously defined. In both cases, notes that itemize the functions of the old element are crucial to the choice.

The definition of elements has been previously discussed in Chapter 4. Most of the text that is devoted to relationships will appear on the two data element sheets that correspond to the two paired associators. Authors are encouraged to avoid placing discussions of domains on the associator pages, even though it is sometimes tempting to do so. Place the discussion of domains on the key pages since such discussions apply to all the associators that cite the key. The discussion of a particular associator (e.g., PERSON TAG OF BENEFICIARY) within a key like POLICY has a remarkable property that every documenter should understand. He has already stated what a POLICY is; he has already stated what PERSON TAG is. The discussion of the associator PERSON TAG OF BENEFICIARY is almost wholly devoted to stating what a beneficiary is. The fact that the associator contains a person tag is almost incidental. If the designer had, as he might, employed SOCIAL SECURITY NUMBER OF BENEFICIARY instead of person tag, only minor changes in the text would be needed, for how a person is identified is incidental to the meaning of "beneficiary." A universal insurance-company-person-identifier-code could also be used equally well. When documenting a relationship, explain the relationship, not the reasons for using a particular associator to connect two keys.

Finally, when appropriate, include copies of policy statements, code lists, instruction sheets ("How Our Policy Numbers are Constructed"), legal documents (a bill of lading), and similar material from the real world. All such documents should be current and they should be dated. While the logical design may not need to absorb these elements of current practice, including them in the documentation enriches the reader's understanding of terminology and gives one an easy way to begin an evaluation of the problem of making a transition to the new system.

## Key-Level Overview

In Chapter 2, we introduced the idea of a key level overview diagram, and provided an example for the New Plants Division data base as Figure 2-4. Recall that the key-level overview diagram only shows the relationships among the keys within the data base; as such it is a summary of the complete set of data base assertions, is derivable from them, and contains no additional information.

Because the relationships among the data base keys provide the major part of the data base structure, the key-level overview permits the designer and others to view the overall structure on a single chart. This view may reveal aspects of the design which are difficult to picture using the individual assertion charts alone; it is certainly a useful aid in introducing someone to the data base who has not previously been exposed to it.

Generally, simple relations between assertion keys are depicted on the key-level overview merely by drawing a line between the boxes representing each key. The nature of the relationships is indicated by drawing arrowheads to represent one-to-many or many-to-many relationships. However, when other than these "binary" relationships are present, nonkey associators will need to be placed on the key-level chart to show the relationship among three or more keys (this is because one line can only connect two boxes).

Rules for creating the key-level overview are as follows:

1. Place a box for each assertion template key on the chart and properly label the contents.

2. For each key, examine the associators subordinate to it. One of two cases will be present:
   a. the associator will have one or more other associators subordinate to it. In this case, place the associator on the key-level overview chart as well.
   b. the associator will not have other associators subordinate to it. If this is the case, do not place the associator on the chart.
3. For each associator now shown on the chart, draw a line connecting it to the key under which it immediately appears in the assertion. If it doesn't appear immediately below a key, then connect it to the associator under which it appears. If this line duplicates an existing one, label the two (or more) lines to show that two different relationships exist.
4. For each associator not shown on the chart, draw a line between the key to which the associator points, and the key or associator under which it appears. If this line duplicates an existing line, do not draw another one. If the line is drawn from a key to itself, put a label on the line to indicate its meaning.
5. Place arrowheads on the ends of lines to indicate one-to-many or many-to-many relationships.
6. Redraw the chart to minimize line crossings.

As an example, consider the following portion of an assertion in the NPD data base:

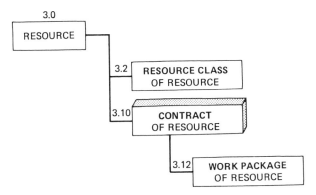

The relevant portion of the key-level overview is:

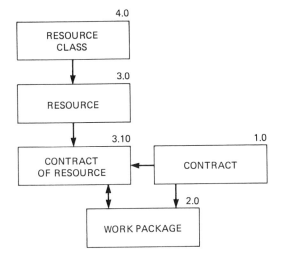

While these rules for creating a key-level overview are for the most part straightforward, some complexity will arise due to the nature of associator reversals in multilevel cascades. The reader will see for example, that the key WORK PACKAGE (2.0), reverses to RESOURCE (3.0) directly (via associator 2.14) and not through CONTRACT OF RESOURCE (3.10). This is primarily because a WORK PACKAGE can only be for one contract. Nevertheless, it would be misleading to draw a line between WORK PACKAGE and RESOURCE on the key level overview; rather the connection between CONTRACT OF RESOURCE and WORK PACKAGE suffices.

Partially because such "overview" charts have difficulty expressing greater than binary relationships (i.e., cascades involving a key and at least two levels of associator subordination), the design process should never begin with the key-level overview. Only when the design is fairly well along should the overview be extracted and used as a part of the evolving documentation.

## Instance Diagrams

Instance diagrams form an essential ingredient of the data base design documentation; they can portray peculiarities and possibilities in the design which are almost impossible to visualize otherwise. For this reason, they are especially useful in logical design walkthroughs. An instance diagram is really a populated example for a portion of the data base. If real, or at least realistic, data can be used, so much the better. In discussing the logical data base design with user representatives, the design can then show how particular cases will be handled, e.g., "Here we show how that troublesome customer with four subsidiaries would be handled in the data base."

There are many forms which an instance diagram can take, and the designer will want to experiment with several to find those most suitable. Generally, instances at the assertion level or instances at the key-level are most appropriate. If the internal structure of an assertion is complex, then several renditions showing different examples will be useful.

In Figure 6-28, an instance diagram at the key level is shown. Notice that each box corresponds to an *instance* of a key, or of an associator. Each box is numbered according to the convention used in the key-level overview. There would, of course, be a complete populated assertion in the data base for each key; nevertheless at this level we are only interested in exploring the example at the key level. The figure shows two contracts, one for Wilson, one for Brown, and two Systems, Electrical and Conveyor. In the Brown Electrical System, there are two Lines corresponding to circuits; circuit number 2 consists of the CONTRACT ITEM INSTANCES: *Junction Box A, Conduit B, and Junction Box C. Also connected via this Line, but not part of it, is the Contract Item Instance Conveyor Control Panel Z. In a similar fashion, this control panel is connected to, but not part of, Conveyor Belt X of the conveyor system. This example can be used to show that a Contract Item Instance can be a part of one and only one Line, or it can be connected to, but not part of, several Lines (of the same or different systems).

There are a large number of key interconnection possibilities which are not readily apparent from a visual inspection of the key-level overview, and their recognition can be facilitated by the use of instance diagrams. For many of these interconnection possibilities, rules will need to be developed stating that they are not allowed in the data

---

*Not to be confused with instance diagrams.

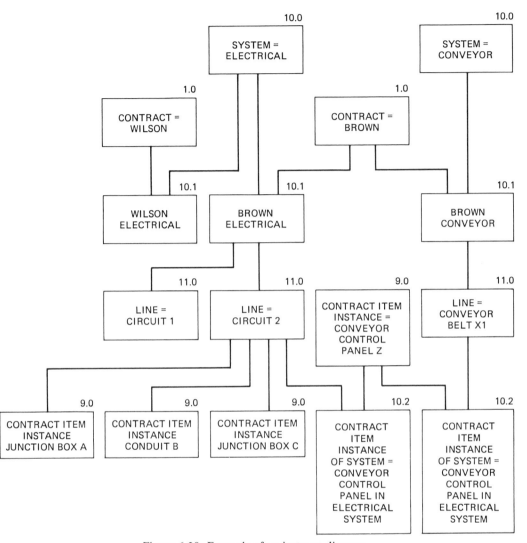

Figure 6-28. Example of an instance diagram.

base, or if allowed, only under given conditions. With the present stage of data base software technology, such "global" interconnection rules or constraints must be implemented through application program logic and not by the data base software itself. Discovering the conditions (with the help of instance diagrams) and documenting the rules is an important data base design function, particularly with more complex designs.

In order to exhibit the interconnection possibilities, the designer should work on one portion of the design at a time. In each portion, several instances of each key or associator should be depicted, and many (if not all) of the possible interconnections shown which are within the constraints of the design. Particular attention is to be placed on keys or associators which have two (or more) superior boxes. The case in which two paths of superior boxes join at a common "ancestor" is especially important for study.

Let's look at two examples, In Figure 6-29, we see some instances of key types similar

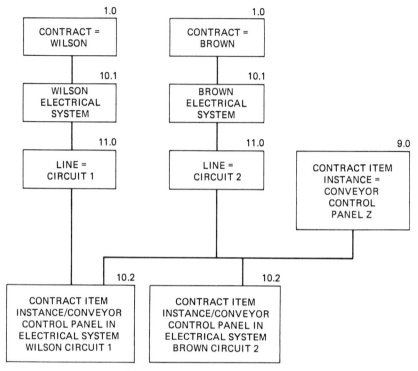

Figure 6-29. An illegal instance.

to those in Figure 6-28. Note in particular we show a Contract Item Instance (Conveyor Control Panel) which is connected to, but not part of, two Lines in Electrical Systems, but these Lines are in systems within two different contracts! It's important to understand that the conditions exhibited in Figure 6-29 are perfectly legitimate and within the logical design as presented so far. Rules or constraints to prohibit these combinations must be explicitly stated: any given Contract Item Instance can only be connected to lines which are all within the same Contract.

A second example contains the common ancestor property referred to above, and is exhibited in Figure 6-30. In this example, insurance companies are chartered in a particular state to insure vehicles; drivers are also licensed to operate vehicles by the state. The instance diagram reveals an interesting question: can a vehicle operated by a driver in one state be insured by a company chartered in a different state? The very process of conjuring up the instance diagram example forces these questions.

## Data Base Evolution Plan

The final aspect of data base documentation to be considered covers planning for the evolution or phasing of the data base. If the data base is large and integrated, it cannot and should not be developed in one fell swoop. Rather, careful planning is needed to phase the development over a period of time.

When pursuing the methodology discussed in this book, there is one approach to data base evolution planning which is recommended. Begin by developing the complete logical data base design for the "most future" implementation. Be sure to carry that design to completion. That is, carefully go through the critical reviews and prepare a final version of the logical data base design documentation. Pay little or no attention to data base evolution planning during this period; concentrate instead on defining and organizing the far future requirements. This is by far the hardest task.

Once the future data base is firm, proceed immediately to the data base evolution planning step. This needs to be accomplished in conjunction with system architects, system planners, and management personnel. The process is one of partitioning the assertion template into chunks, representing the potential phasing of implementation in some orderly and meaningful fashion. Arrange each partitioning of the data base so that the chunks are shown in the most practical time sequence. Naturally, there will be some alternative sequences, in which ABCDE is just as good as ACBDE. Now proceed to debate the merits of these various approaches. Into this debate will be injected other factors that affect the planning. It may be urgent to implement Chunk B as soon as possible since customers are complaining about poor service. It may be equally crucial to implement Chunk C for the accounting area since they can save many dollars with the new data base, or because they have political leverage and control the funding, or because of some new federal regulation, or whatever. These are expressions of corporate priorities, and the planning term will need to consult regularly with management in order to identify the proper plan.

When one or two sequences stand out from all others, the focus of the debate will

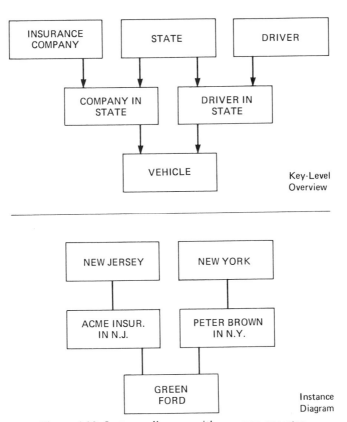

Figure 6-30. Instance diagram with common ancestor.

change from the strategic level to the tactical. The evolution of the data base needs to be aligned with other factors that affect the development of software and even the acquisition of hardware. Resource limitations need to be considered, and the remaining alternatives need to be placed on a tentative schedule. In the worst case, the two plans remain equally matched. One will be finished in two years, but it offers no new capabilities until 18 months have elapsed. The other takes two and one-half years, but it begins to offer new capabilities in ten months. There is no way for a technical group to prefer one of these plans over the other, and it may well be that both sequences are presented, as alternatives, in the data base evolution plan.

Documentation of the resulting data base evolution plans requires a review of the thought process and the various issues considered. In addition to this narrative, there needs to be a section or an appendix which analyzes the logical data base design from the perspective of its sequenced components—the "chunks" that were discussed earlier. Logical data bases are always "carved up" by deciding to include certain keys and to exclude others. Usually this decision encompasses all of an assertion template or it excludes all of it. This is not always true, but when it is, the data base, at a given stage, either includes a provision for data keyed by PART NO. or it doesn't. It is nearly irrelevant, from a data base point of view, that only half the parts will be loaded at that stage: the data base will ordinarily be ready for all of them.

Sometimes assertion templates are split. There are two cases. The first is trivial: various data elements, none of which are associators, are omitted at one stage and are filled in at a later stage. This might be the case if the first batch of parts in the system were of a simpler type than parts in the second batch.

The second case is far more interesting: we decide to include a key and its assertion template in one "chunk," but we also decide to leave related keys out of the data base. That means various associators under the key being retained "point no place." If the associator is *optional,* this way of carving up the data base is completely consistent with the logical design, for no assumption has ever been made that associator must be populated. Whenever the data base is severed entirely at optional links, which is not always possible, the partitioning offers no challenge to the logical design. There is no need even to change the documentation since we are merely making use of an alternative that has already been provided for. Obviously, data bases that are severed along optional associators are to be preferred.

But it is also possible to sever data bases at associators that are mandatory in the view of the final integrated design. When this is found to be necessary, the documentation will need to modified to describe the changes taking place. Under the retained key, where there is a discussion of the mandatory associator that will "point no place" for a time, some statement needs to be made about the plan. There are two possible forms that statement can take:

- During the early stages of data base evolution, before the foreign key is supported, the associator will be regarded as optional: the link to the foreign key will be disregarded. The assertion will be interpreted as if this associator had been omitted from the design.
- Or, during the early stages before the foreign key is supported, the associator will be treated as a nonassociator. The element value will satisfy all the edit checks and will pass all the requirements for an associator value being present. But the

associator will provide no further reference until the rest of the data base is constructed at a later stage of data base evolution.

Observe that these are not particularly troublesome statements to add to the documentation. What is troublesome and requires considerable thought is whether the retained key is really meaningful and useful in the absence of the data in the foreign key. There are no known rules for making that judgment: it depends on the kinds of keys. Two examples will show the contrast.

The first example shows two entities which are so "loosely" connected by a mandatory associator that they can be severed at "X" without undue distress:

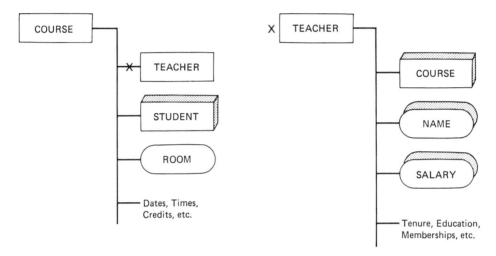

We simply decide to carry the course information in the data base without any indication of the teacher. Or we can treat the teacher as a nonassociator. Later on, perhaps when some open issues about tenure have been resolved, the teacher "file" can be added. Though the associators are mandatory in both directions, there is no great conceptual hurdle in severing the data base at this point.

On the other hand, some entities are very tightly coupled. Reusing an example treated earlier:

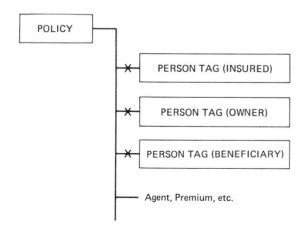

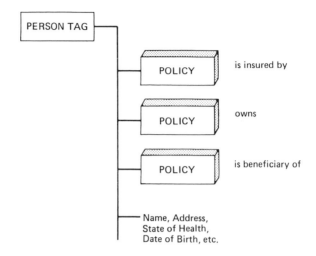

The existence of a record of a life insurance policy that fails to identify the various people (the insured, the owner, the beneficiaries) is very difficult to imagine. The implications are extensive, and they do not depend on the fact that we have shown a triple relationship between the keys. Consider only the named insured. Omitting all data about this person, as hypothesized, includes omitting his state of health. One such state is critical to the administration of a life insurance policy, for the policy is quite different when premiums are being collected from when proceeds are being distributed to a beneficiary. Similar puzzles arise if the other connecting links are severed. In short, this illustrates a case where cutting the data base at a mandatory associator lacks any real attraction.

## COMPARISON TO CODASYL AND RELATIONAL

### Introduction

The primitive elements which have been described in preceding chapters (data elements, domains, assertions, etc.), taken together with rules governing their use and the notational conventions employed, constitute a framework within which the data base designer can construct a logical data base design. There are numerous purposes, most of them obvious, for employing such a framework. It is significant to note that to some degree the framework itself can have an influence on the resulting design. For example, if the framework is difficult to understand and use, then some people who might otherwise have made a contribution to the design may not do so. Or, if the framework permits only the expression of fixed occurrence hierarchical data structures, then obviously the resulting design will have to be in terms of these structures. More subtly, the framework can make certain kinds of data problems stand out, or can alternatively hide them.

While no claim is made that the framework presented in this book is the best possible, the authors do believe it has a number of important features. These can be summarized as follows:

1. Ease of Use (Intuitive)

   The framework as presented contains very few constructs and only several rules. It has proven in practice to be usable by both technicians and nontechnicians alike. We believe this is critical and not just merely advantageous. For the logical design is, in a real sense, a formal encapsulation of user requirements, thereby serving as a communication bridge between user and technician. If the average user cannot readily understand and deal within the framework, these benefits are lost.

2. Powerful

   Easy as the framework has proven to be, there are few cases where its expressiveness was insufficient to handle a particularly complex data problem.

3. Graphical

   The graphical nature of the framework is important because it clearly exhibits the data structures, and also because it allows the designer to deal with large portions of the design at one time. Additionally, the naturalness with which the design can be partitioned (into individual assertion templates) is a great benefit over those frameworks which call for the design to be depicted in a single picture.

4. Rigorous

   The rules of the framework, while not to be blindly enforced, are sufficiently rigorous to guide the designer toward consistent and unambiguous designs. Once certain fundamentals are established (e.g., the entities), different designers addressing the same situation will produce roughly equivalent basic designs (there is always room for embellishment to accommodate history, privacy, etc.). And there would be no ambiguity in interpreting a given design.

5. Extensible

   The framework is easily extensible in a number of directions and we encourage the reader to adopt such extensions he finds useful. However, we caution against making the framework too complex that it turns users off—and this can be done merely be adding many, albeit simple, constructs. We have avoided such extensions (even when they are compelling) in the book to highlight this concern, and to demonstrate how much can in fact be accomplished without them.

6. Free From Physical Constructs

   This, of course, is a mandatory requirement for a logical level framework.

To enable the reader to gain a better grasp of the underlying principles, it will be instructive to contrast the framework presented here with others. In the literature, the term "data model" is used in a close way to "framework" as we use it here. For the remainder of this chapter, we shall refer to the framework as the Associative Data Model.

## The CODASYL Model

The CODASYL model provides constructs which cover both the logical and physical arenas of data base. These constructs were originally included in a single language, called the DDL (Data Definition Language), which served to describe the data base both from a conceptual and internal point of view.* Recent versions of the CODASYL

---

*See Chapter 1.

model have separated out the physical aspects into a Data Storage Definition Language, (DSDL) leaving the resulting schema definition as a potential conceptual or logical level design framework.

The important primitives of the CODASYL model at the logical level are as follows:

- Record—A collection of data elements, including provisions for variably occurring groups of data.
- Data Element—The atomic unit of data.
- Set—The mechanism for interrelating records. The rules are as follows:

  — Each set has one OWNER type record and multiple MEMBER type records.
  — For each occurrence of an OWNER type record, there can be related to it none, one, or many occurrences of each type of MEMBER record.
  — A record type can be an OWNER and MEMBER in any number of sets, and an OWNER and MEMBER in the same set.

A notational convention which is used with the CODASYL model is the Bachman diagram, a sample of which is shown in Figure 6-31. A corresponding design, as it would be depicted by the Associative Data Model, is shown in Figure 6-32.

In contrasting the CODASYL framework to the Associative Data Model, the following may be noted:

1. The Bachman diagram corresponds roughly to what we have called the key-level overview, although there are important differences. Also, both diagrams can be derived from more detailed information provided elsewhere by the framework (schema or assertion templates). Generally, however, the CODASYL designer

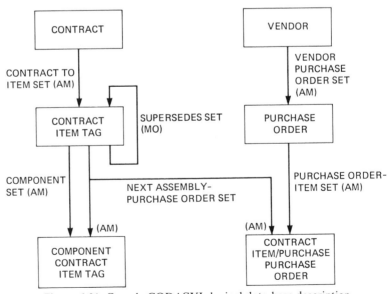

Figure 6-31. Sample CODASYL logical data base description.

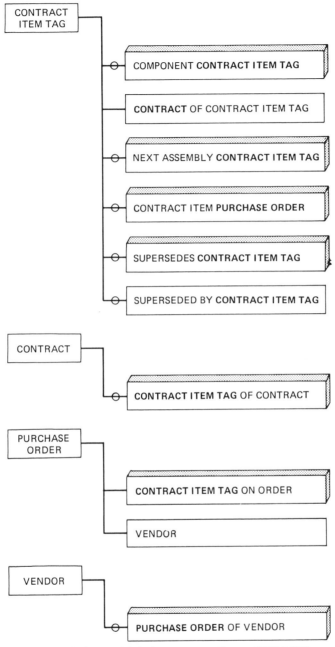

Figure 6-32. Associative model design corresponding to CODASYL example.

will begin at the Bachman diagram level; this is discouraged in the Associative Data Model.

2. The CODASYL framework makes no distinction between data element and domain.

3. Associators in the associative framework have been replaced by sets in the

CODASYL model. From a logical or conceptual point of view, sets have the following disadvantages:

a. The definition of a data relationship within a data base is as significant as the definition of a data element. Yet within the CODASYL model, there is no convenient place to record such a definition. By having each relationship explicitly represented by a data element (i.e., an associator), the designer is forced to give equal treatment to both.

b. A set as defined in the CODASYL framework can have multiple member type records. Each such type record within a set could possibly enter into a different relationship, i.e., a relationship which had a different meaning, with the OWNER type record. Yet with only one set, there can be only one meaning. Thus in our example of Figure 6-31, the NEXT ASSEMBLY PURCHASE ORDER Set is used to relate CONTRACT ITEMS to their NEXT ASSEMBLIES *and* to the PURCHASE ORDERS they appear on, two quite different relationships. While there may be cases in which different record types are legitimately treated in a similar fashion as members of a set, nothing in the CODASYL model suggests when different member types should be included in the same set and when they should be included as members of distinct sets. The difference appears to be devoid of semantic content, and hence the choice does not belong at the logical level.

c. Symbolic keys (data elements which can be used as the access key to a record) may exist within CODASYL records, and reflect legitimate data relationships above and beyond those indicated by sets. Thus there are two ways to indicate data relationships—one known to the DBMS (sets) and one controlled and used by programs and users but unknown to the DBMS (symbolic pointers). Again, this distinction seems unwarranted at the logical level.

d. The reversal relationship in CODASYL is implicit. Thus a set is always defined from the owner to the member, while the reverse relationship, from the member to the owner, is not named. Thus there is no place to describe its characteristics or provide a definition of the reverse relation.

4. With the CODASYL model, a distinct record type must be provided to show a many-to-many relationship between two other records. For example, the Contract Item/Purchase Order record in Figure 6-31 serves this purpose. In the Associative Data Model, many-to-many relationships can be reflected directly.

5. The semantics of an "assertion template" are not implied for a "record type." Thus there is no suggestion that a record corresponds to an entity, or that all the elements in a record be about that entity. There are no rules to discourage the redundant storage of data.

6. Within the CODASYL model, each member type record in a set is declared to have a storage and removal class of membership. The storage classes of membership are:

Automatic—A record occurrence automatically becomes a member of some set occurrence as it is added to the data base.

Manual—A record does not automatically become a member of some set, but can be "connected" to a set later by the action of a program.

The removal classes of membership are:

Mandatory—Once a record occurrence becomes a member of a particular set, it cannot be "discontinued" from the set (unless it is deleted from the data base).

Optional—A record can be "disconnected" from a set without being deleted from the data base.

We have indicated these membership classes for each member of each set in Figure 6-31.* The reader will see that these specifications are concerned with permitting or limiting operations performed on the data base. In contrast, the Associative Data Model contains specifications which enable the designer to permit or limit states of the data base, through the use of the optionality symbol "o." Let us consider some examples. Both models clearly specify that a CONTRACT ITEM TAG *must* have exactly one CONTRACT associated with it. Both also indicate that a CONTRACT ITEM TAG can supersede zero, one, or many other CONTRACT ITEM TAGS, and can be superseded by zero or at most one other CONTRACT ITEM TAG. However, the Associative Data Model design is able to specify that a PURCHASE ORDER must have at least one CONTRACT ITEM TAG. It can also be used to limit relationships to one-to-one although this is not shown in the example.

### The Relational Model

The Relational Data Model has developed from the early work of Codd *et al.* While there are now numerous interpretations of the precise formal aspects of the model, we have taken the principal ideas in what follows.

Relations are built up from *N-tuples*. An *N*-tuple is a collection of *N* data values, where each value has been selected from a particular domain. The data values can be selected from common or distinct domains. For example,

$$\langle \text{ACME, A123, Pittsburgh} \rangle$$

is a three-tuple of values from the domains Vendor Name, Part Number, Factory Location. A *relation* is then a set of such tuples, akin to a table in which the tuples form the rows and the domains form the columns. It is significant to note that "set" is used here with its mathematical meaning; thus the tuples in a relation do not appear in any particular sequence, and relations may not contain duplicate tuples. (Contrast this with the use of "set" in CODASYL.)

The Relational Data Model specifies that relations be in the third normal form. The rules for third normal form depend on the notions of primary key and "functional dependency." A primary key of a relation is the one or more domains (columns) which can be used to identify uniquely each tuple (row). In a particular relation, domain (column) A is said to be functionally dependent on domains (columns) B, C, D, if and only if two tuples each with the same values of B, C, D . . . necessarily have the same value of A. The various levels of normalization are then as follows:

*First Normal Form:* All domains must contain atomic data values only, i.e., relations may not contain relations or repeating groups.

*Second Normal Form:* Each nonkey domain must be functionally dependent on the primary key.

*The membership classes are indicated in parentheses, with the storage class listed first; (AM) means Automatic, Mandatory.

*Third Normal Form:* Nonkey domains cannot be functionally dependent on any other nonkey domains.

Let us analyze these restrictions and the rationale for them with the aid of the example shown in Figure 6-33. This relation R1, is in first normal form, since each domain is an atomic data value (and not a relation itself). However, it is not in second normal form, for a number of reasons. Let us consider the primary key of relation R1 to consist of CONTRACT ITEM TAG and (COMPONENT) CONTRACT ITEM TAG (since there is one tuple (row) for each unique combination of these two columns). The QUANTITY domain is clearly functionally dependent on both elements of the key (there is precisely one quantity for each component item of an item). However, (NEXT ASSEMBLY) CONTRACT ITEM TAG violates the second normal form rule because it is not functionally dependent on the key—there are many (NEXT ASSEMBLY) CONTRACT ITEMS per CONTRACT ITEM, and they don't depend on (COMPONENT) CONTRACT ITEM at all. The same exact reasoning goes for PURCHASE ORDER and VENDOR as well. The CONTRACT domain on the other hand is functionally dependent on only part of the key (CONTRACT ITEM TAG) and not on the other part (COMPONENT CONTRACT ITEM TAG); similarly for CUSTOMER NAME.

The basic problem with relations such as R1 which are not in second normal form is that they involve redundant storage of certain data (e.g., United as the vendor for purchase order P023 is recorded three times). This also provides the opportunity for inconsistent data (e.g., suppose *one* of the tuples reported that American was the vendor for purchase order P023). Moreover, it appears that if we delete the tuple which says that A105 has component A108, we also lose the fact that National is the vendor for P041. The second normal form rules are aimed at preventing these problems.

Let's now examine the several relations depicted in Figure 6-34, which are all in at least second normal form. Relation R2 has the same primary key as relation R1, and quantity remains as the only nonkey domain which is functionally dependent on both elements of the key. This relation is thus in third normal form as well. Relation R3 is in second normal form, since for a given CONTRACT ITEM TAG (the primary key) there is one CONTRACT and also there is one CUSTOMER. However, this relation is not in third normal form because there exists a functional dependency between the nonkey domains (CUSTOMER NAME is functionally dependent on CONTRACT). This is referred to as a transitive dependence of CUSTOMER NAME to CONTRACT ITEM TAG through CONTRACT and

| PRIMARY KEY | | QUANTITY | (NEXT ASSEMBLY) CONTRACT ITEM TAG | CONTRACT | PURCHASE ORDER | CUSTOMER NAME | VENDOR |
|---|---|---|---|---|---|---|---|
| CONTRACT ITEM TAG | (COMPONENT) CONTRACT ITEM TAG | | | | | | |
| A100 | A105 | 50 | A200 | X100 | PO23 | ACME | UNITED |
| A101 | A105 | 30 | A201 | X100 | PO25 | ACME | AMERICAN |
| A103 | A106 | 40 | A202 | X200 | PO23 | SUPER | UNITED |
| A105 | A107 | 20 | A100 | X100 | PO23 | ACME | UNITED |
| A105 | A108 | 15 | A101 | X100 | PO41 | ACME | NATIONAL |

Figure 6-33. A relation R1 in first normal form.

| PRIMARY KEY | | QUANTITY |
|---|---|---|
| CONTRACT ITEM TAG | (COMPONENT) CONTRACT ITEM TAG | |
| A100 | A105 | 50 |
| A101 | A105 | 30 |
| A103 | A106 | 40 |
| A105 | A107 | 20 |
| A105 | A108 | 15 |

RELATION R2

| PRIMARY KEY | | PURCHASE ORDER |
|---|---|---|
| CONTRACT ITEM TAG | (NEXT ASSEMBLY) CONTRACT ITEM TAG | |
| A100 | A200 | PO23 |
| A101 | A201 | PO25 |
| A103 | A202 | PO23 |
| A105 | A100 | PO23 |
| A105 | A100 | PO41 |
| A105 | A101 | PO23 |
| A105 | A101 | PO41 |

RELATION R4

| PRIMARY KEY | CONTRACT | CUSTOMER NAME |
|---|---|---|
| CONTRACT ITEM TAG | | |
| A100 | X100 | ACME |
| A101 | X100 | ACME |
| A103 | X200 | SUPER |
| A105 | X100 | ACME |

RELATION R3

| PRIMARY KEY | VENDOR |
|---|---|
| PURCHASE ORDER | |
| PO23 | UNITED |
| PO25 | AMERICAN |
| PO41 | NATIONAL |

RELATION R5

Figure 6-34. Four relations in second normal form.

is not permitted in third normal form relations. Thus relation R3 needs to be decomposed into relations R6 and R7 as shown in Figure 6-35. Again, redundancy in the data has been removed by the transition to third normal form.

According to the rules, we have broken out the separate functional dependency of VENDORS on PURCHASE ORDERS in relation R5. Finally, relation R4 reflects an interesting case of an "all key" relation. (All three domains must be considered before a unique

| PRIMARY KEY | CONTRACT |
|---|---|
| CONTRACT ITEM TAG | |
| A100 | X100 |
| A101 | X100 |
| A103 | X200 |
| A105 | X100 |

RELATION R6

| PRIMARY KEY | CUSTOMER NAME |
|---|---|
| CONTRACT | |
| X100 | ACME |
| X200 | SUPER |

RELATION R7

Figure 6-35. Decomposition of relation R3 into two third normal form relations.

tuple is identified.) By default, so to speak, this all key relation is in third normal form. However, recent developments in relational data base work have pointed out the problem with relations such as R4. In particular, R4 involves two domains which are multivalued dependent on CONTRACT ITEM TAG—that is, while there is not *one* PURCHASE ORDER for a CONTRACT ITEM (functional dependence), there is a *set* of PURCHASE ORDERS for a CONTRACT ITEM. Similarly, there is a set of (Next Assembly) Contract Items for a CONTRACT ITEM. These relationships are independent in the following sense: CONTRACT ITEM A105's which are on PURCHASE ORDER 23 can be used in *any* next assembly of A105 (A100 or A101); conversely, the CONTRACT ITEM A105's which are used on next assembly A100 can come from *any* PURCHASE ORDER of A105 (PO23 or P041). Yet the rendition of Relation R4 is redundant—to add another purchase order for A105 would cause the addition of two tuples—one for each NEXT ASSEMBLY. Consequently, a recent fourth normal form has been introduced which would cause us to decompose R4 into two separate relations.

We are now in a position to discuss the similarities and differences in the Relational and Associative Data Models. The most significant similarity is that both models incorporate the semantics of the "dependencies" involved in data relationships directly into the data structures supported by the model, i.e., into the data base design itself. However, the rules for doing this in each case, and the resulting data structures which emerge are quite distinct. Examine, for instance, the Associative Data Model assertion templates which correspond to the example under consideration, shown in Figure 6-36. Using this example, we can observe the following:

1. The functional and multi-valued dependencies embodied in the semantics of the data problem are all explicitly reflected in both models. For example, QUANTITY OF COMPONENT ITEM is functionally dependent on CONTRACT ITEM TAG *and* COMPONENT CONTRACT ITEM TAG as given by relation $R_2$ and by the first Template.

2. Except for the rule of reversals, there is no data redundancy in the Associative Data Model, nor is there any in the fourth normal form relational model. Note however that additional information may be provided by the reversal. Consider this simple relation for example:

Primary Key

| Part Number | Vendor |
|:-----------:|:------:|
| A | 1 |
| B | 2 |
| C | 3 |

It is impossible to tell from the definition of the relation, or from an examination of these particular tuples of the relation, whether or not a vendor may supply only one, or more than one, part. In the Associative Data Model, the reversal from vendor to part number would explicitly define the nature of the relationship.

3. There are exactly as many "subjects" in the set of assertion templates (i.e., vertical lines) as there are third normal form relations. Applying the fourth normal form restrictions will result in more relations than vertical lines.

4. More generally, the first normal form prohibition of relations containing relations is omitted from the Associative Data Model. This relaxation results in a much more economical model, coupled with the ability to identify all attributes of an

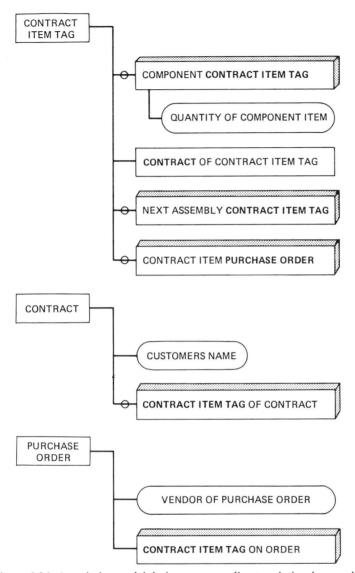

Figure 6-36. Associative model design corresponding to relational example.

entity and its relationships with other entities in a single place (i.e., the assertion template whose key is that entity). This ability to localize what the data base contains about a CONTRACT ITEM TAG, for example, is a significant benefit to the use of the Associative Data Model in providing a conceptual description of the corporate data base. When we consider the necessity to decompose relations involving multivalued dependencies to conform to fourth normal form, then it is likely that an equivalent Relational Data Model will involve many more relations than the Associative Data Model will involve assertion templates. For example, in the sample data base, the single CONTRACT ITEM TAG assertion contains three independent multivalued dependencies.

5. The Associative Data Model emphasizes the distinction between a data element

and a domain. In the Relational Data Model, this distinction is only called for when a relation involves two or more columns defined over the same domain—in this case, the column headings must be further described to identify the particular "roles" which the domain plays in each of the columns. The notion of domain "roles" in the relational model is akin to a data element in the Associative Data Model. In the Associative Data Model, *all* elements in a data structure need to be labeled and defined according to the role or context reflecting their meanings.

## CONCLUSION

Whenever a reversed pair of relationships is declared between two domains, a direct correspondence is established, which the data base system is meant to preserve. Stricter correspondences are included in more permisive correspondences. Correspondences can be compounded serially and vertically. Hence there are indirect correspondences established between pairs of domains as well as direct correspondences. When the indirect correspondence is stricter than the direct correspondence, there may be a design error. Correspondences have update properties that indicate a "natural" ordering of add and delete transactions. These and other detailed properties of individual correspondences can be incorporated directly into the documentation of the data base.

Every data element on the charts should have a separate page of documentation in a documentation notebook. These pages should be cross-referenced to the charts and each other using a locator of the form PSK.L. Documentation should stress the function of each element and why it is present. Data element definitions should not be prepared during the design process; they should be prepared last. Domains should be discussed on the page associated with each key.

Key-level overviews should also be prepared last, as a rule. Instance diagrams, on the other hand, should be prepared when needed, especially when an authoritative opinion on a data structuring problem is required from a user.

Data Base Evolution Plans are also of significant value, and they should be prepared at the end of logical design project. Subdivide the most future design by cutting the structure apart at optional associator links, if possible. This produces "chunks" of the data base that can be assembled in sequence. The sensible sequences provide alternative data base evolution strategies.

The Associative Data Model presented in this book, the CODASYL model, and the relational model all have somewhat different ways of expressing the logical data structure. Some of the differences are noted in the final section of Chapter 6 above.

## REFERENCES

1. Taylor, R., and Frank, R. "CODASYL Data Base Management Systems," *Computing Surveys,* **8**:1, March 1976.

    A complete introduction to the CODASYL data base framework.

2. Bachman, C. "Why Restrict the Modelling Capability of CODASYL Data Structure Sets?" *Proceedings of the National Computer Conference, 1977.*

    This paper contains some proposals for increasing the capabilities of CODASYL sets, including recursive sets and alternate owners, by one of the founders of the ideas behind the CODASYL framework.

3. Chamberlin, D. "Relational Data Base Management Systems," *Computing Surveys,* **8**:1, March 1976.

    A complete introduction to the Relational data base framework.

4. Michaels, A., Mittman, B., and Carlson, C. "A Comparison of the Relational and CODASYL Approaches to Data-Base Management," *Computing Surveys,* **8**:1, March 1976.

An analysis of the similarities and differences of these two frameworks.

5. Wong, E., and Katz, R. "Logical Design and Schema Conversion for Relational and DBTG Databases," in *International Conference on the Entity-Relation Approach to Systems Analysis and Design,* UCLA, December 1979.

Under the proper assumptions, Relational and CODASYL data base designs can be interchanged. This paper shows how it can be done using the Entity-Relationship model as an intermediary.

6. Chen, Peter. "The Entity-Relationship Model: Toward a Unified View of Data," *ACM Transaction on Database Systems,* **1**:1, March 1976.

The Entity-Relationship model as developed by Peter Chen emphasizes the use of the "entity-relationship diagram" to describe a conceptual level data base design. Such a diagram depicts relationships as named lines connecting two or more entity boxes:

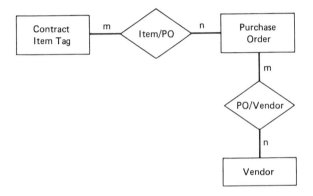

Note the ability to specify many-to-many, one-to-many, or one-to-one relationships. Both entities and relationships can have properties, expressed as attributes and their value sets. The attributes are depicted as named lines connecting an entity or relationship with a circle which reflects the value set of the attribute. Thus:

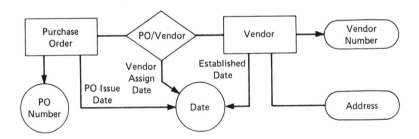

When an attribute and its value set have the same name, the attribute name is omitted. Extensions of these basic notions have been developed, including rules for translation of an E-R diagram into alternative logical and physical representations. Note that for this and similar modeling approaches, a large data problem would necessarily be cumbersome to reflect as a single interconnected schematic.

7. Bubenko, Janis. "Validity and Verification Aspects of Information Modeling." Conference on Very Large Data Bases, 1977.

The process of "information modeling" as used in this article is essentially one of contructing a logical or conceptual data base design. The author suggests that the criteria of validity, consistency, and evolvability be applied to a design, and goes on to discuss a number of potential problem areas. These include

- Lack of understanding of reality
- Erroneous assumptions
- Undetected (or unaccounted for) characteristics of reality
- Unforeseen evolutions
- Misunderstandings of the meaning of names

Some characteristics of underlying data models or frameworks are investigated and analyzed with respect to their impact on preventing the kinds of problems listed. For example, a framework should make a clear distinction between objects and the names of objects (levels of abstraction), since relationships among objects are more stable than relationships among names. Some frameworks depict the design as a single integrated model (e.g., Entity-Relationship Diagram) while others break it up into nondecomposible "statements" (e.g., a set of Relations). Bubenko suggests that the integrated approach is more informative, while the other approach risks missing some important information.

# Subject / Author Index